Fighting for Common Ground

Fighting for Common Ground

How We Can Fix the Stalemate in Congress

Olympia Snowe

WEINSTEIN
BOOKS

Printed in the United States of America.

Library of Congress Cataloging-in-Publication Data is available for this book.
ISBN 978-1-60286-217-3 (hardcover)
ISBN 978-1-60286-218-0 (e-book)

Published by Weinstein Books
A member of the Perseus Books Group
www.weinsteinbooks.com

Weinstein Books are available at special discounts for bulk purchases in the U.S. by corporations, institutions and other organizations. For more information, please contact the Special Markets Department at the Perseus Books Group, 2300 Chestnut Street, Suite 200, Philadelphia, PA 19103, call (800) 810-4145, ext. 5000, or e-mail special.markets@perseusbooks.com.

Editorial production by *Marra*thon Production Services. www.marrathon.net

BOOK DESIGN BY JANE RAESE
Text set in 13-point Perpetua

FIRST EDITION

10 9 8 7 6 5 4 3 2 1

To the people of Maine for granting me their trust and grounding me in the values so essential for public service.

Contents

Part Three

Fighting for
Common Ground

Introduction

WHEN I ANNOUNCED I would not run for reelection to the Senate in February 2012, many people asked me the same question: Was I relieved? The implication was that I was weary of the increasing bickering of recent Congresses and that I was worn down by it.

Nothing could be further from the truth. I've never backed down from a fight and I relish a good debate.

Some of these same well-wishers went on to express the hope that I would finally be able to relax.

No chance.

I have no intention of retiring. I love to work as much as ever.

But the Senate, as well as the 112th Congress, whose term ended in January 2013, was no longer a legislative body where the key issues facing the country could be resolved. I decided not to seek reelection only when I came to the sad conclusion that I could more effectively serve my country from outside the Senate than from within.

What motivated me to dedicate myself to public service for nearly two-thirds of my life was the chance to produce results for those people who entrusted me to be their voice and their champion. I found it exceedingly frustrating that an atmosphere of polarization and my-way-or-the-highway ideologies had become pervasive in our governing institutions, compromising our ability to solve problems at what was a time of monumental challenge for our nation.

The Senate as a whole simply was not doing the job granted to it under the Constitution. The Founding Fathers gave individual senators considerable power and influence, yet we were unable to offer solutions to problems on the floor of the Senate because we were prevented from proposing amendments. Few bills even reached the floor, and when they did, debate was frequently stifled or curtailed by overuse of the filibuster and other procedural gymnastics. Senate committees traditionally prepare bills that can and should be thoroughly talked through in debate, but in recent years that work has been bypassed. All too frequently, a bill was drafted behind closed doors and reported to the floor, then a quick up-and-down vote was forced on the entire proposal.

It was a stunning measure of our dysfunction that we were unable to pass a federal budget. After 2009, the last year in which a budget became law, the legislative branch failed year after year to fulfill one of its most basic functions. And year after year, Congress could only enact temporary provisions to keep the country running, let alone undertake any of the work essential to the nation's long-term economic health like regulatory reform, changes to the creaking tax code, and reducing our crippling deficits and debt. How could we ever hope to balance a budget if we were never even able to pass one?

At the same time, our two parties had become more extreme and more ideologically driven. Fair-minded legislators were reluctant to reach out across the aisle lest they bring on an intra-party challenge like the ones faced by Senator Bob Bennett in Utah, Senator Lisa Murkowski in Alaska, and Congressman Mike Castle in Delaware when he ran for the Senate.

Outstanding colleagues have had their distinguished careers derailed by a tightly organized subgroup within the main Republican Party that is more interested in taking down individuals with whom they don't agree than in electing representatives who will find bipartisan legislative solutions to America's problems.

Democrats were not immune to the new political reality. In 2010 in Arkansas, unions spent an estimated $10 million trying to defeat Senator Blanche Lincoln. She narrowly survived a primary run-off with Lieutenant Governor Bill Halter, but was defeated in the general election. I served with Blanche on the Senate Finance Committee and saw firsthand her tenacious commitment to her state.

Democrats even turned on a former vice presidential nominee when in 2006, Joe Lieberman lost a primary in Connecticut to a more liberal candidate, Ned Lamont, only to run and win as an independent. Joe had built a distinguished record on national security, but was viewed as too conservative and too close to then-President Bush. These were both instances of outstanding public servants being targeted by their own party.

As the same take-it-or-leave-it divisions have been echoed in the media, more and more constituents told me they simply no longer watched the news. I understand why so many Americans are fed up with government. The 112th Congress was almost universally derided as the worst ever. It was the most polarized body since the end of Reconstruction, according to one study, and I grew embarrassed by its partisan bickering, inactivity, and refusal to address the vital challenges facing America. Our job approval ratings were deservedly terrible—in some surveys the percentage of Americans who approved of the Congress's performance plummeted into historically low single digits.

When someone mentioned to Senator Tom Coburn (R-OK) in 2011 that Congress was at a 13 percent approval rating, he replied, "I want to know who those 13 percent are." Senator Michael Bennet (D-CO) published a chart that showed that our popularity was on a par with that of Hugo Chavez and significantly less than perennial favorites like bankers, lawyers, and the Internal Revenue Service.

I'm not a person who tends to rhapsodize about the past and how things used to be better, but I know enough Senate history to understand that the 112th was not typical. Earlier in my own career, and throughout its history, the Senate has transcended its divisions, risen to the occasion as an institution, and earned its status as the "world's greatest deliberative body," a description that in recent times is often tinged with sarcasm.

One triumph was the Senate's rebuttal of President Franklin Roosevelt's attempt to pack the Supreme Court with sympathetic justices in 1937. FDR took it for granted that the loyal Senate, controlled by his vice president, John Garner, would rubber-stamp his legislation that was designed to thwart any Supreme Court challenge to New Deal legislation. Instead, individual senators did what the Constitution mandated them to do and stood up to the President, and the deliberative body did what it was allowed to do when it conducted unlimited debate, both in Judiciary Committee hearings and on the floor of the Senate. Several senators made impassioned speeches in favor of judicial independence, including Josiah Bailey of North Carolina, whose powerful oratory changed other senators' minds. Seduced by his own overwhelming popularity, Roosevelt overplayed his hand and was ultimately thwarted by a bipartisan coalition of Republicans and conservative Democrats.

Historian Robert Caro describes this episode in *Master of the Senate,* part three of his indispensable biography of Lyndon Johnson. In 2005, Harry Reid drew the passage to my attention when he sent me a photocopy of it, along with a handwritten note saying that it reminded him of me. It is the kind of friendly and collegial gesture that senators often make toward each other.

Harry's note coincided with a systematic Democratic filibuster of President George W. Bush's judicial nominees, which was a corrosive force in the Senate. The Republican Majority Leader sought to break the logjam by exercising the so-called nuclear option, by which a "cloture" motion to end a filibuster could be passed by a simple majority rather than a sixty-vote threshold.

A cloture motion ends debate at once and moves the issue straight to a vote. Making this process easier was perceived by many, myself included, to be a severe diminution of the rights of the minority. Fourteen like-minded legislators, seven Republicans and seven Democrats—we were known as the "Gang of 14"—came together in a bipartisan spirit to forestall the nuclear option by agreeing we would support a filibuster of judicial nominees under "extraordinary circumstances." The agreement was the very manifestation of consensus-building and the power of trust. It is not always the rules that require changing but rather how we use them.

When I departed the Senate in 2013, its landscape not only was very different from what it was in 1937, but had even changed substantially from 2005. More recently, legislative outcomes are often preordained, and positions have usually solidified along party lines before a bill even reaches the Senate floor. Today, people rarely rush from Senate offices and cloakrooms to the floor and the galleries to hear a consequential speech. We might take solace from the fact that it wasn't always like this in Congress, nor does it have to be this way in the future. I came to Washington in 1979 determined to make an impact (when I became a member of the House that year, I joined a cross-party women's caucus whose work yielded real practical results), and possessed of the same spirit, I intend to continue this effort now on another stage.

The bottom line is that Congress retains the same potential in 2013 as at any time in its history. But it requires hard work to realize that potential, and legislators have to grapple with the major questions by working with the President, with the other side, and with members of their own party with whom they might disagree. In recent years, the two parties have stood in monolithic opposition; senators collaborate less; they hold separate conferences and caucuses and they meet less often in social settings than in the past.

The Senate's path out of dysfunction leads through increased bipartisanship and cross-party consensus-building. With the same spirit as before, only now working outside Congress, I'll maintain my fight for these improvements and lend my voice and experience as a consensus-builder and act as a catalyst for change. It is imperative we make certain there is a real political benefit and reward to be gained for bipartisanship so we can break what has become the equivalent of the parliamentary gridlock in Congress.

In January 2013, I concluded forty years of service in public office, in the Maine House and Senate and in the United States House and Senate. I know what we have to do to fix Washington, beginning with a call to action to empower the millions of Americans who believe that bipartisanship offers the best way forward at this tipping point for America. Through the power of social media we must mobilize from the grassroots upward to send an unmistakable message to our lawmakers that there is popular support for seeking common ground rather than destructive divisiveness.

Polls in early 2013 revealed that voters wanted their legislators to compromise, but with the parties' deep divisions, and without a receptivity to consensus-building, it is virtually impossible to get anything done in Congress. Power resides with the people through the ballot box, and we must attract and support candidates of both parties who are committed to pragmatic problem-solving.

In order to help ensure that candidates better reflect the ideological pragmatism of most Americans, we should encourage more states to follow the practice of open primaries. Campaign finance reform, including rolling back *Citizens United,* is essential to leveling the electoral playing field, and eliminating so-called Leadership PACs would help to abate the perpetual fund-raising our lawmakers are engaged in, which is a major distraction from conducting legislative business. We will also increase the amount of time members of Congress spend in Washington by instituting five-day workweeks at least three weeks a month, instead of the abbreviated Tuesday-to-Thursday legislative schedule. The other week would be reserved for members of Congress to spend time in their states or districts.

I propose in this book a number of procedural and rules changes that would rightly focus Washington on the essence of public service: working for the people our government was formed to serve. One is to permanently mandate that if Congress fails to pass a budget or appropriations bills are not completed, its members don't get paid—simple as that. We should curtail the ability of Senate leadership to either block or force through legislation without meaningful debate or amendments. The filibuster reforms that were adopted in 2013 were a step in the right direction but they were temporary and more must be done. At the same time we can act on the principles that have helped make America economically strong, which is one of the reasons why I believe a balanced budget amendment is an imperative.

As I said at my announcement that I would not seek reelection, by these and other means I will work from outside the Senate to make sure that the institution, and the government of which it is an integral part, do not continue to be crippled by the dysfunction I felt compelled to leave behind in 2013.

Part One

Chapter 1

The Decision

Over the course of the 112th Congress I came to the regrettable conclusion that the gridlock and ineffectiveness I was witnessing in the Senate and throughout the legislative and executive branches of government were not liable to diminish in the short term and would likely survive the presidential election in 2012 regardless of who won. Each side still had to contend with the pressures coming from its political base that were forcing the parties to extremes that did not reflect the electorate as a whole. Between them, the President and Congress were proving unable to craft bipartisan solutions to the nation's serious problems. My disillusionment grew until I reached a point of circumspection. I started to wonder if I couldn't make a greater contribution by taking my fight in a different direction.

My frustration reached new heights during the year-long debt ceiling fiasco of 2011. We not only failed to resolve real long-term issues of deficits and the national debt, but demonstrated our endemic dysfunction by passing on responsibility for a longer-lasting agreement, first to a so-called super committee and then to a lame-duck session of Congress where the "fiscal cliff" agreement, itself a temporary Band-Aid, was passed. My final vote in the Senate was on this measure, at 2 A.M. on New Year's Day, January 1, 2013.

It wasn't that a light went on in my head and I made an abrupt decision to leave the Senate. As I traveled around my state and the country, people consistently inquired if government was capable of change and what it was going to take to effect reform. I started to look down the road at the prospects for the future and began to consider what the next six years would bring in view of what had transpired over the last few. After every election there were fewer legislators left on Capitol Hill who shared my point of view on consensus-building. The thought gradually occurred to me: perhaps I could make a greater impact working outside the Senate.

At the center of the decision were the people: the people of Maine; the staff who had worked for me so loyally, and their families, who depended on them; and my colleagues in the Senate. All these groups had been like extended families.

Serving in public office is not a job; it involves every element of your existence and consumes all of your waking hours. In the fall of 2011, I was still committed to running for reelection. I was sure I was going to have a primary challenge and I had to be ready for it. Preparing for an election is not something you can set aside—if you stop running hard, you're finished—so I had to consider my future while I was moving full steam ahead. If I was going to serve again, I had to be completely certain it was the right thing to do. I couldn't have accomplished what I had over the last years without bringing the full measure of my devotion to the effort. I knew I had the energy to continue to serve. I was conditioned to serve, it's what my life had been . . . and yet, and yet.

Fortunately, my husband, John "Jock" McKernan, not only knows me, but he is intimately familiar with the unique mix of pressures and rewards that make up public life. He served in the Maine House of Representatives when I was there in the early 1970s. He was a two-term congressman representing Maine's 1st Congressional District from 1983 to 1987 and was twice elected governor of Maine, in 1986 and 1990. I was able to discuss everything with Jock, but for a long time, he was the only person who was aware I was contemplating a departure.

As the holidays approached, the calendar started closing in. If I was not going to run for reelection, I had to announce my decision in time to allow for other candidates to collect the necessary signatures to run, a requirement I had already fulfilled. There were a number of outstanding candidates on our side and there were two Democrats in Congress who could potentially join the race. I gave myself a dead-line—I'd have to decide hard on the heels of returning from the February recess and make a public announcement either way.

This was obviously a life-changing decision for me, and I constantly weighed the pros and cons of leaving or staying. I discussed my thinking with my family and a few close friends; one was Lynn Martin with whom I served in Congress for ten years and who later became secretary of labor for President George H. W. Bush. Having been in the Illinois State legislature, Congress, and in the cabinet, she has represented the best of public service as well as being an exceptional role model for women. Lynn has a breadth of experience in both the public and private sectors so she understood the dimensions of the decision I was making. She offered tremendous insight and perspective, and her advice was invaluable.

On February 21, a week before my self-imposed cutoff, I flew to New York for some fund-raising events. All the while I was preoccupied and immersed in the decision. Before I left, Jock and I talked with his brother Bob, who has been the media consultant for all of my Senate campaigns and most of my House races. Bob has always been an important part of Jock's and my own campaigns, so we wanted to update him on my current thinking. Likewise, I talked with my great friend and adviser Sharon Miller and her husband, Dan. I've known Sharon and Dan for decades, since they rented a ski place I owned at Sugarloaf in the 1970s. Sharon had been Jock's chief of staff and had run his campaigns before she joined me and ran my first Senate campaign. Sharon remained a political adviser for both of my subsequent campaigns, as well as this one. The Millers were surprised to be talking about such a thing with me, but, then, so was I.

Coincidentally, Jock's and my friend David Shaw was on the flight from Portland, Maine, to New York. I saw him at the baggage carousel at LaGuardia Airport and told him I could give him a ride into town. Somewhere on the Grand Central Parkway, his cell phone rang and it happened to be someone I knew, too. David said, "Olympia, Richard says 'hi.'" But I was looking out the window, completely lost in my thoughts. I heard David say, "Olympia says 'hi,' too." (The next day, David, along with his wife, Glenn Close, attended a luncheon sponsored by the organization No Labels, at which I was speaking. I told David I was more focused than I had been the day before.)

After I dropped David at his apartment, I spent the rest of the day going to meetings. At 6 P.M., one of the people I met with said, "My assistant tells me it's your birthday. I hope you're doing something fun tonight." To which I replied, "Well, I'm going out to dinner with someone I've never met before, and tomorrow I have a series of fund-raisers."

The evening turned out to be very enjoyable. My fund-raiser, Claire Holloway, and I had dinner with Nancy Lieberman, a top lawyer in New York who had rebounded with incredible courage from a disastrous, life-altering skiing accident. She hosted us for dinner at the New York Yacht Club. The club is housed in an impressive Beaux-Arts stone edifice in midtown Manhattan. The interior is ornate and grand; sitting in the wood-lined dining room, it's easy to imagine you're having dinner within a large sailing vessel from yesteryear.

I was somewhat taken aback by a turn in the dinner conversation. The three of us had been talking about our jobs, and unprompted by anything I had said, Nancy suggested that I didn't have to keep running, that there were other contributions I could make outside of the Senate. She commented on the corrosive nature of the current political environment. It wasn't that she wanted me to leave Congress, but like so many others, she reflected on how frustrating it must have become for someone like me who is so results oriented.

As she talked I thought, "Wow, this is incredible." Unbeknownst to her, she was voicing many of the things I'd been thinking, and I'd never met her before. Her words underscored the reality that there could be another life for me outside of elective office, one that could be productive and rewarding.

Several weeks later, after my announcement, Nancy emailed me to say she'd miss me in the Senate, but she understood my reasons for leaving. She lamented that there were so few "moderates" left, and said, "I hope it wasn't anything I said at dinner!" I assured her it wasn't, but told her that the conversation had been very helpful to me.

The crowded concourses of New York City's LaGuardia Airport are not places associated with making important decisions. At six o'clock the following evening, a Wednesday, I was there, alone with my thoughts and a few thousand other travelers. I was about to go stand in some line when I saw someone in the middle distance who looked like Jock. I thought, from here, that man looks like Jock. I knew he was traveling himself, but he was returning to our home in Maine from California through another airport. Still, I called out to the man once, twice, and a third time, at which point he heard me and turned around. I saw it was indeed Jock.

I was so happy to see him. I asked Jock what he was doing here, and he said he'd changed his plans and booked a seat on my flight back to Maine to surprise me. We checked our bags, passed through security, and went to look for something to eat. He asked me what I was thinking, and I said I was still going through all of it in my mind. Jock put his arm around me and said, "Why not just run again?" He could tell I needed some respite from the mental machinations I was putting myself through, and in that moment, I felt a tremendous sense of relief.

We went home, and by the next morning I was right back where I'd been the day before, and leaning toward announcing I was not going to run.

Decision day turned out to be Tuesday, February 28. Jock and I had returned to Washington, and I had discussed my conclusion one last time with John Richter, my chief of staff. I had John prepare two statements, one for me running; one not, and in truth, I really didn't decide which one I was going to put out until that day.

My primary concern was that my staff hear the news from me directly, so exactly how the decision would be rolled out was of paramount importance. I concluded that we would inform the staffs in both Washington and Maine, where I had six constituent offices, simultaneously that afternoon. There were Republican primaries that day in Michigan and Arizona and no votes were scheduled in the Senate, so I wasn't going to be called away at an inopportune moment.

The public announcement would be disseminated in the form of a press release. But before it was issued, I made a few phone calls to people I wanted to make sure heard the news from me personally. While I did so, my chief of staff arranged to have my personal staff as well as those on the Small Business, Commerce, and Intelligence committees gather in my conference room, and my staff in Maine to convene on a conference call.

I first called my brother, John Bouchles, with whom I'm close and who has provided great support and counsel to me over the years. He was very sympathetic. He realized it must have been a very difficult choice to make and he was extremely supportive. Quickly, he called me back and said that people would want to know what led to this surprise conclusion. What should he say? I quickly led him through my rationale.

After that, I had to scramble quickly to reach as many of my family members as possible in a very short period of time to inform them of my decision either by phone or email before the news became public. My cousins—Toni Spirounias, Duke Goranites, Georgia Chomas, Kiki Harrington, and Peter Goranites—were like sisters and brothers to me when I was growing up in my aunt Mary and uncle Jim's house, where I lived after I lost my parents. I reached Georgia by phone, and Jock was able to call Peter and email my other cousins. Georgia was concerned about me. "Are you certain this is what you want to do?" she asked, and I told her that under the circumstances, it was. She, too, was loving and supportive. She emailed me passages from Ecclesiastes, the message of which was "There is a time for everything."

Next, I called the Republican Minority Leader Mitch McConnell (R-KY). I've always given Mitch tremendous credit for his preparedness, discipline, and capacity for strategic thinking—especially in managing the divisions within our Republican conference. After I concluded telling Mitch that I would be departing the Senate, the first words out of his mouth were "goodness gracious." He told me that if I stayed, I would be at the peak of my power and could help to build bipartisan support for legislation by reaching across the aisle. But I explained my reasoning and the fact that I'd wrestled with the decision for several weeks. Shortly after, he called me back to find out if it was too late. Was there any possibility that I could change my mind or had I already made any public announcement? By this point, I had. The news was out. Mitch said he was very sorry I was leaving, but respected what I was doing. He was extremely gracious, and he thanked me for my service.

When I told my friend and colleague from Maine, Senator Susan Collins, she said the news was "devastating" but that she understood. Susan and I have similar political philosophies, we have worked closely on issues significant to our home state, and we formed the first (and, to date, only) elected duo of Republican women senators from a single state. I'd actually served with Susan's father, Don, too, in the state legislature. Incredibly, Don, and Susan's mother, Pat, were also both mayors of Susan's hometown of Caribou, Maine, and they were early supporters of mine when I first ran for Congress.

I also spoke with the governor of Maine, Paul LePage. His reaction: "This can't be true!" When I told him that unfortunately it was, he wished me well and said how much I would be missed.

There were other calls I wanted to make but there just wasn't time. We had done a good job of keeping the news in house, but once it started getting out, there was too little time to reach everyone. Jock was able to call his brother Bob; our close friend and Jock's former law partner, Bob Moore; and Sharon Miller to let them know we were making the announcement at 5 P.M. Jock also told my campaign manager, Justin Brasell, about the announcement. Considering what was at stake for Justin, he reacted with grace and professionalism, which I will forever appreciate.

The moment had arrived to break the news to my staff. They were now all assembled in what's called the Ohio Room, a majestic conference room adjacent to my suite of offices in the Russell Senate Office Building. Maine inherited it thanks to the good graces of my friend former Senator Trent Lott (R-MS), who was the chair of the Rules Committee, which has jurisdiction over the assignment of office space. Since Republicans lost the Senate majority with the 2006 elections, Trent's chairmanship was about to conclude. Trent called me and asked if I would like some extra real estate and I said absolutely! Given the limited space available to senators I certainly welcomed and appreciated his gesture. We used the room constantly over the years, but never like this.

The walk down the hallway to the Ohio Room seemed like the longest I'd ever made. As I opened the door, I felt as though I was in a fog. Everyone I worked with on my staff in Washington was seated along the lengthy conference table, and in chairs set against the walls of the room.

"As you all well know, I've been working hard and gearing up for months to run again for reelection," I began. "I frankly never thought twice that I wouldn't be, and that's why I've been going full bore, as all of you have. We've geared up, we've been ready to go, and I have no doubt that we would have been successful, in no small part because of the great work all of you have done on behalf of the people of Maine.

"This is also the point where it comes into sharp focus what it will actually mean to serve for another six years in the Senate. I also just celebrated my sixty-fifth birthday, a sort of milestone occasion that also prompts a lot of soul-searching. And this is very difficult to say, but I've decided that I will not be a candidate for reelection to the United States Senate."

The staff saw where I was headed as soon as I started talking, but hearing the actual words was another matter. I could see looks of deep sadness on their faces as I went on to explain my rationale. I spoke of what a privilege it had been, serving Maine and the country and working on the committees, researching and tackling the issues. And I'd done it with them.

Everyone in the room had made plans assuming I would run. The young people I could see in the room, and those who listened on the other end of the phone in my state offices, were hardworking, smart, and loyal, and as dedicated to public service as I am. Many cried, and I recognized that I was breaking hearts. "I know this is not only a life-changing event for me, but clearly for all of you as well. You are truly the best," I said, "and I will do whatever I can to help you."

When I finished, everyone applauded. As we left the room, one staffer said, "We respect your decision and we stand behind you one hundred percent." Others echoed that sentiment, and I was deeply moved and humbled.

You don't serve in public office as long as I have without outstanding staff, and I have been extremely fortunate to have had extraordinarily talented men and women who truly represented the very best and brightest this nation has to offer. In particular I've benefited from the contributions of four long-standing chiefs of staff with a combined tenure of nearly seventy-three years of institutional experience and dedicated service not only to me, but to Maine and the nation.

In the House, Kirk Walder served me ably, first as my legislative assistant and then as my chief of staff for a dozen years. Kevin Raye has provided me with immeasurable contributions throughout my career. He became my chief of staff in 1995 after I was elected to the Senate. In fact, I first became familiar with Kevin when at the age of fifteen, he wrote me a letter when I was in the Maine Senate offering to volunteer for my first campaign for Congress. In 2004, he was elected to the Maine Senate, and, in 2012, he completed a very successful term as Senate president, where he was hailed for his bipartisan leadership, which produced exceptional results for the state.

Jane Calderwood started with me in my Bangor district office and over the span of more than twenty years became invaluable in leading my legislative staff and, later, my entire operation—she was a master of the process and the art of getting things done. And John Richter began working for me as a staff assistant in my Auburn district office just over six months after graduating from college—continuing on to become my speechwriter and my chief of staff for nine years, providing me with twenty-three years of exemplary service.

Once the press release went out announcing my decision, the phones started ringing. One of the first calls was from our wonderful friend, President George H. W. Bush, who has always been extraordinarily gracious. In this instance, he was no different. Jock and I have known President Bush and First Lady Barbara Bush since before he was Vice President. We visited with them at their summer home at Walker's Point in Kennebunkport and Jock played tennis and golf with President Bush when he was in Congress and then governor and for years after.

We consider knowing the Bushes to be one of the greatest privileges of our lives. They have been tremendous supporters of both of us, frequently hosting fund-raisers for me and Jock during our reelection campaigns. "Tell me this isn't true," he said when I came on the phone. His voice was tinged with disappointment, and I felt badly telling him that, yes, I'm sorry that it is. He added, "Does Jock know about this?" and I said, "Yes!" I also received a heartfelt note from President George W. Bush, which was an extremely thoughtful gesture.

President Obama called and also issued a statement. He was most generous in thanking me for my dedicated service to the country and expressing that he had valued working with me. Vice President Biden, with whom I've had a warm and long-standing relationship, also called, and we had a conversation reminiscing about how much had changed over the years.

I also couldn't have been more pleased to hear from my good friend Hillary Clinton, who is an extraordinary role model for women in America. I've had an enduring respect for our trailblazing former secretary of state ever since Jock and President Clinton were serving as governors and Hillary and I met as members of the National Governors Association's spouses group. Hillary's reaction to my announcement was "Olympia!" and I said, "I know, Hillary. As you can imagine, it was a tough decision." She pointed out that, among the four of us, we had more than a hundred years of public service. We lamented the loss of centrist voices in the Congress, as well as the polarized political environment.

Senator Orrin Hatch (R-UT) called me almost immediately. We'd worked together for years on the Senate Finance Committee; he had crossed the party aisle when he believed in a cause, such as working with Ted Kennedy (D-MA) on the S-CHIP program to guarantee health insurance for low-income children. Orrin told me I would be missed in the Senate and asked if anything would change my mind.

I was very gratified to hear from a number of other colleagues with whom I'd had a long and productive bipartisan legislative relationship, including Barbara Mikulski (D-MD), Dianne Feinstein (D-CA), Lisa Murkowski (R-AK), and Mary Landrieu (D-LA). Senator Jay Rockefeller (D-WV) told me he was "mournful," a characterization he's repeated many times since. Many colleagues also wrote to me following my announcement, including Majority Leader Harry Reid, who sent me a nice note, which I very much appreciated.

I received a very gracious call from former Senate Majority Leader and Maine congressional delegation colleague George

Mitchell, whose seat I won after he chose not to seek reelection in 1994. Even as he was leading the Senate, there was no issue critical to Maine that was too small for his attention. George is exceptionally talented and highly accomplished, and not surprisingly has had a remarkable and distinguished career. It was also gratifying to hear from other former Senate colleagues as well, including Don Nichols, who had added me to his Whip team to ensure diverse voices were heard within the party, Chris Dodd, with whom I worked closely over the years in both the House and Senate, Max Cleland, a true American hero, with whom I served on the Armed Services Committee, and George Voinovich, who garnered a record of fiscal responsibility at all levels of government in which he served. In a subsequent visit to my office, Trent Lott assured me that, yes, there is life after the Senate! Governor Mitt Romney also left me a nice message, which I very much appreciated, as he was in the midst of a difficult primary season.

The following Tuesday, I spoke to my fellow Republicans at our weekly policy lunch. I said, "I know this has come as a great surprise, and I didn't intend it to be. Indeed in many ways it was a surprise to me, too. But in reflecting on the fifty-six years of combined public service Jock and I have given and contemplating the next six years, I felt that at this point I could best contribute in other ways."

In these days, I was overwhelmed by the responses I got from people in Maine, and the tributes that described my leaving as a loss for the state and the country. There is no greater gift than the honor of trust that Mainers had placed in me. When I went to the Senate floor for the first time after my announcement, it was uncharted territory, and I was immensely gratified by the graciousness and warmth with which I was received by many of my colleagues.

So many people said they expected me to be in the Senate for many more years, and although I have never taken electoral success for granted, for a long time, so did I. During my first post-announcement press conference in Maine, I was explaining my decision to a packed room, with my family on the dais. In the midst of the questioning, Kim Block, an anchor for a local news broadcast in Portland, said she had a question. "Actually I have two questions," she said. "First, are you sure?"

I was.

I would stay only for as long as I could fulfill my responsibilities as a problem-solver, and that wasn't possible anymore. CBS *Face the Nation* host Bob Schieffer summed it up that Sunday morning, March 4, when he said, "What does it say about the state of our government and politics when serious people [like Olympia Snowe] conclude that serving in the United States Senate is no longer worth their time and effort? That's the part that should worry the rest of us."

It was imperative we return Congress to something more closely resembling the institution I joined in 1979. Clearly, something was terribly wrong in Washington.

Chapter 2

2011 and 2012—
Two Very Bad Years

For most of our history, despite crises and difficulties, Congress, with its diverse and even conflicting viewpoints, has found a way to compromise and find the means of solving the major challenges facing our country. The rules of the House and Senate have required the two parties to come together through meticulous consideration and debate. But recently, and especially in 2011 and 2012, those rules were used to drive the two sides apart and therefore make problem-solving impossible.

When the Constitution was written in 1787, James Madison and the other founders worked out a specific vision for each chamber of the legislative branch. The Senate and the House of Representatives would carry out the will of the people, but each chamber was carefully constructed, with different forms that matched their functions.

Article I, Section 2 of the Constitution created a House of Representatives designed to be, as *Federalist* No. 52 noted, a "scheme of representation as a substitute for a meeting of the citizens in person." Madison regarded it as "particularly essential" that the House "have an immediate dependence on, and an intimate sympathy with, the people," to have, as *Federalist* No. 55 noted, one body comprising a "class of citizens" that will sympathize most with the "feelings of the mass of the people."

They had a very different goal for the Senate and took a very different approach. The requirements of Article I, Section 3 were deliberate: equal representation, statewide appointment (changed by the Seventeenth Amendment in 1913 to elections), six-year terms, nine years of citizenship, and at least thirty years of age. *Federalist* No. 62 explained that the equality of representation in the Senate was the "result of compromise between the opposite pretensions of the large and the small States," and that the statewide nature of the office would ensure that unlike representatives, who would be elected by "the crowded inhabitants of a small district," senators would be less subject to the "infection of violent passions, or to the danger of combining in pursuit of unjust measures."

I've witnessed the proper functioning of our government work firsthand, as it was adapted for the Maine House of Representatives and Maine Senate, and later in the U.S. House of Representatives and U.S. Senate. The House could react more quickly under the pressure of events, but the Senate acted as a corrective, the check and balance, to ensure any legislative response was more measured.

It was a system derived from the belief that thoughtful, well-intentioned legislators could, and would, look for ways to bridge differences. I often think of the famous saying that there are two things you never want to see made: laws and sausages. But at least laws did get made at one point, even if you didn't want to see how!

In the 112th Congress, the institution's rules and procedures were utilized selectively as one side tried to push through its legislative agenda and the other endeavored to do what it could to block it. Congress became a place of burned bridges and scorched earth when we should have been finding common ground to fix the country's real and continuing economic problems, such as high unemployment, low growth, and the massive debt that is threatening to smother us. Yes, there are often legitimate concerns—from the majority that the minority is all too frequently threatening filibusters, and from the minority that the majority won't allow amendments to a bill and too often moves to cut short debate on the first day the bill is filed. However, it's critical that both sides make a good-faith effort to make the Senate work as an institution.

Here's how much things have changed: We had 161 procedural votes to forestall a filibuster during my first term in the Senate (1995–2001) and 164 during my second term (2001–2007). In my third and final term (2007–2013) we had 276, a 71 percent increase in filibusters from my first term to my third term. There are essentially two reasons to employ this tactic: because the minority (which has been the Republican Party since 2007) is opposed to the legislation in general, and as a result of the Majority Leader not providing assurances that he or she will allow a sufficient number of minority amendments to be considered to the bill on the floor.

On a number of occasions I have not joined with my Republican colleagues in supporting filibusters that I believed were not warranted. However, any Majority Leader can circumvent the open amendment process by a practice known as "filling the amendment tree." When he is filling the tree, the Leader handpicks all amendments to be considered on the floor and either disregards the minority's amendments entirely or preselects which ones they can offer. Prior to Majority Leader Reid, who took the office in January 2007, the previous six Majority Leaders combined filled the tree 40 times over the span of 22 years. Through the end of the 112th Congress, Majority Leader Reid had filled the tree 70 times since 2007. As a result, millions of Americans represented by the senators from the minority party were effectively being silenced in the legislative process. Therefore, often the only means left for these senators to have a voice is to threaten a filibuster. In those cases, I joined with Republicans to support the cause of an open amendment process—which I believe is essential to the appropriate functioning of the Senate.

That's why it's imperative that both sides step back and figure out how to make the process work, especially as these votes typically occur in conjunction with the most important matters facing our nation. To make matters worse, when we contort the rules of the Senate, we instigate a vicious cycle, because today's majority can become tomorrow's minority and vice versa, and when the change occurs, each is tempted to employ the other's tactics.

To lend some historical context, the first "cloture" rule to end a filibuster, in 1917, called for a two-thirds majority, that is, 67 votes, and in 1975 this was revised to 60. The idea of a majority vote for cloture was raised in the "nuclear option" proposed by the Republican Majority Leader, Bill Frist, in 2005. At the time, then-Minority Leader Harry Reid said, "If there were ever an example of an abuse of power, this is it. The filibuster is the last check we have against the abuse of power in Washington."

Seven years later, now-Majority Leader Reid announced in the lame-duck session in November 2012 that he intended to use the Senate rules in the next Congress in order to reduce the power of the minority by making cloture votes a simple majority. In response, Minority Leader Mitch McConnell said, "If this is such a reasonable rule change, why not work to try to propose it on a joint basis, subject to [a] sixty-one-vote threshold?" He said that the tradition is for rules to go from Congress to Congress. "How would you feel if two years from now I have your job and my members say, why don't we get rid of the filibuster with just fifty-one votes?"

This is why rules persist from Congress to Congress.

I have another example from the 112th Congress of the perversion of Senate rules and norms. Just three months into the new session, on April 14, 2011, I had a disagreement with Majority Leader Reid on the Senate floor over an amendment I offered to a reauthorization bill on small business investment research. I had asked that we include provisions to examine the effects of any regulatory reform on small businesses. Senator Tom Coburn and I had introduced a bill—the "Small Business Regulatory Freedom Act"—in March. As former chair and then ranking member of the Small Business and Entrepreneurship Committee, small business is one of my areas of expertise, and the small business investment research had passed through the committee, so I was managing this bill for the Republicans on the floor of the Senate.

I was informed by my Small Business Committee staff director, Wally Hsueh, that there was an agreement that ten amendments to the bill—five Democratic and five Republican—would be considered and voted on when we returned from the two-week recess due to start the next day. My amendment was listed among them.

But then something unusual happened.

About twenty minutes before the Majority Leader took to the floor to formally request the unanimous consent of the Senate to concur with the agreement, he came over to tell me he was removing my amendment from the list. He mentioned that several Democratic senators, including committee chairs, did not want to take a vote on regulatory reform. A discussion followed about whether to have a Democratic alternative, but none was forthcoming. And when the Majority Leader asked for unanimous consent for which amendments would be considered and voted on after the recess, there was no mention of my measure.

It was highly unusual for a ranking member of a committee of jurisdiction not to be accommodated like this. My intention was to promote debate on regulatory reform as it affected small business— that is, considerably—and it didn't have to be my measure that facilitated it, but this was my opportunity to initiate the debate, and I wanted to take it.

The President of the Senate asked if anyone objected to the Leader's request. I had a flight that night to return to Maine for the recess, but I was determined to stay there and argue for my amendment's inclusion.

I stood. "Mr. President, I reserve the right to object," I said. "I thought we had an agreement that there would be an even number of amendments offered on both sides. And now I understand that in the request that is put forward by the Majority Leader, there are five amendments for Democrats and four amendments on our side." It should be noted that it is common practice to split the number of amendments equally, so the imbalance was all the more suspicious. "I thought my amendment would also be included in the agreement. So I am asking unanimous consent that the order be modified to include Snowe amendment No. 299."

The Leader arose and said he objected to my request. "The legislation of my friend from Maine is not relevant or germane to this legislation," he said. "In addition, her legislation has not had a hearing."

I was incredulous.

"I appreciate the comments that have been made by the Majority Leader," I said. "But to the contrary, this is very relevant to the underlying legislation," which, after all, was a small business bill—and if anyone were to ask the business community exactly what their major priority is, it would be regulatory reform. "You don't have to take too many Main Street tours to figure out what is happening on Main Street. They are struggling to survive. . . . [So] what could be more important at a time when we are struggling to create jobs in our economy, where we need to create millions of jobs if we are ever going to turn around this serious unemployment rate that is plaguing our nation today and critically affecting the personal financial well-being of all Americans?"

Moreover, I observed that we had numerous hearings within the Small Business Committee in which regulation was discussed. In fact, we'd held a hearing five months earlier specifically titled "Assessing the Regulatory and Administrative Burdens on America's Small Businesses." Moreover, the Small Business Administration's own Chief Counsel of Advocacy testified before the Small Business Committee in November 2010 that, "[a]s Chief Counsel, my top priority is and will continue to be ensuring that the voice of small business is heard in the regulatory process."

"As I look through the number of amendments that are going to be offered to vote on in the Majority Leader's [request], many of these amendments have not had hearings, either; they have not been the subject of very specific hearings. The point is, everyone has had the opportunity and would have the opportunity to review this legislation and debate it amply," I said. "I am just surprised that there is a new standard here," because hearings had never been a prerequisite for voting on amendments.

I also pointed out that in the fall of 2010, we had a small business jobs bill, part of which was a $30 billion lending program that was seriously flawed, but it had not been the subject of one Senate hearing. "If members of the Senate don't want to vote for the amendment, they don't have to vote for the amendment," I said. "[I'm] just saying: please allow us to have a vote on this specific amendment just like the others that are in the Majority Leader's unanimous consent request. That is all I am asking."

Ultimately, because the Majority Leader was not able to secure unanimous consent for his plan, he postponed the entire bill until we returned from recess. We had nothing but time, but apparently the Leader hadn't been prepared to utilize it and allow consideration of an important issue.

When the Senate resumed consideration of the small business innovation research legislation on May 4, I again spoke on the Senate floor and lamented what I called the "disturbing trend [in the Senate] over the past several years of disregarding the minority rights and flat out disallowing votes on amendments." "Voting is our primary responsibility," I said, "as are amendments to flesh out the legislative process. We should have had a vote on the legislation I was offering as an amendment . . . to reduce the burden on our nation's small businesses."

But regrettably, that vote would have to wait. When it was finally held a month later as an amendment on another bill, it garnered support of the majority of United States senators. Yet, believe it or not, because of the quirks of the process, it still didn't pass the Senate.

In early June of 2011, Mitch McConnell, the Minority Leader, asked me if I wanted him to offer what was essentially my regulatory reform legislation as an amendment to the Economic Development Revitalization Act. An open amendment process had become a rare occasion, but in this instance the Minority Leader had right of first recognition after the Majority Leader, so he could get the measure considered. Regulatory reform was a priority for Republicans given its critical importance to small businesses, which are central to creating desperately needed jobs.

With my concurrence, the Minority Leader called up the amendment on my behalf on June 8. The next morning, the Majority Leader called me to say he was calling for a vote on my amendment at noon, which was about two hours away. "Why would you do that?" I asked. Harry said that I'd had opportunity to speak on my amendment but hadn't done so, so he was moving to table, or kill, it.

I didn't understand the sudden hurry, or why my amendment had been targeted since there were other amendments pending that had not been debated or voted on. I realized I would only have a few minutes at most to discuss my amendment, so I ran over to the floor of the Senate and argued my case with the Majority Leader and his staff.

As we were talking through the issue, Joe Lieberman (Ind-CT) joined the discussion. Joe was chairman of the Homeland Security Committee, which had jurisdiction over regulatory reform, including my proposal, and he provided assurances that his committee would hold hearings on the issue and I would be able to testify on my legislation. At this point, the Majority Leader relented, but only partially. He offered me a choice: I could have a majority vote at noon on a tabling motion to my amendment, which under the rules is not debatable—or have a debate, but then be subject to a cloture vote on the legislation at two o'clock, which would require sixty votes to pass. I chose the latter, which at least provided an opportunity to secure support during the lunchtime break.

An issue is elevated and highlighted when it is discussed on the floor of the Senate. I wanted to make my points into the record, which I did, and there was healthy bipartisan debate. Mitch McConnell came onto the floor while I was speaking and sat at the Minority Leader's desk and listened intently to the debate. It was a signal of his support and that of the Republican conference.

My amendment garnered a majority vote, 52-44, but the amendment itself was not adopted because we did not reach the sixty-vote threshold. The good news was, we got the majority of the Senate on record in favor of the amendment. The bad news was, it was defeated. This was all the more unfortunate because I supported the underlying legislation for the Small Business Innovation Research Program, and had done so since the program's inception in 1982. Chairman Lieberman upheld his promise to schedule a hearing along with the ranking member, Senator Susan Collins, which took place in June 2011. A number of different measures were discussed, and also testifying that day were Senators Mark Warner (D-VA), David Vitter (R-LA), and Pat Roberts (R-KS), as well as Cass Sunstein, who was administrator of the White House Office of Information and Regulatory Affairs. But no further action was taken on the Senate floor by the time I left the Senate in January 2013.

The system of making legislation has regressed in other ways. We also no longer have a series of items on the agenda that both parties have agreed to address in concert with the President. More and more, bills are brought to the floor for votes with very little real work having been done in the committees. Committee hearings have become more theatrical rather than practical, designed to convey more of a political message than develop concrete solutions.

Senate Finance Committee Chairman Max Baucus (D-MT) and I had a number of conversations over the past several years to discuss

topical and critical issues like tax reform and entitlement programs. These subjects are squarely under the purview of Finance,
and Max has always fought to ensure that the committee would remain at the forefront of developing legislation in its areas of expertise. That the relevancy of the Finance Committee was even a topic
for discussion is a sad commentary on the state of affairs in the Senate, given that it has jurisdiction over about two-thirds of the federal
budget, including taxes, Social Security, and Medicare. In fact, I recall
in early 2011, at the beginning of the 112th Congress, Max and I
were scheduled to meet one-on-one, and my staff and I anticipated a
discussion of specific priorities for the year. As it turned out, we also
talked about the Congress in general and the importance of main-
taining the integral role of our committees in the legislative process.

In the summer of 2012, Chairman Baucus and ranking member
Orrin Hatch agreed to work on reducing tax "extenders"; that is, tax
provisions that were continually extended only for temporary periods of time, which meant that they had to be constantly revisited,
instead of providing individuals and businesses certainty with perma-
nency.

Max, with whom I've had an excellent working relationship
over the years, met with me on this issue on June 27. I said I wholeheartedly agreed we should move forward with a committee debate
and vote (otherwise known as a "markup") on an extenders bill. But
I also wondered why the leadership hadn't asked the committees of
jurisdiction to at least begin working through relevant portions of
the considerable list of items we would have to deal with later in the
lame-duck session—something I had urged the Majority Leader to
do in a letter back in April.

On August 2, the Finance Committee held a bipartisan markup
and sorted through changes among the members to make the whole
bill acceptable to the majority of the committee. The bill was voted
out by a wide margin (19 to 5), with Orrin Hatch stating, "This legislation isn't perfect, but it is an essential step towards the ultimate
goal of comprehensive tax reform." Chairman Baucus was hopeful of

getting the legislation to the floor of the Senate, yet the bill was never placed on the Senate agenda, as would have been customary in sessions past on such a major initiative.

The tax code was last overhauled in 1986 and thousands of changes have been made since, with the result that the code is now more than seventy-two thousand pages long. Here, and with so much other legislation, we fashion short-term Band-Aids to avert crises. The temporary nature of our fixes is in danger of becoming a permanent feature of legislation and the tax code is a massive paper monument to what one witness before the Finance Committee described as our permanent, temporary tax code.

In his book *The Debt Bomb,* my Finance Committee colleague Senator Coburn describes how exasperated we were during the 112th Congress. He quotes me as saying, at our end-of-year meeting in 2011, "Are we even going to fix this? . . . We've known all this was coming. . . . It's preposterous. We should use this occasion to do something right so we aren't embarrassed we wasted the last two years of America's life." But I'm chagrined to say we couldn't do anything, and once again we entered what Tom called the "annual holiday train wreck," when bills were delayed to the very last minute or shunted aside entirely.

These strategies and tactics have created a historically inactive Congress. The 112th Congress passed only 283 public laws. The 80th Congress (1947–49), which President Harry Truman decried as the "do-nothing Congress," passed 906. I hesitate to think how Truman would have described us! We had devolved into an ever-more partisan stalemate.

As far as the disposition of the 112th Congress was concerned, the writing had been on the wall for some time. Health care reform, which dominated the 111th Congress, certainly exemplified the partisan breakdown, and the package that came to be known as

"Obamacare" eventually passed the House and Senate with no Republican support at all.

President Obama was able to utilize a sixty-vote Senate block, until the election of Senator Scott Brown (R-MA) in January 2010 ended the Democrats' filibuster-proof majority. Elections in 2010 left the House in Republican hands and the Senate with a Democratic majority. With little chance of cross-party agreement, legislating became guerrilla warfare, marked by cloture motions and filibusters, legitimate devices in the senatorial arsenal but hardly the path to well-crafted legislation to attract bipartisan support.

Nevertheless, after the election, the lame-duck session in December 2010 did signal some encouraging progress. In fact, a December 22 article in the *Atlantic* called it "the most productive lame duck session since World War II—and maybe ever." I was one of the thirteen Republicans who joined with Democrats to ratify the "New START" Treaty with Russia on nuclear missile reduction. I was also one of a smaller group to vote in favor of repealing "Don't Ask, Don't Tell." Both votes seemed likely to indicate that with more collegiality and bipartisanship, we'd get off to a strong start in 2011, focus on the debt ceiling, and pass a budget resolution.

But the lame-duck session was in the end a false dawn, because what emerged over the course of the next session was a political sideshow. The debt ceiling crisis that dominated the legislative agenda of the first eight months of 2011 was a manufactured scenario around which everyone could politically posture but which jeopardized nothing less than our entire economy. This was an episode that, more than any other, demonstrated to me that government was broken and required drastic change.

The federal government's debt has been governed by a statutory limit since the Second Liberty Bond Act of 1917 financed the country's entry into World War I. This debt limit or ceiling has been raised in other times of national crisis (near the end of World War II, in 1945, it was set at $300 billion). It has been raised more than seventy times since 1962 and has been raised every year since 2001, as the federal government has routinely spent far more than it takes in in revenue. Borrowing grew to such an extent that by mid-2011, in the midst of the debt ceiling crisis, the government borrowed 40 cents of every dollar it spent.

In January 2011, Treasury Secretary Tim Geithner informed Harry Reid that the debt limit, set in February of 2010 at $14.29 trillion (!), currently stood at $13.95 trillion. If Congress did not extend the limit by March 31, Secretary Geithner warned, the Treasury would be unable to borrow more money to meet existing obligations. Such a default would have far greater impact than the government shutdowns of 1995 and 1996, which occurred after Congress failed to enact appropriations bills. The default would create, in Secretary Geithner's words, "catastrophic damage to the economy, potentially much more harmful than the effects of the financial crisis of 2008 and 2009." The cost of all borrowing would rise; stock prices and home values would fall; job losses and business failures would increase. The "safe-haven status" of U.S. Treasuries and the standing of the dollar would be damaged and the government would soon be unable to cut checks for military and government salaries, veterans' benefits, Social Security and Medicare payments, or pay the bills to keep the country running. Secretary Geithner called a default "unthinkable."

And yet, with March 31 less than three months away, no sooner had the Senate reconvened on Wednesday, January 5, than we went on recess as scheduled on that Friday, and we stayed home through January 24. On March 17, another temporary spending measure bought a few more weeks. Secretary Geithner wrote a second letter to Congress in April and a third in May asking for an increase in the debt ceiling. Despite widespread agreement in the Senate that legislation was needed to reduce spending while increasing the ceiling, on May 16, as anticipated, the Treasury announced that the ceiling of $14.29 trillion had been reached. Secretary Geithner said that the country could get by on "extraordinary measures" until August 2, but if no action was taken by then, the United States would default for the first time in its history.

That we were even at this point was proof of a broken system. We weren't passing budgets, reducing our spending, or even approving appropriations bills to fund the government on time, which led us to the brink of a government shutdown in April 2011 because, four months into the year, we still hadn't finalized the budget numbers for our federal spending, which should have been completed by October 1, 2010, the beginning of the fiscal year!

I had the benefit, or some might say the burden, of knowing how difficult jobs could get done when legislators from both sides actually sat together around a table. I had experienced such a process when I was first in the House. In the early 1980s, America was experiencing double-digit inflation, double-digit unemployment, and an astronomical prime lending rate of 20 percent. President Reagan recognized the value of building a coalition of moderate Republicans and conservative Democrats to pass a budget that was a cornerstone of his bold economic recovery plan.

Republicans were aware of President Reagan's efforts to reach out to a number of Democrats—the conservative-to-moderate group that was known as the "Boll Weevils," and to those of us as moderate northeast Republicans, called the "Gypsy Moths" (somewhat playfully named after the insects that were plaguing the northern parts of the country), who had joined together as a counterweight to get our voice in the room.

As a result, we negotiated budgets together to help reconcile our political and regional differences and ensure that no one region bore a disproportionate burden of spending reductions. We had to scale down spending in the face of mounting deficits. Driven by the uncertain economic times, we felt an urgency and an obligation to act given America's perilous position.

For months an interesting cross section of members of the House from both sides met in Leader Bob Michel's office suite almost daily, along with Trent Lott, who as the whip was responsible for building the bipartisan coalitions necessary to secure the votes essential for passing President Reagan's economic recovery plans.

Among those on our side was Jack Kemp, an architect of the Kemp-Roth tax cut of 1981, and the ranking member of the House Appropriations Committee, Representative Silvio Conte, a moderate Republican from Massachusetts. Also in the room were legislators like Congressman John Breaux (D-LA) and then-Democratic Congressman Buddy Roemer, as well as Congressman Bill Green, a moderate Republican from New York, and Congressman Carl Pursell, a moderate Republican from Michigan.

For the meetings, the long table would be piled high with stacks of papers and we'd literally roll up our sleeves and go through every point of the budget, line by line. Office of Management and Budget Director David Stockman would present different policy options on every budget "function," such as education, national defense, and transportation, so we could agree to targeted spending reductions that were acceptable to a majority around the table.

In reaching an agreement, we would engage in vigorous economic debates. As I mentioned in a speech at the time, "I met with budget-conscious Democrats and fellow Republicans to hammer out a workable, bipartisan budget." So open was the process that I was able to put my points directly to the President with a phone call. I urged that the Defense Department exercise self-discipline. "We'll keep our budget commitments on defense spending—all we ask is that the White House do likewise." We managed to conduct extremely substantive deliberations, the likes of which are rarely seen today.

After the budget resolution passed, the respective authorizing committees were then charged with determining how they would adjust their policies to reach the figures required for each function. The committees could develop their own alternatives so long as the bottom-line numbers in the budget resolution were ultimately achieved.

Reaching the bottom line was achieved by means of a thorough and vigorous legislative process. It required reconciliations that would modify major parts of entitlement programs, but the rounds of debate that preceded these negotiations could build the coalitions that made it possible to pass the final budget through the House and Senate. We were all involved and invested in the process, and had experienced how the measures were assembled.

Fast-forward thirty years.

Through the spring and summer of 2011, the rancorous posturing on both sides obscured what, in my opinion, were the real issues surrounding the debt ceiling. While the President had requested that the ceiling be raised another $2.4 trillion, there was no plan to reduce deficits and debt over time. No mechanisms were established to ensure that Congress would actually tackle this issue if we were to raise the debt ceiling.

Even as the debt ceiling deadline approached, we had failed to address any substantive solution in either the House or the Senate. Consideration was forestalled in anticipation of the potential of a proposal emerging from the "grand bargain" negotiations between President Obama and Speaker of the House John Boehner (R-OH). Even the President's own Simpson-Bowles Commission Report, released in December 2010, and which outlined ways of reducing the debt by $4 trillion, was all but ignored when it fell short of the supermajority required for it to be reported to Congress for a vote. The President and the leadership could have agreed to make Simpson-Bowles a basis for congressional action.

By the end of July, the country was running out of money. A well-publicized factoid made news: the computer company Apple had more cash in the bank than Uncle Sam.

There was significant disappointment that a grand bargain wasn't achievable, but both the President and the Speaker were facing political cross-currents and deep divisions not only within the country, but within the Congress. These forces regrettably created a situation on both sides which quashed any potential for agreement.

I served with John Boehner in my final two terms in the House and know he is solutions oriented. When he said in November of last year that he is the "most reasonable, responsible person here in Washington," I believe he was truly dedicated to reaching an accord. But in truth, both sides of the aisle face problems whenever you're trying to steer an institution with a significant number of new members and a fractious caucus. That's one reason why the grand bargain attempt is a prime example of where vigorous and sustained public input has the potential to produce a more positive outcome. If Americans weigh in and speak out overwhelmingly in "real time" to demand results while negotiations are occurring, that gives substantial impetus to overcome the natural tug from those at each end of the political spectrum and chart a course for constructive compromise.

The President and congressional leaders of both parties finally came to an agreement on July 31. The House passed a Budget Control Act, which ratcheted back spending by $917 billion, increased the debt ceiling by $900 billion to $14.694 trillion, and set up the Joint Select Committee on Deficit Reduction—known hereafter as the super committee. It was charged with agreeing on a package to reduce the federal budget deficit by at least $1.5 trillion. If it failed, automatic spending cuts of $1.2 trillion, balanced between defense and domestic programs and otherwise known as "sequestration," would be triggered on January 1, 2013. When your remedy to head off disaster is to form a committee, you know you're in trouble. The House version formed the foundation of the final act, which passed the Senate and was signed into law on August 2.

I was in a state of disbelief at the cavalier attitude that prevailed on Capitol Hill following the vote. The crisis had been averted at the eleventh hour, but we had not forged a solution that would foster confidence with the financial markets and the American people. And incredibly, as soon as the debt ceiling was raised, it was as though the smell of jet fumes permeated the Capitol, beckoning senators and House members to Reagan National Airport for flights home for the monthlong August recess.

The day following the vote I was in the Republican Senate Cloakroom, a long, narrow, and ornate room leading off the back of the chamber and lined with wingback chairs. It is normally a place of considerable activity and conversation during votes. But that

Wednesday, no one was there. The silence and empty rooms were jarring and incongruous with the monumentality of what still had to be accomplished.

The 112th Congress had plenty of things left on its agenda, and the blame for its inattention can be shared. We still hadn't adopted a federal budget, our yearly appropriations bills, or a host of additional measures critical to the functioning of the government. For instance, the latest extension of the law authorizing the Federal Aviation Administration (FAA), which had lapsed in 2007, expired on July 22. As a consequence, 4,000 FAA employees were furloughed, 74,000 private sector jobs were placed at risk, and the FAA lost $30 million per day in revenues from fees it could no longer collect on airline tickets. But the House and Senate blithely dispersed for the August recess, recklessly ignoring the plight of workers at a time of 9 percent unemployment. It was another example of how divorced from reality Congress had become.

It wasn't until the media brought a firestorm of attention to the issue that we passed an additional extension on August 5, and we finally reauthorized the FAA in 2012. For five years, it had been critical to enact this legislation that, among other things, was required to install the next generation of aviation technology at our airports—but we always said by the time we would get around to passing the bill, we'd only be installing "present" technology.

Republicans still had our traditional policy lunch at twelve-thirty on the day we were all taking off for recess. I stood up and expressed my exasperation. "We still have so much more to do. Where are we going? We should be individually and collectively embarrassed to be leaving. We should be staying and forfeiting recess to tackle what remains. Raising the debt ceiling was just the beginning, not the end. Let's give up our recess to show how committed we are to finishing the job."

Of course that didn't happen, Congress left town, and late on Friday, August 5, Standard & Poor's downgraded America's sterling AAA rating for the first time in history.

After that policy luncheon, I engaged in a conversation back in the cloakroom with Senator Jeff Sessions (R-AL), the lead Republican on the Senate Budget Committee, about what we had just discussed. I expressed the thought that perhaps we should have a refresher course on how a bill becomes law, because it seems that the art of legislating has been largely forgotten.

The super committee met for the first time on September 8 and was made up of an equal number of Republicans and Democrats, chosen by House and Senate leaders. It worked against the clock but failed to report out a package by the deadline in November. Each side blamed the other for intransigence over tax cuts or revenue increases but the differences between the two sides were irreconcilable. My impression was that if leadership wanted members of the committee to reach an agreement, it would have been possible.

The committee was composed of people of quality and good intentions, many of whom had long-standing legislative experience. But the mission they were charged with, in the time frame that was established, and bearing in mind that they were discussing entitlement savings and raising revenues, was almost impossible to accomplish. It was unrealistic to expect that a twelve-person Washington commission could achieve in less than three months what 535 members of Congress had failed to do in more than three years. Instead, we should have set in motion a process for deficit reduction that would have instructed the existing standing committees to determine how to reach specific goals and report their recommendations as part of a package that the full Senate could debate and vote on by a specific date. In that way, we would have been compelled to address this major question. To my mind, the super committee was a diversion, a false trail on the road to nowhere.

The stakes were extraordinarily high, and still we could not act decisively. The Bipartisan Policy Center found that the higher interest rates triggered by the debt ceiling showdown will cost taxpayers $18.9 billion over ten years in additional interest payments. Throughout it all, consumer confidence plummeted and the markets fell as our national creditworthiness was jeopardized. Businesspeople I spoke with in Maine told me a wall went up, and customers simply stopped spending money. In all areas, confidence in government was shattered.

A study by the American Enterprise Institute showed that the debt ceiling crisis caused a higher level of policy uncertainty than did any event since at least 1985, surpassing the Persian Gulf War, the Iraq War, Lehman Brothers, the TARP bailout, and even the terrorist attacks of September 11, 2001. (Policy uncertainty occurs when outcomes cannot easily be predicted and leads to, among other things, reduced spending and investment and stifled growth.) And, worse, it could have been avoided. To take the country to the brink of default was political and financial brinksmanship of the worst kind. It was unimaginable and unconscionable.

The consequences of Congress's failure to fulfill its legislative functions reverberated throughout the entire country in multiple ways, and the people of Maine suffered along with their compatriots elsewhere. Dairy farming is a vital component of the state's economy, and our failure to replace the 2008 Farm Act as it expired at the end of September 2012 had serious implications for milk producers in my state. Dairy farmers were hit hard by low milk prices caused by an oversupply, and the Farm Bill included the Milk Income Loss Contract (MILC) program to assist with a safety net of protection. The Senate passed a new farm bill in June, but the legislation was held up in the House. As the date of expiration loomed, a bipartisan group of sixty lawmakers from both houses urged that a temporary fix be found.

While Congress dallied, dairy farmers were suffering from rising feed costs and the effects of drought. When I addressed the Fryeburg Fair in Maine at the beginning of October, I explained that I regretted this inexcusable inaction and the impact it would have on Maine dairy farms. If no legislation had passed by January 1, dozens of programs would have expired. Agriculture would have fallen off its own cliff, reverting to the provisions of the Farm Bill of 1949, and milk prices may have doubled.

Under these circumstances, I've wondered what motivates people to seek public office. If you arrive in Congress with high expectations and a reforming zeal, the reality, where little is accomplished despite what is at stake, can be disillusioning. We are creating a new generation of lawmakers who are familiar only with the disharmony of the last few years.

In speeches I've delivered I've sometimes quoted David McCullough, who once addressed a House of Representatives retreat and discussed the milestones achieved by Congress when its members worked together. McCullough's list was impressive: the Homestead Act, the abolition of slavery and child labor, the building of the Panama Canal, the transcontinental railroads, and the Interstate Highway System. Congress created Social Security and passed the Voting Rights Act. We sent Lewis and Clark to the West and Americans on voyages to the moon, and in times of crisis we passed the Marshall Plan and Lend-Lease. On the floor of the Senate I once asked if we were going to act in this economic crisis. History awaited our answer, I said.

History is still waiting.

Chapter 3

Childhood

I WAS BORN IN AUGUSTA, MAINE, in 1947. My parents, George and Georgia Bouchles, ran a diner close to the state capitol and when the legislature was in session, politicians would eat in our restaurant. I received an email recently from someone whose mother still recalls that when I was a baby, patrons, including Republican and Democrat legislators, would hold me in their laps while my parents served meals. Perhaps this was where I absorbed the spirit of bipartisanship!

We lived across the street from the diner in a first-floor apartment, and I spent a lot of time between the house and the restaurant making my own entertainment, like the time I helped my brother, John, who was four years older, build a snow tunnel outside our building. Back then there was a farm just below the state capitol and someone sent me a picture of my brother and me standing in front of the barn. My brother looked immaculate while I looked as if a comb hadn't been put through my hair in years!

In an open space next to the diner were some cement culverts, and one day I was sitting on one with a friend and holding her pocketbook. The next thing I knew, I was attacked by a swarm of bees and stung from head to toe. My father was in the kitchen cooking and I ran in, screaming. I must have been quite a sight. He took me outside and found a patch of dirt and covered me in mud to salve the stings. What I remember vividly is being worried that I had dropped my friend's pocketbook. She had let me hold it as a treat, and I didn't want to lose it.

My father was more than twenty years older than my mother. He had been married before he met my mother and he had six children from that marriage. I learned from a registry of Greek-Americans one of my cousins showed me that my father owned a hat and shoe-cleaning store in Lewiston, Maine, in 1920, and later on he operated a restaurant, so when we moved back there, it was familiar territory to him.

He and his brother came to the United States from Greece in 1908, when he was fifteen. He was part of a large family from Mytilene, the biggest town on the island of Lesbos. His brother returned home but my dad stayed. Once when Jock and I were at an event on Ellis Island, Jock found my father's name on the American Immigrant Wall of Honor, spelled differently. By a happy coincidence, Mytilene is also a sister city to Portland, Maine. Members of the Greek community in Portland had forged an alliance with the old country. I've been to Greece a couple of times but never to Mytilene, and I'm determined to go with Jock.

My mother, Georgia Goranites, was also Greek, but she was a first-generation American. Her parents were from Sparta, as were her brother and sister, but she was born in this country and graduated from high school in Lewiston, one of the first in the Greek-American community to do so.

Around the time I started kindergarten, we moved to Lewiston, about twenty-five miles from Augusta. There, my parents worked in a restaurant, and I remember its swivel stools and soda fountain and tables laid out against the window. I have few other recollections of us all being together in Lewiston. Our neighbors Priscilla and Francis James were wonderful to me. Priscilla would fix my hair and have me over for lunch, and I played with her children, who were around my age.

When I was around six years old, my mother became ill. She was sick for some time before she was diagnosed with breast cancer, and after that, she was in and out of the hospital. I was aware that my father wasn't well, either, but he continued to work while my mom was being treated. He had his hands full, and I worried about him constantly. I canceled outings that had been planned with our neighbors if I knew he was feeling sick. I didn't dare leave.

When we were together, my brother and I would listen to the radio in the kitchen waiting for our father to come home from work. When dad was at the restaurant one day I heard a report that a hurricane was on its way. We didn't have a phone at home, so I walked up to Main Street to a variety store where they had a telephone booth, then called my dad at work and told him he had to come home.

I tried to be helpful around the house if I could. My mom must have been in the hospital the day I filled the bathtub with water and soap, washed all the towels I could find, dragged them outside, and hung them on the line without rinsing them. When my father came home, he wasn't exactly enthusiastic about my efforts. I wonder if he ever got all the soap out. With all the hours he worked, we didn't have much time to do things together. When he could, he'd take me on the bus to the beach on a lake in Auburn, which must have been a respite for him, too, however brief.

When my mom was home I'd talk with her about her illness as she lay in bed. I was fraught with worry, trying to understand what was happening. I knew enough to ask her about dying and if she was going to die. I can only imagine what it must have been like to be asked these questions by your young daughter. Treatment for breast cancer was brutal in the 1950s and she was tormented by the side effects, as well as the pain. She wrote letters to her friends setting out her worries about her sick husband and two kids and what the future held for all of us. I have some of those heart-wrenching letters. In one, she wrote to a close friend named Nellie Constantine on October 3, 1953, after she had her major operation.

> I'll never forget the day I left to have the operation. I knew that I might never come back if it was an advanced case. . . . Olympia kept

telling me that she would take care of me when I came back. It was pouring rain and they stood outside in the rain watching me while I was leaving. [The children] looked so lost and lonely that I thought my heart would break. I couldn't cry as the pain went deeper than that.

Even though I was very young, I thought I needed to be grown-up and I told my mom not to worry. But the cancer was bigger than either of us. Near the end I went to the doctor's office with my mom. The doctor saw her in the waiting room and said, "Georgia, what are you doing back here?" and she said, "I'm not feeling well."

On July 2, 1955, I was scheduled to visit her in the hospital with my brother; but the plans were changed and I ended up going to the beach with the Jameses and their two kids. I now realize my mother must have been too sick to see me. When I arrived home, my dad was upstairs with the landlady (who also happened to be Greek) and my brother, and that's when he told me my mother had died. My mom was thirty-nine, my brother twelve, and I was eight. I was beside myself and utterly distraught. I remember I ran next door to tell the Jameses.

My dad had to keep on working and he continued to put in long, late hours at the restaurant. It was very tough for him. He was sick, he'd just lost his wife, and he had my brother and me to look after but very little means with which to do it. Even when he was barely getting by, however, he made sure we didn't feel deprived. He loved to cook for us and made great meals, with plates of cantaloupe and scrambled eggs and, if we were lucky, steak and eggs for breakfast on the weekends.

It was clear something was up when I came home from school for lunch one day, as I always did, and saw a whole set of bedsheets and clothes and shoes and socks in my size laid out in the living room. I raced back to school, which was practically in my backyard, and got my friends to come with me to look. My dad had mentioned the possibility of my going away to school, but I hadn't thought much of it until I saw the clothes I was going to take with me. I told my friends, "It's true, I'm going to be leaving."

My father had learned about St. Basil Academy from our Greek Orthodox church, Holy Trinity, where I have been a lifelong member, and which has been a constant wellspring of strength for me. The church-run school is situated along the Hudson River in Garrison, New York, and offers residential facilities for out-of-town students and those who are in need. My dad and I were very close and I knew what a difficult decision it must have been for him to send me away to school. He looked very sad but he did what he thought was best, so I was determined not to cry when the time came for me to leave.

I vividly remember being dropped off at school for the first time, in April 1956. Our family didn't own a car, so my dad hired a local couple, the Maloneys, to drive me down from Maine. The Maloneys were very kind to me and coincidentally, many years later Mrs. Maloney and I were reunited when we were both members of the Androscoggin County Republican Women's Club. When we arrived in Garrison, they couldn't find the school, and I sat in the backseat of the car holding my breath hoping they wouldn't. But they stopped at a gas station to get directions, and we found our way to the big black iron gates of the school.

In 1944, the church had purchased the four-hundred-acre estate of Jacob Ruppert, the brewer, politician, and onetime owner of the New York Yankees, and established the school. The estate was magnificent, with a long, winding road that made its way down from the gate to the main house. As we drove down we could see a giant eagle cast in metal that I later learned had stood at Grand Central Terminal, and I wondered what we would see next. We drove past lovely Japanese ornamental bridges and reached the main house, a large Tudor-style building. The house was high above the river and directly across from West Point. Behind it, children were playing softball in the fading light of early evening.

I settled in to school life well. To make things easier for my dad, I wrote him a letter six days a week. Did he read them? I don't know.

(Given my penmanship, he probably couldn't anyway.) When the mail was delivered, a big bell was rung. I was there every day to hand over my letter for my dad. I don't recall if he wrote back, but writing to him helped me to feel connected to him.

When I arrived back home that June, the couple who had first driven me to Garrison dropped me off at the restaurant. It was past dinnertime, and my Dad was still working. When I walked in he was just beaming—he was so excited to see me. I sat at the counter, and with a big smile on his face, he said I could have anything I wanted. So I had a hot fudge sundae, and then he let me have another one right after that.

One day soon after I got back, I was standing on the sidewalk in front of my old school, Wallace Elementary, when I saw my teacher from third grade, Miss Tewksbury. She was so nice to me, she said, "Olympia, what are you doing home? You have to come visit us. Your desk is still there." The school was still in session, so I went back and sat in class the whole day. I loved every minute of it, seeing my friends; Wallace was such a warm and nurturing environment, where I had innumerable positive experiences.

Over the summer, I hung out with my old friends from school and from our street. I paid a special visit to my next-door neighbors, who had often written me wonderful letters keeping me abreast of what was going on. Everyone in the neighborhood was very support-ive, and I was in and out of their homes.

I returned to St. Basil's in September. That November, my dad's heart gave out at nine o'clock one night at the restaurant while he was sitting in a booth talking with our Greek Orthodox priest.

The residence supervisor at the school, who was a nun, called me down to her office the next morning to tell me that my dad had died. He was sixty-three, and I was an orphan at the age of nine. I was beyond bereft. I didn't want to believe it, so I took off for the main building and found a phone booth to make a collect call to my father's restaurant. Such a call required an operator and when she reached someone at the restaurant she said, "I have an Olympia

Bouchles on the line trying to reach her father, George Bouchles." The man on the other end of the line paused and said to the operator, "I don't want to tell her that her father is dead," obviously not realizing that I was listening on the other end of the phone. Well, he needn't have worried. I heard what he said and threw the phone against the wall, screaming. I ran up the hill back to the dormitory, where I was sent to bed. My next-door neighbor later mailed me my father's obituary, which was very important for me to see.

It must have been decided that it would be best if I didn't attend the funeral, so I stayed at school until Christmas. Then I returned home to Auburn, where my aunt Mary and uncle Jim became my guardians. My brother, John, went to live with a half brother, Jim Bouchles, also in Auburn, who was married and had no children of his own.

I was so young, but there was nothing I could do except carry on. My uncle owned his own barbershop on Main Street in Lewiston, and my aunt worked the looms on the third shift in the Continental Mill. As it turned out, my uncle had health problems too, but when he died in 1963, it was a shock. Experience didn't make any of these losses easier to handle, but once again, I was in tragically familiar territory, and to survive I had to keep going. There didn't seem to be any point in wondering why terrible things happened to our family.

My brother, John, was in education for thirty-two years, all but six of which were as assistant principal at Lewiston High School, the second-largest high school in Maine. When students from Lewiston High visited me in Washington, they'd often say that they'd heard I was Mr. Bouchles's sister. I'd say, yes, I am, and I'd kiddingly ask them, "Exactly how well do you know him?" because part of my brother's responsibilities included discipline! In fact, John described to me a meeting he had in 1989 with one of his students, who had apparently just seen the announcement on television that Jock and I were getting married, which also mentioned that John was my brother. The student, sporting a leather vest and tattoos, came into John's office and said, "Mr. Bouchles, I didn't know Olympia Snowe was your sister." John kidded him and said, "Yeah, where have you been the last three years?" The kid shot right back, "In the ninth grade!"

———— ⨎ ————

The greatest gift my father gave me was sending me away to school. As much as I had loved going to school in Lewiston and playing in the streets around our home and riding my bike, going to St. Basil's infinitely expanded my horizons. I emerged from St. Basil's fortified with the central ideas of our culture, better able to cope with the personal challenges that lay ahead, and imbued with a grounding in my faith that remains the bedrock of my life today.

I also now realized there was a larger world out there and I loved it. The first time I was in New York City I was awed. It was an amazing place to take in for a young girl from Elm Street in Lewiston, Maine. Soon after, I sought ways to explore the city, going on real adventures at a much younger age than most people.

After the first couple of trips to school, when my dad hired the couple to drive me to Garrison, I traveled between St. Basil's and Lewiston by train. I traveled to and from Maine through Grand Central Terminal in New York City, sometimes on an overnight train. A couple of times on my return trips, my aunt's nephew and his wife, who lived in New Jersey, met me at Grand Central and put me on the train to Garrison. On one occasion, they drove me home to Maine in a snowstorm for the Christmas holidays.

I took these train trips by myself, the first of which was when I went back to school after my father died. My uncle put me on the night train, and I stationed myself behind a couple who seemed elderly to me. I asked them what time it was and what time we were getting in. When they told me we would arrive at 6 A.M., I said my uncle had told me the train got in at 2 A.M. I was immediately fearful that I was going to miss my stop or get off at the wrong station. I sat up all night in a state of agitation, worrying about the time and where we were. I took my shoes off and couldn't get them back on because my feet were swollen. I squeezed my feet back into my shoes when the train arrived, and the rest of the trip passed uneventfully.

It was necessary for me to be resourceful when I made my trips in and out of New York. I'd leave school in the evening so I could get home the following day, but the connections never seemed to line up. I have no idea how the school and my family communicated, but I didn't want to worry my aunt Mary and uncle Jim, and I ended up spending a considerable amount of time on my own in Grand Central. On more than a few occasions that meant I stayed there the whole night—certainly not circumstances I would recommend for a ten-year-old. I was in Grand Central some years ago with Jock and I pointed out the benches off the Main Hall near the restroom where I used to sleep; they looked exactly the same!

I slept on the bench all night one time and when I was ready to make the connection, instead of getting a skycap, I dragged most of my luggage to the platform and then went right back for the last case. As I returned, I ran into a friend from St. Basil's and I was excited to see her. We chatted, time passed, and by the time I got to the track, my suitcases were gone. I lost all but the one suitcase I'd left by the bench. I was horrified. What I don't remember is why every time I traveled I seemed to take everything I owned with me. People who know me now might say that some things never change!

On another occasion, the school asked me to put a girl who must have been even younger than me on a train to Chicago. I enjoyed taking on these responsibilities. After I made sure she was safely aboard, I hung around the station waiting for my train, which didn't leave until after midnight. While I was waiting I was stopped by the police. I had so much luggage they assumed I was running away from home or school with all my worldly possessions. I assured them that I wasn't on the run and asked them to make sure I wasn't going to miss my train because I was looking forward to going home for Christmas. They took me to Travelers Aid, the volunteer service that assists people like a ten-year-old girl on her own in Grand Central.

Travelers Aid called the school and my aunt to verify that what I was saying was true. The police told me next time I was coming through, I should be sure to contact Travelers Aid. I said that I would, but I know that I didn't. I knew I could take care of myself.

When passenger train service to Portland was canceled in the early 1960s (service to Lewiston had been discontinued even earlier), I had to take the bus to Maine. I spent time at the Greyhound bus station in New York, and that was a very different proposition from Grand Central. On the first occasion, I sat on a bench all night and watched as the police approached people who were sleeping and tapped them on the soles of their shoes with their billy clubs to wake them up and move them along if they didn't have a ticket.

I had attempted to buy my ticket earlier in the day with a check, but no one at the bus station would cash it. I tried nearby banks to see if any of them could help, but they couldn't, either. It occurred to me that a number of students from Garrison would be coming into Grand Central in the morning, and I was confident one of the parents coming to meet them would be able to cash my check.

I decided to take a cab over to Grand Central, and a man outside the station asked if I wanted help hailing a taxi. I told him I was fine but he got me a cab anyway. When I got in, a man was already in there, and the guy leaned in and told both of us we owed him a dollar. I said, "A dollar? I asked you not to get the cab. I can get my own cab." He didn't look very friendly, so I crouched down in the corner of the backseat. The man next to me gave the guy a dollar. When I asked him why, the guy reached across and would have tried to grab me when the driver, who'd made no move to help me and was obviously in on the scam, got the guy's attention. At that moment, a police officer was coming around the corner, the hustler faded away, and the driver took off.

If I could, I'd call my friends who lived in the city ahead of time and delay my trip to Garrison and visit them. I'd put my suitcases in a locker in Grand Central and either take the bus to the West Side, or the subway out to Jackson Heights. Before I went to Queens for the first time, I asked my friend to provide a description of her house and when I walked to the end of her street, I stood there and every single house for as far as I could see looked the same. I found a phone booth and called her and got her address. It was so exciting for me to explore the city like that.

I was probably twelve at the time this happened. When you're that young you're endlessly resilient, and you adapt when you have to. After my first train trip, I overcame my nervousness and became thoroughly independent. There was enough support around me at home and at school that I never felt abandoned, and my family's support and my successful early self-sufficiency were both invaluable to me later in life.

My first trip to Washington, D.C., was when I was in fifth grade at St. Basil's and I was selected to make a presentation at a big Greek-American dinner for AHEPA, the Hellenic men's philanthropic organization, in the ballroom at the Mayflower Hotel. St. Basil's was owned by the Greek Orthodox archdiocese and strongly dependent on financial support not only from the church but also donors throughout the national Hellenic-American community. I was to deliver the speech in Greek to help demonstrate the success of the school to its supporters, and I rehearsed and rehearsed. A teacher drove me to Washington, along with an older student, who was a backup in case I was unable to perform.

We did a little sightseeing and rode the streetcars. When we arrived for the event, the ballroom was huge—there must have been more than a thousand people there, with a large dais up front for dignitaries including the Orthodox Archbishop Iakovos, the spiritual leader of our church, who at that time was the archbishop of North and South America. I sat at the table, too nervous to eat, constantly rehearsing my speech in my head until an official came over to my table and informed my teacher I wouldn't be able to deliver my remarks since the program now was going to run past midnight.

My first reaction was to be relieved—now I could I eat my ice-cream cake, at least—but then I was very disappointed, given all the work I'd done. But I feel I've made up for it with plenty of speeches I've given and listened to since then. I have attended the same AHEPA event in Washington many times, and in 1996 I was honored for my service and presented with a statue of Pericles that I cherish —even though Pericles was an Athenian and my family roots lie in Sparta!

Over the years at St. Basil's, I increasingly demonstrated maturity and dependability. I took on as much work there as the administration would give me. One day in the ninth grade the dean of the school took me aside for a walk, and asked me if I would be willing to assume responsibility to supervise the dormitory while they searched for a replacement for the full-time supervisor, who had left. I quickly agreed.

One of my responsibilities was to assign the weekly chores to each student. We had Sundays off but during the rest of the week our duties included cleaning our dorms, waxing and buffing the dining room floors, and taking care of the property around the dormitories. I'm certain that plenty of my can-do spirit was developed at St. Basil's.

We broke one rule when we went out and explored the whole place, which we weren't supposed to do. There were snakes, including venomous copperheads, which I'd almost lose my mind over if I thought about them. We'd check out the waterfalls and hike down to the Hudson River. We even took a boat out once, even though I couldn't swim.

Given the dormitory environment, it was essential that we got along with one another. Fortunately, cliques weren't the norm at the school. There was, however, one girl who intimidated the others and I decided she needed to stop. I stationed myself in a room she had to pass through on the way to the other wing of the school. I was so nervous I manically chewed on a piece of licorice. She duly came along with her friends and I was sitting with mine.

When she got close, I made a comment that would get her attention, and she said, "What did you say?" and she came up to me and stood as close to me as possible and we faced off. Still chewing away, I said she had to stop what she was doing. I managed to break the ice by confronting her about her behavior. She later told me she respected me for what I did and we actually became good friends. The atmosphere lightened up a lot after I stood up to her. I felt I was compelled to act and thankfully it turned out well as a life's lesson. I have never been one to let a bad situation fester. And it wasn't the last time I surprised someone by standing up to them.

Classes at St. Basil's didn't go beyond ninth grade, but the administration gave me the option to stay and live at St. Basil's and attend a high school in nearby Highland Falls. I discussed the idea with my aunt and uncle, and they offered me the choice to come home. Even though I'd been extremely comfortable at the academy in New York, I ultimately determined I should try to reestablish my roots in Maine, so I returned to Auburn for high school.

My brother, John, had graduated from Edward Little High School by the time I arrived there for my sophomore year. Although one of my five cousins, Kiki, was still there for her senior year, she was the only person I knew and all the other students were from one of two local junior high schools. I didn't fully anticipate what it would be like adjusting from a tiny boarding school and walking in cold to a large public high school. Yet again I was facing another hurdle in life, something else I needed to get on with and adjust to. I toughed it out and eventually made friends.

I'd thrived at St. Basil's, where the classes were small and we took half our lessons in modern Greek. At Edward Little High School in Auburn, there were more than three hundred students in my class, which seemed enormous because it was more than three times the entire size of St. Basil's.

At Edward Little, there were teachers who had a profound influence on me. I loved Mrs. Whipple, my English-literature teacher, and in fact her son, Jim, has been a lifelong friend. She was funny and animated, and she brought to life the writing and the authors with her passion for the subject. I received a Christmas card from her three years ago, when she was ninety-six. She kiddingly wrote, "I taught you, that's why you're so smart today!" Mr. Chick, another English teacher, was a wonderful and inspiring man who encouraged me to go on to college. I've also stayed in contact with my social studies teacher, Frank Cooper. One of my nieces later attended Edward Little and he enjoyed pointing out my seat to her. "That's where Olympia used to sit," he said. "I remember how much she loved government and politics," which I did.

In the fall of 1964, I rode the same school bus as a fellow student named Sue Hathaway. It turned out her father, Bill, was running for Congress, and she talked about his campaign. I was extremely intrigued by this very impressive notion: running for elective office. She described a world far removed from mine, and it sounded exciting. I wondered what it was like and wanted to hear more. Hathaway, a Democrat, won the election for Maine's 2nd Congressional District. In 1972, he ran against the legendary Margaret Chase Smith for her Senate seat and won. Hathaway ran again in 1978 but lost to Bill Cohen.

In time, the steps in my own political career would intersect with Hathaway's like pieces in a congressional jigsaw puzzle. I was working in Bill Cohen's office when extraordinary circumstances intervened in my life and I ran for the Maine House. In 1978, I, too, like Bill Hathaway, and Bill Cohen before me, ran for Margaret Chase Smith's 2nd District seat. Over a very short period, the high school student who loved politics had an intense, and unforeseen, political education that was centered on the Maine State House in Augusta, only blocks away from where I spent the first four years of my life.

Chapter 4

Why I Ran

THE LEVEL OF DYSFUNCTION I witnessed at the end of my third term in the United States Senate would have been unfathomable to that twenty-six-year-old rookie legislator who first showed up at the State House in Augusta in 1973. On my first day in elective office, after I'd been sworn in by Governor Kenneth Curtis, the same governor I had interned with five years earlier, I took a moment to stand in the ornate House chamber of the historic capitol in Augusta to take it all in. I saw the legislators whom I knew by name and local reputation, if not personally. This was my hometown, and I had already had a very eventful life. I remember thinking, "Okay, so now what?"

The Senate Majority Leader, Bennett Katz, came up to me. As if he'd been reading my mind, he said, "Olympia, I know right now you're probably looking around and wondering how you got here. But let me tell you, in six months you'll look around this same chamber and wonder how everyone *else* got here!"

My state's legislature is a scale model of Congress. Maine's bicameral body has existed since 1832, with a people's House and a discerning Senate similar to those mandated by the United States. Just as in Congress, we had two political parties, and when one had a majority, it could prevail, but usually representatives on both sides of the aisle came together to tackle the state's problems. Once elections were over, my colleagues and I largely put campaigns and party labels behind us and worked together to enact laws that genuinely improved the lives of the people in the state. A high level of consensus-building and bipartisanship meant that the place functioned properly.

The Maine legislature is supposed to be a part-time body, but it meets every year. In the second year of any two-year term, business is usually concluded by July unless the session takes up emergency measures. Given the finite number of days we were in session, our deliberating was meant to be brisk. Apparently, before my time, someone would put a blanket over the clock if the session was in danger of running beyond its mandated limit. I quickly had the experience of serving in both the majority and minority. In 1973 the Maine House was controlled by Republicans, but the following year, in the wake of Watergate, Democrats took over. Three years later, when I was elected to the Maine Senate, it was controlled by the Republicans.

My years in the Maine legislature were an extremely positive experience. Making laws was a hands-on process. The number of legislators was small—151 representatives and 33 senators—so it was possible to be personally acquainted with all your colleagues. Every bill had a hearing in committee, there were joint House and Senate committees, and the House and Senate committee chairs had to account for every piece of legislation and dispose of it in both chambers before the legislative session could adjourn. Even in those days, the Maine legislature had a somewhat higher percentage of women compared to other state legislatures and the Congress, and the body as a whole demonstrated a great work ethic. I focused on the issues and learned how we could work together as legislators to help our constituents in practical ways. There was cross-party voting, and although we had fights, we were usually able to work through our political differences and find solutions.

We had one of our major and instructive cross-party successes early in my career when we abolished the Executive Council. It was an unelected, anachronistic holdover from 1820 that confirmed gubernatorial appointments in the state. Many previous sessions had tried and failed to dissolve it. As one paper, the *Toledo Blade*, reported, "In recent years the Maine council—appointed by the combined House and Senate—has been chiefly criticized for attempting to usurp gubernatorial powers, and flouting legislative intent."

In the waning days of our session in 1975, the Speaker of the House and the president of the Maine Senate assembled a bipartisan, bicameral group, with three members from the House and three from the Senate. We worked hard at reaching a solution. Our first meeting took place at the restaurant of the Senator Inn, after a day in the legislature, and was run by the Senate and House chairs of the group, Ted Curtis and Mike Carpenter, respectively. We huddled over our plates to start sketching out a plan and then returned for the legislative session, which was running late into the night.

Ultimately, we recommended a new confirmation process to our caucuses. After the measure passed both chambers with the required two-thirds majority, an amendment to the Maine Constitution went on the ballot in 1975 and passed comfortably. This successful effort had an important influence on me. I saw that anything is possible, even under difficult circumstances and time constraints, as long as you put forth a good-faith effort to solve a problem and have enough legislators who share a spirit of cooperation.

I ran for the Maine Senate in 1976. For that race I employed a decidedly low-tech campaign vehicle: a bicycle. The Senate district I was seeking to represent included Auburn and the more rural areas surrounding the city, so I thought I'd ride a bicycle to get out to voters, knock on doors, and introduce myself.

One of the doors I knocked on was at the vacation cottage of the future chief of staff to President George W. Bush, Andy Card. In 2002, I spoke at an event in Washington, D.C., honoring Andy as Boy Scout Citizen of the Year, and I relayed this story, saying he was probably surprised by my visit because, being from Massachusetts, he'd never actually seen another young Republican before—let alone one on a bicycle!

After I was elected, I received a call from the president of the state senate, Joe Sewall, who had been an instrumental supporter of mine, to discuss my preferences for committee assignments. Before I was even able to finish my response, he said he intended to appoint me chair of the Health and Institutional Services Committee. He said that committee would be dealing with one of the most controversial issues of the next session: deinstitutionalization, which included closing one of the two mental health hospitals in the state.

I said, "Joe, I'm not sure; that's not exactly what I have in mind. I don't have any expertise in health issues." But Joe wouldn't take no for an answer. "Don't worry," he said. "You'll learn quickly." He was right.

In the state legislature, if my committee had jurisdiction, I'd do the research—there was one staffer assigned to my committee—and hold a hearing. As Senate chair of the committee, I was responsible for probably one hundred bills that were introduced in that session, between January and July. All of them had to be disposed of on the Senate floor, whether by passage, defeat, or postponement for consideration in the next session.

The consolidation of the mental health facilities was a controversial plan, but also the centerpiece of the governor's agenda, so this was a major undertaking. When I started looking into the idea, I didn't know where the journey would take me, but as I did my research, held hearings, and followed where the facts led me, I came to the conclusion that the proposal wasn't going to work. I didn't see any way that we could close the hospital, because there weren't enough mental health services for the people who were going to be released into the community. Without a strong family support system or community health centers, they might be abandoned and forsaken.

One Sunday morning prior to the announcement of my decision, I received a call from the governor, Jim Longley. He was a man of strong and passionate convictions, and a forceful advocate for what he believed was right, which I highly respected, and we had a spirited conversation. I began to explain my fundamental concern: that patients discharged from the hospital would face a lack of services. His response: "Why don't you leave it up to the experts. They're the ones who know best."

"But, Governor," I said, "if that were the case there wouldn't be any need for a legislative branch. We weren't elected to be experts, we were elected to examine the question—that's *our* responsibility." In the end, my position prevailed, and did so overwhelmingly.

As the Senate chair of a committee, I was well aware I had the authority to influence the outcome of a bill and I thrived on taking hold of a problem and finding the best solution. These formative political years influenced my whole approach to public service: problem-solving grounded in a strong political philosophy. And that was rewarded when as a freshman, in 1977, I was tied for fifth among outstanding legislators in the Maine Senate. According to a column written by longtime Maine political reporter, John Day, in the *Bangor Daily News,* one of the factors the survey took into account was "effectiveness." He went on to say, "There are some very competent legislators who have failed because of a lack of understanding of the give and take of politics, to be effective in gaining passage of their legislation."

Building a consensus involving both parties made for the best law. We were respectful of the traditions and practices of the institution. My years in the Maine legislature reinforced for me the infinite possibilities for making the process of governing work for the common good.

My decision to run for election almost forty years ago was a hard one, born of the most tragic of circumstances. I had been married a little more than three years when my husband, Peter Snowe, a recently elected member of the Maine House of Representatives who had also served in that body several years earlier, was killed in a car accident. I was twenty-six, and Peter was thirty.

Peter Snowe had been a childhood friend and classmate of my cousin Duke, so I'd known him for many years. Peter and I initially dated for a few months when I first attended the University of Maine. We then took a break. We started dating again a few years later. One summer after college, I lived with his parents, Barbara and Carlie Snowe, who always treated me like a daughter. Barbara died in 2011, and to this day I continue to maintain a very close relationship with Carlie. At the time I stayed with them, they owned a gift, antique, and interior design shop. Peter persuaded them to allow us to open a sandwich shop for the convenience of their customers, which I would run for the season in a building they also owned just across the street.

I was in my early twenties, and I'd always thought I'd probably get married later, perhaps when I was about thirty. By the time I got to college I was very self-sufficient and used to taking care of myself. I had my heart set on a career. Soon I read Betty Friedan's *The Feminine Mystique,* and I was struck by Friedan's discussion of the choices women make between family and work. I struggled with my decision. I wanted to turn my passion for politics into a job, and during college I built a résumé that would help fulfill my burning ambition to get a job in Washington.

As part of a study program, I worked for the governor of Maine, Kenneth Curtis, a Democrat, for two summers. During the first I worked in the Office of Economic Opportunity, formulating Head Start programs, and during the second I was in the governor's office. Charlie "Chick" O'Leary, who was later president of the Maine AFL-CIO for two decades, interviewed me for these positions in Augusta. I didn't have a car, so a friend offered to give me a ride to the interview, and by coincidence, my friend's brother was good friends with Charlie. I was originally assigned to the Treasurer's Office for the city of Augusta, but during our conversation, Charlie asked me, "What's your major?" I told him it was political science, and he asked me if I'd prefer to have a job more suited to it. I said I would, and he told me he had an idea.

That's how I ended up working for a woman who was a technical assistant for Head Start, and as we traveled the state, I saw firsthand the value of the program. I witnessed how children who would otherwise be at tremendous risk of falling behind from the beginning were thriving. The program ensured they could start school on an equal footing with more advantaged kids. The way these children were responding made a big impression on me, and was one reason why I became a staunch proponent of Head Start years later in Congress.

Charlie O'Leary said he'd secure me a position in the governor's office the next summer. It was a coveted assignment, and I hardly expected it to actually materialize. But Charlie followed up on his promise and I received a letter the following spring confirming that he'd found me a place. His generosity made a lasting impression on me. For years I kidded Charlie, the union stalwart, for being such a big help at the beginning of a Republican politician's career!

During that second summer I spent a month reviewing legislation other states were considering or had enacted. Then I worked with Albert Mavrinac, an extraordinarily accomplished professor from Colby College who'd been assigned to help set up the new State Planning Office. My responsibilities included interviewing officials at the various state agencies to assess the effectiveness of initiatives like the Bulk Food Program, a forerunner to Food Stamps.

During these months, I absorbed valuable knowledge about the workings and responsibilities of the governor's office. For the first time I visited the governor's residence, the Blaine House, named for the famous nineteenth-century Maine politician James G. Blaine, when I delivered the results of my study of other states' legislation. Later that summer, Governor Curtis hosted a luncheon at the residence for the interns, including a personal tour of the Blaine House.

Twenty years later, I was living there as the state's First Lady, as well as a congresswoman, and was about to enter the U.S. Senate. This was another one of those echoes from the future that would have knocked me over if I'd had any intimation of them at the time.

At the end of that summer of 1968, I received a letter from Professor Mavrinac. "I enjoyed having you around this summer," he wrote. "It was pleasant and a comfort to have someone who would cheerfully accept any assignment however vague or however loaded down with questions, sub questions, and sub-sub questions—who would promptly return a neat and fully researched paper on the issue at hand." I've always prided myself on being thorough. I left this second internship even more determined to go to Washington, and eventually I did, just not by the route I anticipated.

⸻⸺◇◇◇⸻

In 1969, after I graduated from the University of Maine, Peter and I were married. He had already served in the state legislature for two years. In 1966 he'd run in Auburn, during the city's at-large election. It was a difficult seat for a Republican to win. In fact, the result was so close that the state's Supreme Judicial Court declared it a tie, and Peter won a special election in February 1967. He thus became, at twenty-three, the youngest member of the legislature. He lost his next two races, for the Maine Senate in 1968 and for the Maine House in 1970. When he ran for the House again in 1972, I told him, we're not going through this again if you lose. But this time he won.

I continued working in politics. While Peter ran for the State House, I had a part-time position as a Republican member of the Board of Voter Registration for the city of Auburn. It was during that period that I met Bill Cohen, who was running for Congress for Maine's 2nd District seat. On the day that Bill announced his candidacy, he made a stop at City Hall, where I was working. City Clerk Leroy Linnell came over and said, "You are the only Republican here. Would you be willing to be in a photograph with the candidate for Congress, Bill Cohen?" So I "volunteered" for the job, and I appeared alongside Bill Cohen and his wife on the front page of the paper the next day. The future was calling again—within a few years we were serving together in the Maine congressional delegation.

In 1973, Peter joined the legislature, and I helped set up Bill's first office in Lewiston, which a friend and I ran together. On April 10, 1973, a cold, snowy spring day, I was at work in Congressman Cohen's office. I was talking with a constituent on the phone when

Dick Ray, a senior employee of Peter's, came in with a stricken look on his face. He told me I should put the phone down. I knew instantly that something terrible had happened, and without saying anything, I hung up the phone. He then delivered the crushing news: my husband's vehicle had flipped over on an icy road as he was driving from a legislative session back home to Auburn. He was killed instantly. Now I couldn't breathe, paralyzed by shock and devastation.

The days that followed were consumed by grief, disbelief, and going through the motions of having to make all the necessary arrangements.

Shortly after the funeral, friends and political leaders approached me about running for Peter's seat. I had never before considered running for office myself. I had worked, very recently, on elections for Peter and for Bill Cohen, and I'd campaigned and hosted coffees for other congressional and gubernatorial candidates, so I knew what being in a campaign entailed. As much as I loved politics, was this what I wanted to do?

The special election was only weeks away, on May 21, and I was struggling with my personal trauma and grief. The easy thing would have been to decline, but Peter had always said, "Olympia, you have an opinion on everything. Maybe you should run for office!" Now I recognized there was a certain logic to the idea. In what tragically proved to be foreshadowing, my husband had also told me very specifically, "If anything ever happens to me you should run for my seat."

In the history of American politics, other widows had taken over their husbands' seats, but not many of them had made it a career. However, I was already involved in the local Republican committees, and I did feel I could make a contribution. In the days leading up to my decision I had many long conversations with friends and family. Some asked why I'd want to run for office now, that it would seem the least likely time to assume an additional burden like this. Most said if you want to do it, then do it.

One of the people from whom I sought advice was Chris Potholm, professor of Government at Bowdoin College. Chris had been a classmate and very close friend of Bill Cohen when they were undergraduates at Bowdoin, and Chris had been the strategist of Bill's 1972 congressional campaign. It was Chris who asked me to help set up newly elected Congressman Bill Cohen's office early in 1973. When I found myself faced with this decision on whether to run, I knew Chris would give me the best advice. I went to see Chris and his wife, Sandy, for an overnight visit to talk through the various elements of this decision. As usual, Chris was able to lay out the important considerations and by the time I left, I had decided I would give it a try, saying to myself, if it doesn't work out, I won't do this again. But I made my mind up to run.

The result was by no means a foregone conclusion. We had to circulate petitions to get my name on the ballot, and I had to address the Republican City Committee and make my case for why I should be nominated for the special election. Someone stood up and asked if I was up to it, given the circumstances. I didn't like the inference and replied that I was well aware of what I was getting into, having been previously involved in Peter's campaigns. I was prepared to live up to my obligations and work hard running a full-fledged campaign. Others spoke in support of my effort, and I was nominated and ran against the Democratic nominee, Fred Brodeur.

In the election, I was rallied by some wonderful people who had just worked on Peter's campaign and volunteers who gathered from throughout the state. We started from scratch, doing everything Peter had done—door-to-door canvassing, speeches, radio ads—only this time I was the candidate. I discovered that it was one thing to be behind the scenes, working with Peter or Bill Cohen, and another thing altogether to be the focus of attention, asking people to entrust me with their votes. The circumstances were very emotionally charged. I was mourning my husband, and I had to reach deep within myself and focus hard on the campaign and everything it required of me.

I won the election. When Peter had been sworn into the state legislature on the opening day of the session in January, the local paper wanted to take a photograph of the two of us on the floor of the

House. Peter and I went back and forth over who should sit at his desk. He insisted that I should sit and he would stand next to me, and the photo was taken that way and published in the paper. Five months later, I was sitting at that same desk.

I served out Peter's first year and a second-year special session. I was reelected to the legislature in 1974 and won a seat in the Maine Senate in 1976, my last stop before I ran for Bill Cohen's U.S. House seat in 1978, when Bill entered the U.S. Senate race.

It would have been easier to decide not to run in 1973. When Peter died, I was struggling with the enormity of his sudden loss, and with my decision I heaped yet more pressure and responsibility on myself at a time when it would have been normal to refuse. Instead I chose to take on the challenge, to bring some order and control to my life after it had suddenly been upended once again, as it had been after the deaths of my mother, father, and uncle. I didn't want to be impetuous, or act prematurely, given the circumstances. But ultimately I was convinced that the discipline and the focus that the campaign would require would be good for me, and once I started running, I certainly did not want to lose.

When I was struggling through my own grief, my thoughts naturally gravitated to those others who shared similar tribulations. It occurred to me, what do other young widows do, especially those who have children? Seared into my consciousness was the understanding of how quickly events can change one's circumstances, and how horrific it is for those less fortunate with families to care for. This realization became the driving force behind my early legislative focus in Congress and fueled my sense of responsibility to champion issues of importance to women.

In my instance, I was at least fortunate in that Peter had been fastidious about making sure I was taken care of in case something happened to him. Just days before his death, in fact, he asked me to meet him at the bank and sign some papers. It was a Friday afternoon, and I was clear across town in Bill Cohen's office, but he insisted I come over before the banks closed to sign some paperwork involving some apartment buildings he owned. He had everything set up, just in case.

When I was elected to Congress, I discovered there were egregious inequities about pensions and benefits that were denied to women upon the death of a spouse. Women could face extreme obstacles if they did not have the support system I had. This was one specific area I felt a special obligation to act on in Washington. I came from reduced circumstances and was acutely aware that Peter's death could have easily left me in a very different situation.

After Peter died, I didn't languish in bitterness or anger about my situation. Fate can hand us terrible tragedies, but you have to work with what you have and try not to make your predicament any worse. In my darkest days I held out hope in the belief that life would get better tomorrow, and that I just had to wait it out, as hard as that was. I believed that the tough time would pass. Did I know it would get better? No, but I believed it would. This spirit is what carried me forward, and I always persevered in driving in that same direction.

That is a philosophy that would have to sustain me once again when the unimaginable occurred. In January 1991, my stepson, Peter McKernan, with whom I had become very close, died unexpectedly at age twenty during baseball practice from an undetected heart condition, while a sophomore at Dartmouth College.

I had experienced other tragedies in life but nothing could prepare me for this unspeakable loss. Jock and Peter had a beautiful father-son relationship, and what a blessing that Peter was able to spend a year with us at the Governor's Residence when he was attending Kents Hill School, a college preparatory school located nearby, before he attended Dartmouth. What a priceless gift that year would become.

The love and support we received from so many of Peter's extraordinary friends at Dartmouth were also extraordinary gifts. We drew tremendous strength and comfort from these young people during the most challenging of times. Among Peter's very finest traits was that he treasured friendship, and that's the gift he would bequeath to us at a moment when it would make all the difference. In particular, we have maintained a very close relationship with his best friend and roommate from Dartmouth, Jay Gonzales—which brings us indescribable joy. We are exceptionally proud of Jay, who recently served in the cabinet of Massachusetts Governor Deval Patrick as his administration and finance secretary.

The following June, President George H. W. Bush and First Lady Barbara Bush hosted the annual White House picnic for members of Congress and their families. I brought along one of Peter's best college friends, Jimmy Young, and as we were leaving the White House by way of the Rose Garden, I happened to encounter Ethel Kennedy and her son, Joe, with whom I was serving in Congress. I introduced them to Jimmy. He was quite excited to meet them and they were both extraordinarily gracious. As Ethel and Jimmy walked out together, Joe Kennedy and I were ahead of them and he expressed his sympathy at the loss of Peter. He said he had heard me speak recently on the floor of the House. "I watched you debating on the floor, and I thought it was great you still had the fighting spirit." That meant so much to me coming from someone who had experienced his own profound losses and understood the depth of despair. I've never forgotten it.

Part Two

Chapter 5

The Functional Congress

W HEN I WAS SWORN IN as a member of the 96th Congress in January 1979, it was my debut on the national stage. I represented Maine's 2nd Congressional District, the nearly half-million people living in the state's northern section, roughly 85 percent of the state's area and the largest congressional district east of the Mississippi River.

All freshmen in Congress bring to Washington their own particular bundle of personal beliefs and life experiences. My world and the world around me changed considerably, but my convictions did not alter radically during my tenure. I have never been one to follow the crowd. In my thirty-four years in Washington, the Republican Party drifted away from the mainstream, first in the House, and then in the Senate. Where I was once a cochair of a Republican National Convention and mentioned as a possible vice presidential running mate, I left the Senate in 2013 very concerned about the direction the party was headed.

Throughout my career I traveled the bipartisan road and was consistently a consensus-builder. When I joined the Senate in 1995, moderates on both sides of the aisle still made concerted efforts to maintain bipartisan links. For a long time that made me a valued member of the Republican caucus when it had a general interest in building bridges with Democrats. I persevered, finding common ground on vital fiscal and social concerns, until the partisan politicking took over and success became rare.

I was elected to Congress as a legislator, a Republican, and a woman—not necessarily in that order—with a commitment to help my country, my state, and my party. Above all else, in my view a legislator is a problem-solver. He or she has the ability and capacity to help constituents in large ways and small. There are myriad reasons that people run for a legislative office. Some are more interested in focusing on a narrow universe of issues, while others become involved in a wide range of legislative efforts. But to be successful, no legislator can neglect the full array of responsibilities and demands of the office, and that includes helping her constituents—someone trying to obtain her Social Security check or a veteran seeking his rightful benefits—who struggle with a powerful governmental bureaucracy. It's as critical for a legislator to be effective in these matters as it is in foreign policy or taxes.

My constituents were confident that I would go to bat for them to right a wrong. In 2006, *Time* magazine named me one of the ten Best Senators, calling me "The Caretaker" and noting that I was at the center of every policy debate in Washington. "She is also known as one of the most effective advocates for her constituents," the piece went on. "She goes back to Maine nearly every weekend, often stopping in a small town for what she calls a 'Main Street tour'—walking the streets and visiting shops to ask people what they're thinking about." In 2005, I ferociously fought alongside the rest of the Maine delegation for our state's military facilities and their exemplary workforce—and, remarkably, we were able to save two of the three installations slated for closure. And I secured funding to assist low-income Americans in paying their heating bills—a program I was instrumental in establishing.

Ultimately, I was driven to use the power, potential, and auspices of public office to move heaven and earth to do good and help others. I feel that commitment today as strongly as ever, and it drives me to now focus my energies outside the Senate, to fix what is now America's blocked and dysfunctional system.

In 1979, I was typical of Maine Republicans, both voters and legislators. I was independent-minded, fiscally conservative, and socially centrist, believing that government has a role in ensuring that the least fortunate Americans have an adequate safety net they can depend on when necessary. These views, even as they may have differed in small ways from those of my colleagues, as theirs did from mine, were recognizable as those of a moderate northeastern Republican. This breed is much scarcer today, as there are fewer centrist Republican legislators in total, and fewer still, in relative terms, from the Northeast.

Being a Republican did not preclude my willingness to work with legislators who were at different points on the political spectrum. Often a bill would be written off by some legislators because of who was presenting it. But that was never a factor in my thinking on an issue when I was looking for an essential legislative partnership. It was the issue that was paramount.

I worked with Jeff Sessions on honesty and transparency in budgeting, I supported Rand Paul (R-KY) on an amendment to force debate on U.S. military involvement in Libya in 2011, and Jim DeMint (R-SC) on advocating for a balanced budget amendment. I've also worked with the late Paul Simon (D-IL) on student loans, Ted Kennedy on a number of issues like the patient bill of rights, Ron Wyden (D-OR) on prescription drug coverage and a host of issues when we both served in the House, and Dianne Feinstein on landmark legislation requiring greater fuel economy for America's entire automobile fleet, to promote a healthier environment and reduce our dependence on foreign oil. Jack Reed (D-RI) and I partnered on home heating assistance, and pairing with Barbara Boxer (D-CA), we passed an airline passenger bill of rights. Why did we collaborate? Because we were in agreement on the particular piece of legislation. If a legislator is prepared to build a consensus to solve a problem, there is no limit to what he or she can achieve.

Consistently the Republican principles of limited government, lower taxes, individual freedoms and opportunity, and a strong national defense have been the basis of my political philosophy. But no party has a monopoly on good ideas. More often than not, when a solution is grounded in those fundamental Republican tenets, I have applied what might be described as a Republican formula to a problem. But not always. While holding strongly to my beliefs, I have never been rigid. This was the case in 1978 and it's true today.

In addition to the paramount concerns of my country, constituency, and party, I decided from the beginning of my career in elected office that I had a unique and overriding obligation to improve the lot of women in this nation. I took this responsibility seriously when I joined the legislature in Maine, but in the national arena I had more opportunity to make a significant difference.

In the 1980s, discrimination against women in society was still pervasive—in pension and wage inequality, in weak legal remedies for domestic violence, in negligible levels of funding for affordable and accessible child care, and in nonexistent child support enforcement. I was determined to play my part to make women's independence and survival more achievable within the law.

In 1979, there were only sixteen women in the House and one in the Senate. We recognized that we had to unite to fight for women's issues. We certainly didn't agree on everything, but we couldn't afford to draw political lines in the sand when it came to matters of importance to women. So when we spoke on these issues, we spoke as women, not as Republicans or Democrats. This esprit de corps and bipartisanship are still at work among congressional women, and a camaraderie and mutual respect transcends our political differences.

It is as a Republican consensus-builder, rather than as a woman legislator, that I have experienced the most change in my own role in Congress. In 1982, to the surprise of many and in what would be unheard-of today, House Minority Whip Trent Lott appointed me, as deputy whip, with the job of helping to run legislation through the House. It was a notable appointment because I was the first woman deputy whip to serve in history, but also because Trent wanted his whip organization to reflect the diverse political views represented within the party—including moderate northeastern Republicans. Just imagine the likelihood in 2013 of a deep-south Republican inviting a far-north Republican to join his whip team!

In later years, it was abundantly evident that my position on the political spectrum isolated me from the majority of the party. In April 2009, when Arlen Specter (R-PA) left the Republican Party, I wrote in an op-ed in the *New York Times*, "It is true that being a Republican moderate sometimes feels like being a cast member of *Survivor*—you are presented with multiple challenges, and you often get the distinct feeling that you're no longer welcome in the tribe." The common ground I had worked toward all of my career seemed to have fallen fallow.

Reflecting on the development of my political beliefs, it's difficult for me to pinpoint precisely when they coalesced, and there was no single "a-ha" moment that captured my Republican loyalty. Being orphaned at the age of nine forced me to become an extremely self-sufficient little girl and this undoubtedly formed the way I look at the world. I believe in individual responsibility and the notion that you do what you can for yourself. My concept of government's role in people's lives is that it is limited but legitimate, and essential when people have nowhere else to turn.

Every day I witnessed the tremendous sacrifices both my parents and my guardians—aunt Mary and uncle Jim—made to bring me up at a time when my aunt and uncle had five children of their own. After my uncle passed away, my aunt relied on very little other than herself. At that point she was working as a seamstress for a men's clothing store, and received small Social Security checks as a result of her husband's death.

My aunt Mary was instrumental in inspiring my drive to excel, the will to endure, and the tenacity to persevere. Particularly memorable were the words of wisdom she imparted one day when she saw me relaxing: "Olympia, while you're sitting, you should be thinking about what you could be *doing*." I admit there are times when I wondered if, throughout the years, that advice has proven more of a curse than a blessing! But that approach to living—the idea of forging excellence whenever possible and striving for success—has been essential to my ability to surmount otherwise impossible challenges. Aunt Mary also instilled in her children and me a sense of the importance of education. My aunt was a great source of strength and courage in my life, and she meant everything to me. She was a limitless source of inspiration.

People from Maine share a hard-earned reputation for independence. The coastline is rugged and often battered by an angry ocean. Most of the state is covered with forest, much of it remote, and the people toil on the land as loggers and farmers, or on the ocean fishing and lobstering. The men and women of Maine are hard workers who have had to adjust to the loss of thousands of textile and mill jobs that have mostly left New England. Many times they have rebounded from tough times like the ones we are in now, aided by their Yankee frugality and the robust self-sufficiency and determination with which they adapt to life's inevitable challenges.

When they go to the polls, Mainers have a tradition of electing candidates with similar traits who go on to be independent-minded legislators. Republican Senator Margaret Chase Smith is a prime example, and the state has a history of putting independent governors in the Blaine House, the governor's mansion in Augusta. One was Jim Longley, in 1974; another was Angus King, who succeeded Jock in 1995 and who succeeded me as senator in 2013. As further evidence, Ross Perot, in his 1992 run for the presidency, had his strongest showing in Maine, garnering more than 30 percent of the vote in the 2nd Congressional District—which I represented at the time and ultimately for sixteen years.

Every member of Maine's congressional delegation is very conscious of the legacy of Senator Margaret Chase Smith, the first woman elected to both the U.S. House and the U.S. Senate. Smith represented Maine's 2nd District from 1940 to 1949, and then was senator from 1949 to 1973. In her independence and integrity, Senator Smith personified the values of Maine people. She consistently did what she thought was in the best interests of her state and her country, unfailingly following her conscience.

On June 1, 1950, Senator Smith stood before the Senate and delivered an excoriating indictment of the red-scare tactics of Senator Joseph McCarthy. Not only was McCarthy a man of great power and influence, but he was a member of Smith's own party. Smith was taking a huge risk, but she felt compelled to speak out because McCarthy's false accusations were destroying lives and fueling paranoia and fear across the nation.

Smith never mentioned McCarthy by name, but the intent of her speech was obvious, beginning with its title, the "Declaration of Conscience." Smith upbraided any Senate colleague who would abuse congressional immunity to make unsubstantiated attacks on American citizens and reminded the senators that they had sworn to uphold the Constitution, which allows free speech and trial by jury, not accusation. She argued that the country would suffer if the current Democratic administration remained in power, but if Republicans won without "political integrity or intellectual honesty," it would be equally disastrous. "I don't want to see the Republican Party ride to political victory on the Four Horsemen of calumny—Fear, Ignorance, Bigotry, and Smear."

I have often tried to imagine what it must have been like for Senator Smith to make that speech. It was an extraordinary act of courage to publicly slay a giant of demagoguery when her ninety-four male colleagues would not (there were forty-eight states in 1950). McCarthy exacted revenge by removing Senator Smith from his Permanent Subcommittee on Investigations and organizing a primary challenge to her, but Senator Smith far outlasted McCarthy, who was condemned by the Senate in 1954. Smith's speech exemplified the essence of leadership, which in another age might have propelled her to greater national prominence. As financier and presidential adviser Bernard Baruch said, "If a man had made the Declaration of Conscience, he would have been the next President of the United States."

The state of Maine used to further demonstrate its singularity by holding elections in September rather than November, a quirky tradition that continued for more than a hundred years until it ended with the 1958 vote. From this oddity rose the saying, "As Maine goes, so goes the nation," the election seen as a predictor of the rest of the country's intentions two months hence. Maine was true to its spirit with that last September vote in 1958, returning Edmund Muskie to the Senate. Muskie was the first Democrat elected to the Senate from Maine, and Democratic gains in the governor's office and Congress foreshadowed national GOP losses in November.

In 1960, two years after that election, I was thirteen and at school at St. Basil Academy in New York when I had the first political experience that I remember as an early marker for my interest in politics. Before the national election, it was decided there would be a straw poll at St. Basil's for the presidential race, and for some reason I volunteered to lead the poll on behalf of President Eisenhower's two-time vice president and Republican candidate for the presidency, Richard Nixon. I confess that I don't recall precisely why I backed Nixon over Kennedy, but it was clearly indicative of my nascent Republican predisposition. I also know that my mother had been interested in politics and she wrote to the governor or the secretary of state, but I don't know whether she, or my aunt and uncle, for that matter, considered herself Republican or Democrat.

In high school, my academic interest in current affairs and politics took shape. During my junior year at Edward Little High School in Auburn, President Kennedy was assassinated. I opened the door when I got home from school and saw my aunt standing right in front of me with tears in her eyes. She told me in a quavering voice that President Kennedy had been killed. I ran to the television to see for myself and I couldn't believe it. Later I made my way to the local library to do some homework and to find others to connect to at this unimaginable moment. I asked the librarian, Mrs. Cody, if she had heard the devastating news as the rest of the country had. She had, and we talked through it together for some time. Like every other American, I was glued to the TV coverage for days after.

Our family had just suffered the recent loss of my uncle Jim; we were still in a state of mourning, and now so was the entire nation. I was awed by Jackie Kennedy's grace, poise, and courage as she confronted these horrific circumstances. They left a lasting impression on me and I tried to draw on her example and image of strength as I struggled through my own ordeal ten years later.

When I was attending the University of Maine, there was not a heavy Republican Party presence on campus. I was a self-described Republican by this time, but not an activist.

It was as a senior in college, on my second visit to Washington, that I met Margaret Chase Smith. It was January 1969, and I was attending President Nixon's inauguration with my fiancé Peter Snowe. We stood by the Capitol's East Portico in the freezing cold and went to the inaugural ball that evening. The Lewiston paper published a picture of me in my long dress. Senator Smith knew Peter from campaigns in Maine so we were able to visit her in her Senate office and I sat in front of the legendary senator's desk. It was another political connection that, at the time, I didn't know I had made.

In 1970, on my first visit to the party's state convention in Portland, Senator Smith spoke. The county delegations were seated according to how they reached their fund-raising goals and my county, Androscoggin, had surpassed our target so we were seated in the front row. As a woman who was dominant in a man's world, the Senate, Smith mesmerized me and I couldn't wait to hear her speak. The senator commanded the audience's attention with her presence. When she stated simply and powerfully, "I tell it like it is!" the place erupted with applause.

When Senator Smith lost an election, in 1972, she was heartbroken. I attended a Republican women's group luncheon for her at a small restaurant outside Auburn shortly after. She addressed the group with sadness, but it was inspiring to see her so stoically honoring her commitment.

In 1976, while I was in the Maine Senate, there was significant speculation that Bill Cohen would run against Senator Ed Muskie, and that Jock was thinking about running for Bill's 2nd Congressional District seat. At that point Jock and I were serving in the legislature together, where he was assistant minority leader. Jock described his itinerary as he traveled across the district attending Republican dinners and events and laying the groundwork for a potential campaign. I said to him at one point, "Well, I'm glad you're doing it because I wouldn't want to!" But that year, Bill Cohen ran for reelection to the U.S. House. Subsequently, Jock moved out of the 2nd Congressional District to join a law firm in southern Maine.

In July 1977, I was in the throes of shepherding all of the bills in my committee in the final days of the legislative session. It was a beautiful summer day and I was driving between Auburn and Augusta, listening to the radio. A late-breaking news item was announced: Congressman Bill Cohen would not be seeking reelection to the United States House of Representatives. There was nothing in the broadcast about Bill running for the Senate, but I recognized that it was implicit in his decision.

I understood that this was potentially a watershed moment for me. If I wanted to take on the challenge of running for Bill Cohen's now-vacant seat, the ball was in my court. I took an immediate detour on my way to Augusta and drove to the cottage I was renting during the final months of the legislative session with two of my friends and fellow legislators, Barbara Gill and Angela Aloupis. Barbara wasn't there, but as soon as I saw Angela, who was a childhood friend (and would later become my district director when I was elected to the House), I said, "Did you hear the news?" She said, "Yes!" Angela was very excited. "I hope you're going to do it." She assumed I was going to run, but that was something I needed to figure out for myself, and quickly.

The first person I saw when I arrived at the State House was Jock, who greeted me by saying, "You have to run, and I will do anything you need to help!" I knew he had given a great deal of thought to how to run for the 2nd Congressional District seat, and so we decided to have dinner and discuss the best way to proceed.

It was at that dinner that we agreed I would begin to solicit support from my fellow Republican legislators in order to dissuade others from considering a run. Jock agreed to write the campaign plan and to have his mother (a well-known Republican activist) begin to organize the city of Bangor—Jock's hometown and the hub of eastern Maine.

Jock's plan called for establishing an exploratory committee and travelling around the district, testing the waters by meeting with opinion makers and key members of the local Republican organizations. The effort worked as planned. We avoided a primary, and in January 1978, I announced my candidacy for Bill's seat. Bill was exceptionally encouraging of my efforts. He set a standard for all of us who followed him into elective office as a leader of courage and conscience—who was willing to make the challenging decisions even as a freshman in the House and a member of the Judiciary Committee, where he broke with his party to vote for the impeachment of President Nixon. He went on to have a distinguished career not only as a United States senator but as secretary of defense under President Clinton. Bill's popularity in Maine was undeniable; and he, like Jock, came from Bangor, where coincidentally, they were both high school basketball stars. I admired him greatly, and his support meant the world to me.

Jock was unquestionably of tremendous help at this pivotal juncture in my life, and it wouldn't be for the last time. Little did I know that the passion we shared for public service would lead to a wonderful life together.

We eventually began dating, and when Jock was elected to the U.S. House of Representatives in 1982, in what was a unique situation, since Maine has only two districts, between us we represented the entire state. In 1987, after two terms in the House, Jock became the first Republican governor of Maine in twenty years. At this point, circumstances had changed—it was becoming more and more difficult to spend time apart, so we made the decision that we would get married. In 1989, after going out for a decade, we became the first governor and member of Congress (and later senator) to wed. I added the title of "First Lady" to my existing position as "Congresswoman." As we used to joke when we were both in public office, our idea of quality time together was listening to each other's speeches!

The first time you seek office, you're introducing yourself to the electorate. Following Bill Cohen's example, I walked the congressional district from west to east, from Bangor to Washington County, and north to Aroostook County. I didn't cover every mile on foot, but enough over a period of months to meet people and get a sense of their communities. The most important question to face the first time is, why do you want the job? You have to establish your identity and credibility, and what you want to accomplish. My campaign strategy was that I was "not one of the boys," meaning that I wasn't going to go to Washington to go with the flow of things and become another member of the club. I also focused on how I could bring my state experience to bear in Washington.

The campaign generally went well throughout the race. We had the right plan, the right media, the right message, and the right staff, led by David Sparks, my seasoned campaign manager. Jock continued to be the strategist and my sounding board, as he has been for more than thirty years now.

I also had the advantage of being a well-known Republican who had been elected to the statehouse from a Democratic stronghold. I won comfortably with 50.8 percent of the vote in a seven-way race, with the second-place candidate, Democrat Mark Gartley, garnering 40.9 percent. I was thirty-one, and to this day, I remain the youngest Republican woman ever elected to Congress.

The incoming Republican congressmen and women in my class met for orientation sessions at a Marriott hotel near Washington's Dulles Airport. The hotel is in northern Virginia, and far enough outside the city that you can see the Blue Ridge Mountains. Clearly the leadership wanted to isolate us so there would be no distractions. We were a large class of incoming Republicans, including Dick Cheney (R-WY) and Newt Gingrich (R-GA). It was an exciting time and this was an enthusiastic group that was determined to get things done in Congress. We weren't going to be satisfied warming seats in the minority—the position Republicans had found themselves in since 1954 in the House. We wanted to make our mark.

As a first-term congresswoman, I diligently responded to the concerns of my constituency, which is essential in building connections with voters and potential voters. In the first piece of legislation I introduced, I opposed the Dickey-Lincoln hydroelectric dam on the pristine upper St. John River in the very north of my district. For part of its course, the river marks the border between the United States and Canada. I thought the project would produce power only intermittently, and even then at relatively low levels; create few permanent jobs; but cut a wide swath through miles of scenic country and flood thousands of acres of land. My position was opposite to that of Maine Senator Ed Muskie—who was a legislative giant in Maine and in our nation, and who remained in the Senate until 1980, when President Carter appointed him secretary of state.

Jock and I became good friends with Senator Muskie and his wife, Jane, and we hosted them, their family, and twenty-five of their friends for his eightieth birthday celebration at the Blaine House. We derived great joy in spending that occasion with them, and he considered his tenure as governor of Maine his most enjoyable time in public service. I couldn't help but think how important gatherings like the one we organized that night are to the functioning of our government.

In the end, our campaign against the plant was successful. The project was never built, and the dam was finally deauthorized by Congress in 1986.

Even after you've been elected, you're still very much trying to define yourself. In preparing for my reelection, I had a conversation with my pollster, Robert Teeter, who later joined Market Opinion Research and worked on multiple GOP presidential campaigns. He said to me, "Of course we'll also have to run ads telling voters about who you are." I said, "But didn't they just elect me?" "Yes," he responded. "But they still don't really know you." He was right, and I never forgot that lesson. It's essential to remind people what you stand for and what you've accomplished, and to never take anything for granted.

***

On arriving in Congress, I was surprised by the conservatism of some members of our caucus. Most Republicans in Maine would have been categorized as being from the more moderate wing of the party. We were what were called "Rockefeller Republicans," by and large, practical fiscal conservatives and not the more ideological or social conservatives I encountered in the House and who made up a significant percentage of our number. As a group, however, we as Republicans didn't pigeonhole ourselves and we could usually work together on legislative issues. While there were differences, they were narrower than they are today, and we were not consumed by them. It was similar to the situation back in Maine. Republicans of a similar frame of mind, like Bill Cohen, and Jock, when he came to Congress in 1983, experienced primary challenges from conservatives, but political reconciliation within the party was still possible, and almost always occurred, once the challenge was overcome.

In the early 1980s, the House, as I mentioned earlier, was the home of the Gypsy Moths and Boll Weevils who were prepared to at least consider a bipartisan approach to solving a problem as it presented itself. In addition to the consensus-building route to legislative solutions, an individual representative had the considerable potential power to introduce an amendment to a piece of legislation making its way through Congress.

The Government Operations Committee, which I served on during my first year, was chaired by Jack Brooks (D-TX), already a legendary figure in Congress. Brooks, who died in 2012 at the age of eighty-nine, represented two House districts in Texas for more than forty years. I once had the temerity to read back the chairman's own words to him on some issue he'd expressed differing views on. I think he appreciated my moxie; he was smiling as I spoke!

In 1980, my second year in the House as a member of the Government Affairs Committee, I proposed an amendment to legislation that was designed to distribute money to economically distressed regions of the country as part of President Carter's commitment to urban policy. The money came in two forms, $200 million as "Targeted Fiscal Assistance" to cities with higher-than-average unemployment and lower-than-average growth; and $800 million of "countercyclical" assistance that was to be made available in the event of a recession (defined as two consecutive quarters of a decline in gross national product).

According to the original proposal, the money was allocated according to a complicated formula under which New York City would receive $37 million and other municipalities in the state $15 million of the allocation of Targeted Fiscal Assistance—26 percent of the total. California was also awarded significant help, so much so that to these two states, vital as they are, and comprising 18 percent of the country's population, were supposed to get 40 percent of the money. States like Maine were losing out; Washington County, Maine, with severe unemployment and low wages, wasn't going to get a dime. I thought the money was being split inequitably and the imbalance needed to be addressed. So I went into battle.

In contrast to the Maine State House, I now had a staff to assist me. From the beginning I told them to think like Sherlock Holmes. Presented with an issue, they had to get to the bottom of it, thoroughly learn the ins and outs, and figure out a solution. In my office, at whatever level, we've always immersed ourselves in every detail of any given subject.

In this case, I circulated a list on the floor to every member, highlighting which states would stand to benefit and which were going to lose out. Since every state except New York and California would be allocated additional money under my plan, I thought I would have most members on my side, and I did. After a heated session on the floor, led by the eighty members of the New York delegation, I prevailed. My amendment refashioned the formula so that no one state could get more than 12.5 percent of the money, making the whole package fairer to smaller states. The bill passed by 214 to 179 in the House, with most Republicans opposing. The legislative process, including the acceptance of amendments, had been allowed to work. Today, this scenario couldn't even be contemplated in the House and it is increasingly rare in the Senate. But back then a freshman minority member like me could have a substantive impact on legislation.

As of the beginning of 2013, the last time there was an "open special rule" allowing for an open amendment process was while the House was debating the 2013 Defense Department appropriations bill on June 29, 2012. The Woodrow Wilson Center in Washington went back to look at House data over the years and found that there has been a significant reduction in the use of an open rules process on the floor. During the 96th Congress (1979–81), 161 bills (75 percent) were considered under "open rules." In my last session in the House during the 103rd Congress, the number had dropped to 31. And in the 110th Congress, the House considered 23 bills under "open rules" (15 percent).

It's my belief that today the leadership tries to protect members from voting on sensitive matters that could jeopardize their reelection. Much of what is done in Congress is designed for a thirty-second ad, the purpose of which is political leveraging, no more, no less. Advancing a policy position or disadvantaging the other side is more important than solving a problem, which can be done by means of a vote like we had on Targeted Fiscal Assistance. The ability to offer an amendment is critical, especially for a member of the minority party, as was the case with my House experience. I didn't run my idea past the party leadership in 1979, and I took advantage of the open amendment process. Then, a single representative could offer her idea, work with others in both political parties, and her amendment was allowed to proceed to a vote where it was judged by the House on its merits. This is what we did in the Maine legislature, when I had acted on my principles, came up with ideas to solve problems, and designed legislative solutions.

Now, in Congress, I was taking on larger, more entrenched interests. New York City's share of the money was scheduled to fall to $15 million and I made the front page of the *New York Times* in February 1980, where Mayor Ed Koch said the amendment was "very, very unfair."The headline in the *Portland Press Herald* was "Olympia Makes 'em Mad in Gotham," which had not been my intention. The *NewYork Times* quoted me as saying, "I love NewYork, as we all say," and I tried to prove the point when I wore an "I Love NewYork" button the day after the vote. And it's true, I do, and I would have proposed my amendment had it been Kansas City and the state of Florida getting a disproportionate share of the money.

This wasn't the only time I had an impact even as a single, minority voice in the U.S. House. In my freshman year, Congressman Silvio Conte, then-ranking member of the Appropriations Committee, informed me about a hearing being held concerned with creating the Low Income Home Energy Assistance Program (LIHEAP) in the midst of our country's major energy crisis. In 1973, the retail price of gasoline was just 39 cents per gallon. By January 1979, the price had jumped to 68.2 cents, by May that year it was 80.3 cents, and by August the price was 96.3 cents per gallon. Representative Conte asked if I wanted to testify along with Speaker of the House Tip O'Neill. So I joined the Speaker that afternoon in championing this program to assist less fortunate Americans in paying their heating bills at a time of skyrocketing prices.The program exists to this day.

In 1986, the Department of Energy recommended two sites in Maine for study to be considered as a nuclear waste depository. In the aftermath of a public outcry that followed, I was one of the leaders of a bipartisan effort to support the House chairman of the then-Interior and Insular Affairs Committee, Congressman Mo Udall (D-AZ)—who was a legendary environmental defender, to amend the Nuclear Waste Policy Act of 1982 to designate one facility,Yucca Mountain in Nevada, as the single nuclear repository. Mainers united in their opposition to the proposal. Commenting on the public hearings on the 1986 proposal and the thousands who turned out in protest, Governor Joseph Brennan was quoted in the *Philadelphia Inquirer* saying, "There has been nothing like it since theVietnam War."

Critically, in those days, my independent-mindedness did not lead to my ostracism in the House. To the contrary, it garnered me a position in Trent Lott's whip organization as deputy whip, and as cochair of the Republican National Convention in New Orleans, where I was also honored to speak at First Lady Nancy Reagan's luncheon. Geographic and ideological distinctions existed within the caucus as they always have done. Newt Gingrich, my fellow member of the class of '78, was always a man of action whose driving ambition was to return the party to power in Congress. As a young man, Gingrich had been a Rockefeller Republican, having worked for the Rockefeller campaign in 1968 when he was a student at Tulane University. In Congress he was a maverick. In 1979, he was one of thirty Republicans to vote for the creation of the Department of Education, and his ideas of an "activist" government were anathema to some in our party.

So in 1983 Gingrich founded the Conservative Opportunity Society. Two years later, I helped cofound the 92 Group with Representative Tom Tauke (R-IA) and thirty-five colleagues. Our name referred to 1992, the year we were targeting to become the majority party by developing positions that would achieve electoral success. Both groups aspired to the same goal: the return of Republican ideas into the center of government. But if the groups were working toward a similar destination, they were taking dramatically different routes. The COS was more partisan and confrontational; the 92 Group looked to bring Republican ideas onto common ground with the Democrats.

The existence of both the 92 Group and the Conservative Opportunity Society showed the diversity of ideas, strategy, and tactics that existed within the Republican caucus. And they mirrored its regional distinctions: the 92 Group was largely northeastern and midwestern; the COS, with its leader from Georgia, more southern and western.

In 1989, after Trent Lott was elected to the U.S. Senate, he was briefly succeeded as Minority Whip by Congressman Dick Cheney, but after Cheney was appointed secretary of defense, Congressman Newt Gingrich won the election to replace him by two votes over

Representative Edward Madigan (R-IL). Newt had called me at around nine o'clock the night before the election to ask if I would second his nomination, so I knew what was at stake and that the race would be close.

I hadn't decided until the final days to support him, but by the time he called I'd made up my mind and so I agreed to speak on his behalf. It was my belief that a coalition of Gingrich's group and that of more moderate Republicans of the 92 Group, whose style and outlook was mirrored by Minority Whip candidate Bob Michel (R-IL), would help us reach the Republican majority we all coveted.

In my speech, I said that I couldn't help think of Newt Gingrich and Bob Michel as the "Odd Couple," referring to the Neil Simon play, movie, and seventies sitcom about the very fastidious Felix and the very untidy Oscar. My only question was, which one of Newt and Bob would be Felix and which would be Oscar.

But for Republicans to become the majority party, an odd couple was what we needed: the "experience, patience, and understanding of Bob Michel's leadership," and the "dynamism, fresh ideas, and vision that Newt Gingrich can bring." I described my voting record and Newt's as "something quite short of carbon copies," but we could have differences and still be good Republicans. It was consistent with the aims of the 92 Group to support Newt Gingrich's nomination, I said, because he should be part of the coalition that could "shatter the yoke of the status quo."

I was far from the only moderate to support him—he was nominated by another, Bill Frenzel of Minnesota, and seven of the ten New England Republicans supported him. I had meetings with Newt over his candidacy and I thought we had basic agreements on key fiscal issues that all Republicans could agree on for reducing spending and balancing budgets. I knew that in seconding his nomination, I was going to get a lot of credit if it went well, and a lot of blame if it didn't.

When Newt was working within the Republican conference during my time in the House, he always tried to build consensus, and

I thought he was one person who could take us to a majority. In 1994, he did—and became Speaker of the House in 1995 as I took up my seat in the United States Senate. I had found success through consensus-building in the House and hoped to replicate that experience in the upper chamber. And one of my abiding and continuing priorities was the well-being of women in American society.

Chapter 6

Women's Issues

WHEN I FIRST CAME TO WASHINGTON, I was struck by how few women there were in Congress. In the Senate, Nancy Kassebaum (R-KS) was alone, and only sixteen women served in the House, among them Millicent Fenwick (R-NJ), Geraldine Ferraro (D-NY), and Pat Schroeder (D-CO). Barbara Mikulski was in the House, where she served from 1977 to 1987, and she has represented Maryland since then in the Senate, making her the longest-serving female senator and the woman with the longest overall tenure in the entire history of the United States Congress. The percentage of women in Congress was relatively unchanged from the 1950s through the 1980s. In fact, women's representation had been almost negligible since the first woman representative, Jeannette Rankin, was elected in 1917 until the "Year of the Woman" in 1992, when the number of women in Congress almost doubled.

I was one of the women senators who wrote a book together in 2000, *Nine and Counting*. With our effort, we wanted women and girls to know that their voices can and must be heard—not only in the halls of Congress, but in classrooms and boardrooms; on ball fields and in all areas of endeavor. As I joked at the time, we often said we made our male colleagues suspicious every time the women in the Senate got together; so we could only imagine what they would have thought if they had known we were writing a book—goodness knows what we'd say!

I'm pleased to say the 113th Congress has twenty women (and counting) in the Senate, less pleased that only four of them are Republicans! And where there were 16 women in the House of Representatives in 1979, in 2013 there were 78. Still, while women make up 18 percent of Congress, we are 51 percent of the U.S. population. Progress, or the lack of it, is measured by more than numbers alone, and in the House no women were appointed committee chairs when assignments were made for the 113th Congress. In the Senate, by contrast, there are eight committees chaired by women.

Congress hasn't always been the most welcoming of places for a woman. (In the early days we encountered simple practical problems like the number and location of restrooms.) I was nominated by a colleague to become a member of a discussion group within the Republican Party but a male colleague shot me down, saying, "We can't have women here."

But that was nothing like the shameful treatment Pat Schroeder endured when she joined the House Armed Services Committee in 1972. As she recounts in her autobiography, Pat wanted to be part of a body that controlled 65 cents of every dollar spent by Congress. No woman had ever served on the committee and the chairman F. Edward Hébert, a Democrat from Louisiana, preferred it that way. When Pat got her wish and was appointed, Hébert told her, "I hope you aren't going to be a skinny Bella Abzug," a comment intended to insult both Pat and the feminist Abzug, a representative from New York. Unforgivably, Hébert also objected to the committee's first African-American member, Ron Dellums, and when the committee met, he made Schroeder and Dellums share one chair because, Hébert said, they were only worth half a seat each. Dellums and Schroeder got their own seats, Hébert eventually lost his chair, and I joined the Republican Party discussion group a few years later.

A woman often brings a different perspective to decision-making in government. We all have our own backgrounds and viewpoints, of course, but I believe that, in general, women are more relationship-oriented and more collaborative. Perhaps it's because many of the skills women develop in life are particularly applicable to an institution like the Senate, where collaboration is required to achieve results.

The severe underrepresentation of women in Congress contributed to the legal discrimination we faced in the past and face today, albeit to a lesser extent. While there were certainly many male colleagues who had joined the battle to "right" these "wrongs" enshrined in laws that were working against women, it was also apparent there could be no substitute for having women in the arena to drive the agenda.

Women like Pat Schroeder, who joined the House in 1972, and Geraldine Ferraro, who was in my freshman class after the 1978 election, were indicative of changes that were taking place in the workforce. (As an illustration of how the political environment has evolved, I once attended one of Geraldine's fund-raisers, which even then was highly unusual.) Pat and Geraldine were both mothers with school-age children when we started working together: Pat had two children in grade school and Geraldine three in high school. It is crucial that our political institutions reflect American society; that they include working women and mothers, people from ethnic and religious minorities, and representatives of all shades of legitimate political expression. Perhaps because we have always been an underrepresented group, women in Congress have more often than not been more resistant to partisanship than our male colleagues. We do have disagreements over policy, but if I approached a female colleague to garner her support or asked her to join me as a partner on an issue, I would invariably find a willing participant and an active listener, someone who would help construct a viable solution.

One of the initiatives I am promoting in my post-Senate career is the Women's Leadership Institute, which I have established in Maine. Our aim is to develop life skills and leadership capabilities in young women in high school in the state, making them aware of their assets and how they can be translated into opportunities later in life. It's essential for women to recognize their own strengths and develop plans and not set limits on their goals. Our aim is to find leaders who can be a positive force in all areas of business and society, but if we can nurture women legislators, so much the better.

My friends in college were amazed that I was so enthusiastic about my political science major and singularly focused on eventually going to Washington to work in some capacity. That kind of passionate calling is an important trait to cultivate in girls early on, and the sooner they can get on track the better. High school is difficult enough to begin with, but it can be easier once a young woman recognizes her own potential and understands that she can make a significant contribution in the larger world.

In 1979, I joined what was then called the Congresswoman's Caucus, which would later change to the Congressional Caucus on Women's Issues, an organization 125 members strong that I cochaired for more than ten years, beginning in 1983, with Democrat Pat Schroeder, who was a great colleague and partner in our mutual zeal for our cause. We presided over what Women's Policy Inc. called some of the group's "most historic achievements." I was the fourth member to serve as cochair since the caucus was founded in 1977 by Congresswoman Elizabeth Holtzman, a pro-choice Democrat from New York, and Congresswoman Margaret Heckler, a pro-life Republican from Massachusetts. They understood that despite their differences, they couldn't afford to draw lines in the sand on issues of importance to women when we were so drastically underrepresented in Congress.

In 1981, when some of our male colleagues expressed interest in being part of the caucus, the group decided to rename the organization the Congressional Caucus for Women's Issues, so the men could join. That change helped to build and broaden support for the bills and initiatives we were championing.

The caucus met in a beautiful little oasis in the U.S. Capitol accessed by a door between two statues right off the old House Chamber (now Statuary Hall). In 1848, John Quincy Adams, who served in the U.S. House after he was President, collapsed on the floor of the House. He was brought to this room and it is where he died two days later on a sofa that still remains there. At that time, it was the Speaker's office; eventually it became the Congresswomen's Reading Room, and by House resolution in 1991 was renamed the Lindy Claiborne Boggs Congressional Women's Reading Room, in honor of the esteemed congresswoman, the first woman to be elected to Congress from Louisiana, and longtime secretary of the caucus.

At one point when Speaker of the House Tom Foley's wife wanted to incorporate the reading room into expanded offices for the Speaker, I prepared to write a letter to circulate among all our female colleagues vigorously opposing that takeover, but Lindy said, "Listen, Olympia, let me see if I can just go take care of this. If not, then we can consider the letter." And she did take care of it, in the way only she could, in her genteel but persuasive manner.

In 2012, the photographs of all of the 228 women who had served in the 216-year history of the United States Congress were displayed in the room, and whenever I saw them, it always struck me that all the women who ever came to the House or Senate fit onto just a few small walls! By the 113th Congress, the total number of women senators and representatives who had ever served reached 296. They could all sit in the House of Representatives with 139 seats to spare. (The total number of individuals who have served as representatives and/or senators was 12,099, so the ratio of women is very low.)

The number and scale of issues that women in America confronted was daunting, but the legislators representing them worked to address and solve the problems methodically. In President Ronald Reagan, we found a chief executive who was willing to listen and, in various instances, to act.

The results of the 1980 presidential election revealed that Ronald Reagan had an eight-point "gender gap" between women and men voters. The party's support among women was eroded by the dropping of its endorsement for the Equal Rights Amendment from the platform and President Reagan's stance opposing *Roe v. Wade.* When President Reagan performed even worse with women voters in subsequent polls, he recognized that he had a problem. Following the 1982 midterm elections, I arranged a private meeting with White House Chief of Staff Jim Baker to encourage that Elizabeth Dole and former Representative Margaret Heckler be nominated to cabinet positions. Elizabeth, who married Republican Senator Bob Dole of Kansas in 1975, had served as White House consumer affairs aide for President Nixon and a consumer advocate for the Federal Trade Commission.

In 1983, I organized meetings between all of the House Republican women and President Reagan to garner his support for a proactive legislative agenda that targeted major inequities that posed obstacles to women and their families. We sat down in the Roosevelt Room of the White House with the President and Vice President Bush, and I was particularly gratified to see both Elizabeth Dole, now secretary of transportation, and Margaret Heckler, the President's choice for secretary of health and human services, at the table.

We discussed issues like workplace discrimination, child care, and child-support enforcement; more top-level talks took place over the coming months. I remember that the President was very attentive with a quizzical look on his face, as if he were thinking, "Why would I have a problem with women voters? I care about their issues!"

Following these meetings, President Reagan championed enforcement of child support payments, which was controversial, incredibly, as many in the administration believed government should not become involved. Indeed, child support enforcement had been assumed to be a woman's problem, not society's; but now it's a matter for the courts to enforce.

In 1983 the caucus bundled a comprehensive package of reforms, including child support enforcement, into the Economic Equity Act, which was designed to redress some of the worst legal imbalances, grouped under two main headings: work and family. They represented areas where women's roles in society had changed: as working women, single heads of households, as caregivers, or as elderly women living alone. The act was introduced by Pat Schroeder and me in the House and Alan Cranston (D-CA) and Dave Durenberger (R-MN) in the Senate. It also included a provision that for the first time allowed homemakers to contribute to an IRA and gave single heads of households the same tax status as married couples. In addition, expanding the dependent care tax credit assisted millions of working families struggling with child care or elderly dependent care.

We sought pension reform, when far fewer women than men had private pensions but were also often denied survivor's rights. One day a woman testified before the House Permanent Select Committee on Aging, a special committee chaired by the legendary Democratic Representative Claude Pepper of Florida, who was an iconic figure particularly to America's seniors. She described how she had been denied a share of her husband's pension: He had worked for a company for twenty-nine years and died of leukemia thirteen days before his fifty-fifth birthday. In those days, a woman could lose her pension if her husband canceled his benefits without informing her, and Congresswoman Ferraro led the effort to end this injustice.

By no means was every legislative goal reached at the first attempt or, in some cases, ever, but the caucus was entirely successful in raising questions about women's issues in an organized and concerted manner that had not been attempted before. As a result, the changing roles that women were finding and aspiring to, and our attempts to create legislative solution to discriminatory injustices, were highlighted.

President Reagan discussed women's issues in his State of the Union addresses. In his 1982 address, the President highlighted the launch of the Task Force on Legal Equity for Women and a Fifty States Project, which sought to review state laws for discriminatory language. He also hailed Sandra Day O'Connor, whom he had appointed

as the first woman U.S. Supreme Court justice in history. It was for-
tuitous that they hit it off so exceptionally well in their first meeting,
as her landmark selection could not have been a more superlative example and role model for women across the nation, and the world.
In his 1984 State of the Union address, Reagan noted that women
had filled 73 percent of new jobs in the managerial, professional, and
technical fields the previous year.

In retrospect what was so unusual about our meetings with the
President was that they took place at all. It never occurred to me that
President Reagan would not agree to our requests. Yet they would be
almost inconceivable in the current political discord between
branches of government.

I first met Ronald Reagan at a dinner in Portland, Maine, in
1978, when he was on a speaking tour. At that point I was serving in
the Maine Senate. I sat at the head table, directly to the right of the
former California governor, whose last term in that office had ended
in 1975. In his address he spoke about reforming the welfare system,
which became a prominent theme in his national campaign. He concluded his speech with a question-and-answer session.

When he was finished, Governor Reagan sat down and then
leaned over to me and asked, "Do you happen to know the name of
the woman who asked the last question?" I said, "No, but I can find
out. Why would you like her name?" "I don't believe I gave her a sufficient answer," he said. "And I want to follow up with her." I was very
impressed that he cared enough to rethink how he responded, and
that it was important to him. That left a lasting impression on me.
He was intensely committed and passionate about his view of the
world and his vision for the country. There was speculation that Governor Reagan was going to run against Jimmy Carter in 1980, but I
just wasn't expecting him to be President, or that our paths would
cross again in the U.S. House of Representatives.

Throughout my tenure in Congress, I have often promoted
President Reagan's way of interacting with the Congress as a model
of how cooperative relationships can be established across party lines.

Reagan was relatively accessible himself and had an exceptionally disciplined and professional liaison team that assiduously operated in both chambers. They were a familiar presence on Capitol Hill, constantly patrolling the hallways and buttonholing members of Congress. Before a major meeting between President Reagan and Canadian Prime Minister Brian Mulroney in March 1985, when Jock and I were both serving in the House, we were granted a meeting with the President to discuss concerns we had about major cross-border trade issues, primarily Canadian potato crops (since potatoes are a major crop in Maine). In Volume One of his *Diaries,* Reagan noted the purpose of our coming to see him and showed the lengths to which he would go to be responsive and attentive to lawmakers:

> Reps. Olympia Snowe & John McKernan (Maine) came by to plead their case re Canadas dumping subsidized potatoes, wood products & fish on Maine to the great detriment of those same products produced in Maine. I've promised to take this up with P.M. Mulroney when we meet in Canada next week.

President Reagan was engaged in the process of lawmaking, but there was a limit to his support for our initiatives. He was opposed to ratification of the Equal Rights Amendment, a measure I was vehemently in favor of. (The ERA had overwhelmingly passed Congress in 1972 but required a supermajority of states to ratify it within seven years, a qualifying standard it narrowly failed to meet by 1979.) In 1976, support for the ERA was still part of the Republican Party platform, which shows how far the party has moved. After it was removed from the platform in 1980, I called the action a tragic setback for the Republican Party. Still, popular support for the ERA remained high, and I long and wrongly, it turns out, believed that its passage was possible.

In 1983, rather than scheduling an extensive debate on the ERA, the Democrats abruptly called for a vote in the last week of the House session, with less than twenty-four hours' notice, by placing it on what's called the suspension calendar. This was usually reserved for noncontroversial issues, and the time for debate was restricted to forty minutes. It fell six votes short of the two-thirds majority necessary for a constitutional amendment, passing by a 278-147 vote. The fate of the ERA was determined down in the trenches of the culture wars of the mid-1980s, and I remained a committed supporter.

In my comments addressed to the Atlanta Conference on Women and the Constitution on the occasion of the Constitution's bicentennial in 1988, an event that was sponsored by the former First Ladies Mrs. Carter, Mrs. Ford, and Mrs. Nixon, I related in my speech that,

> looking back at 200 years of women under the Constitution, what stands most distinct is the degree to which women have fared differently than men, differently and to the disadvantage of women. I'm quite confident that a three day conference reviewing women's rights at the time of ratification of the Constitution would have been about three days more than needed . . . there was not much to review.
>
> As a result of being left behind at the starting gate, American women have faced legal, social, and cultural challenges throughout our nation's history. It is an unfortunate American heritage that is still being encountered today.

I went on to explain:

> A basic question for our purposes here today emerges as this: Are the problems women face a function of law or of societal attitude? Are they engrained in people's minds or enshrined in the Constitution? To get at the answer, and to better consider women's experiences under the Constitution, it is useful to recall the nature of the Constitution itself.

Our Constitution is not a wholly self-executing document. Many of its provisions and guarantees must be put in place through enactment of law by legislatures . . . So, to a great extent, the Constitution thus must be implemented, and rights defined, through the political process.

I said that the silence in the Constitution on women's rights—beyond the Nineteenth Amendment, which guarantees women the right to vote—troubled me. The ERA's passage would have been an important advance for the country. Nevertheless, there is a certain irony in the fact that the ERA ultimately played such a central role in changing the nature of the debate on women's place under the Constitution, yet did so without itself becoming a part of the Constitution. Yes, we failed to attach the ERA to the Constitution, but the debate over the ERA helped, to a significant degree, to bring forth for the public the existing limits on constitutional equality for women. It gave the American people a new understanding of the overt and subtle discrimination women faced. And by injecting this awareness into the American consciousness, the ERA debate provided the backdrop of acceptance for many of the legislative and judicial changes that would follow.

Realistically concluding that the ERA was dead, those of us as women in Congress proceeded to work on legislative redresses to the kind of discriminatory laws and practices I've enumerated. One vital area of concern was women's health, which I have described as "a missing page from America's medical textbooks," one that was for decades chronically unaddressed and unresearched.

In the mid-1980s, the Women's Caucus discovered that some health studies funded by the National Institutes of Health (NIH) included only men. When we dug a little deeper, we were horrified to find that *all* federally funded research was being carried out exclusively on men. A coronary disease risk factor study, for instance, used a pool of fifteen thousand men. It was called "Mr. Fit." Such exclusivity meant that a drug that was deemed effective in a clinical trial had never been tested on women. A breakthrough finding of a study on physicians' health established the connection between coronary disease prevention and aspirin, but the 22,071 doctors studied were all men, and any similar benefit for women was unknown. Apparently, someone forgot that heart disease is the leading cause of death among women. As I've said in the past, scientists at that time clearly agreed with the sentiments of Henry Higgins in the song from *My Fair Lady*—"Why Can't a Woman Be More Like a Man?"

For years, scientists treated more than half of the population— women—as medical anomalies. They complained that health research could endanger or would be affected by women's reproductive systems. Women have been bearing children for quite some time, and are likely to continue doing so in the future! So I questioned why medical research, rather than ignoring that fact as an inconvenience, didn't work instead to accommodate it. We were fortunate to have Congressman John Dingell (D-MI), the chair of the Energy and Commerce Committee, which had jurisdiction over the NIH, as a major champion. Dingell is the longest-serving House member, having first won election to the House in 1955 (Dingell succeeded his father, John Sr., who took his seat the same day FDR was inaugurated.)

In 1987, the Women's Caucus persuaded the NIH to change its official policy to include women and minorities in its medical trials, an acknowledgment of scientific reality, finally. Pat Schroeder and I, along with Henry Waxman (D-CA), who chaired the Commerce Committee's Subcommittee on Health and the Environment, asked the General Accounting Office (GAO, and now known as the Government Accountability Office) to document any inequities in medical research at the National Institutes of Health. As a result, the GAO discovered that the NIH was violating its own policy.

In response, I introduced legislation to create the Office of Research on Women's Health at the NIH—Barbara Mikulski passionately championed the issue in the Senate with the late Senator Ted Kennedy. The office was established administratively at NIH and made permanent by statute in 1993.

Furthermore, Pat Schroeder and I, on behalf of the caucus, introduced and fought for legislation to establish comprehensive equity in women's health research, while Barbara Mikulski was doing the same in the Senate. At a pivotal juncture, Senator Mikulski launched a key panel that also included Connie Morella (R-MD) to explore the shocking discriminatory treatment at the NIH, which further galvanized national attention. And in the end, together with the Women's Health Equity Act, we produced watershed policy changes that mandated that trials include the unstudied sections of the population. To this day, these efforts are resulting in lifesaving medical discoveries for America's women.

In 1991, President George H. W. Bush made the historic appointment of Dr. Bernadine Healy as the first female director of the NIH, a significant sign that his administration would take women's health issues seriously. After just a few weeks with Bernadine Healy at the helm, the National Institutes of Health launched the groundbreaking Women's Health Initiative (WHI) that studied the postmenopausal health of nearly 162,000 women, aged 50–79, over a fifteen-year period. The studies focused on preventing heart disease and breast and colon cancer as well as fractures from osteoporosis. The WHI was prompted by the revelations unearthed by the Women's Caucus, and we helped usher in the most far-reaching clinical trials in women's health ever undertaken in the United States.

Many of the results have been and continue to be released— and guess what they are saying? In one area, that of hormone replacement therapy (HRT), the conventional wisdom for decades has been that HRT might have a protective effect for women. In fact, according to the studies, it increases risk of cardiovascular disease. And even when women discontinued the therapy, their risk of developing breast cancer remained about 27 percent higher, and their risk for any cancer was 24 percent higher. When this link was established in

2002 between hormone use and breast cancer, millions of women stopped HRT. Breast cancer rates fell 7 percent the next year, meaning thousands of lives saved.

⸻ ∞∞∞ ⸻

Nineteen ninety-two was the "Year of the Woman" in the Senate. Four new women were elected that year, including Dianne Feinstein and Barbara Boxer, making California the first state to have two women senators. In the previous Congress, there had only been two women senators out of one hundred, and as Feinstein had noted in her campaign, "two percent may be good enough for milk, but it's not good enough for the United States Senate."

The caucus had a very significant year in 1993. We enacted thirty bills on women's issues in the first session, at least five times that of any of the previous six sessions. We effected changes in the areas of education, health, defense, taxes, family leave, abortion rights, and childhood immunization. Just after President Clinton was sworn in and he appointed First Lady Hillary Clinton as his point person on his then-controversial effort to reform health care, the caucus met with her to build an alliance on issues impacting women. We made vital gains, but we still had a long way to go in Congress despite our record numbers of 7 senators, 48 representatives.

I was a fierce proponent of the Family and Medical Leave Act, which eventually was passed in 1993, the first piece of legislation signed by President Bill Clinton. The FMLA provides for twelve weeks of protected leave for situations like the birth of a child or a medical emergency. It was a key issue for the caucus at a time when women were entering the workforce in even greater numbers. When a working woman had to make a choice about being with a child, a spouse, or a parent in time of need, all too often that choice meant losing her job.

The compromise legislation was designed so that women are no longer penalized for their unique childbearing roles, and to address the legitimate concerns of employers. I showed that Maine's own

FMLA proved that it wasn't a hindrance to small businesses with more than twenty-five employees. Still, it was a long haul to get the act passed and in a speech on the House floor, I lamented that it had sat on the shelf longer than most canned goods.

I can recall sitting in the front row of the House of Representatives with Pat Schroeder, who had championed the effort for years along with my good friend Congresswoman Marge Roukema (R-NJ), as we watched the members vote on the bill. We agreed that if we didn't drive these kinds of issues, who would? I've stayed in touch with Pat over the years and we reminisce fondly about those days and how we forged significant advancements for women.

Our biggest disappointment in 1993 came when the House and Senate banned Medicaid funding for abortions except in cases of rape, incest, or when the woman's life was endangered. Over the ensuing twenty years the Republican Party's position on abortion would be a crucial part of its increasingly damaging emphasis on social issues.

The Women's Caucus was one of the most effective of a number of similar groups in Congress and I viewed it as a template for achieving bipartisan success. In 1995, the new Republican leadership in the House of Representatives prohibited the funding of caucuses such as ours, effectively eliminating them. This was unfortunate for a number of reasons, not the least of which is that it dissipated the collective expertise we had accumulated in the course of our history. In the 1980s and early 1990s the actions of the Congressional Caucus for Women's Issues made the lives of millions of women better in large and small ways. The benefits of our efforts continue to reverberate.

Some encounters in life, when reflected on years later, are recalled with such clarity, it's almost as if they'd been engraved on the mind for the future. When I was honored to receive the Susan G. Komen for the Cure's Betty Ford Lifetime Achievement Award at the Kennedy Center in 2012, I said in my remarks that my first meeting with Nancy Komen Brinker, in 1983 in my office, was just such a moment. She was just beginning to lay the groundwork for a foundation in memory of her beloved sister that would transform the way we fight breast cancer nationally and internationally. She has become a great friend over the last thirty years and achieved far more besides establishing her foundation. She shouted to the entire world, Enough is enough! I'm taking on breast cancer, and who's with me?

As it turned out, millions of people were with Nancy. Just think how far we've come. When my mother died of breast cancer when I was eight years old, prevention and screening weren't even in our lexicon, and the last thing a woman diagnosed with breast cancer thought she'd become was a survivor. Today, we've reduced breast cancer deaths by 25 percent, and it's largely because Nancy's organization has raised $2 billion, leading to peerless strides in research and prevention.

Constituents should never underestimate the influence that a single letter among thousands can have. If there is any skepticism about the potential power of the pen, or what would today be the keyboard, consider this illustration.

In the early 1990s, I received a note from a resident of Maine named Bonnie Lee Tucker. Breast cancer was rampant in her family; her mother had died of the disease at age fifty. Bonnie wrote: "I'm a third generation [breast cancer] survivor and as of last October I have nine immediate women in my family that have been diagnosed with breast cancer. . . . I want my daughter to be able to live a normal life and not worry about breast cancer. I want to have the BRCA test [the genetics test for breast cancer] done but because of the insurance risk for my daughters' future I don't dare."

The NIH was offering genetic testing but nearly a third of women were refusing it for the same reason. Bonnie Lee Tucker's query prompted me to work on legislation to prevent a health plan or insurer from discriminating against someone on the basis of their genetic information or because they had requested or received genetic services. The law was eventually extended to bar discrimination on these grounds in the workplace, too. The importance of the law was underscored when the Human Genome Project succeeded in mapping all the genes in the body in 2003. More and more genetic markers were found for diseases, and until there was law forbidding it, Americans could be fired or dropped from insurance even if they only sought testing for a genetic predisposition.

The Genetic Information Nondiscrimination Act (GINA) was a decade-long endeavor, demonstrating once again the virtue of patience, but it was eventually signed into law in May 2008. The senator who was most instrumental to GINA's enactment was Ted Kennedy. Just a few days before the signing he disclosed his illness, and we had only just heard the tragic news that he was fighting a malignant brain tumor. Ted was the lead Democratic cosponsor of the legislation and as chair of the Health, Education, Labor, and Pensions Committee, he marshaled it through Congress. On two occasions, we forged an agreement on the nuts and bolts of the bill so that it could pass the Senate, as it did unanimously, in 2003 and 2005. On each occasion it took sixteen months to prepare the legislation and we spent a year at the end working toward an accord with Senator Tom Coburn so he would release his hold on the bill in the Senate. Eventually we reached an agreement and GINA was enacted.

When President George W. Bush signed the bill, among those present were Congresswomen Louise Slaughter (D-NY), a Democrat who was the lead sponsor of this legislation in the House, and Judy Biggert (R-IL), the lead Republican co-sponsor; Republican Senators Mike Enzi of Wyoming (the ranking member of the HELP committee) and Judd Gregg of New Hampshire (who had served as chair of HELP); and Dr. Elias Zerhouni, director of the NIH. Former Democrat Majority Leader Tom Daschle (D-SD) also had championed the law during his time in the Senate. This was a truly bipartisan effort for what Senator Kennedy called "the first major civil rights act of the new century." Discrimination on the basis of one's genetics is now just as unacceptable as discrimination on the basis of race or religion.

I look back with pride on the array of accomplishments that were achieved by us women in Congress. I was extraordinarily honored to chair the Small Business and Entrepreneurship Committee for the 108th and 109th Congresses (2003–2007). (The only other woman to chair a Senate Committee in that period was my Maine colleague Susan Collins, at Governmental Affairs for the 108th Congress.) Geraldine Ferraro became the first woman to appear on a major ticket, as the Democratic candidate for vice president in 1984. Nancy Pelosi (D-CA) was the first woman to serve as the Speaker of the House of Representatives. When she held this office, from 2007 to 2011, she became the highest-ranking woman in the history of the Congress.

I am confident we will have a woman President in this country sooner rather than later. Condoleezza Rice met with me in 1986 when she was a professor at Stanford and considering running for Congress. As she was describing her background, it didn't take long to discern she was highly accomplished and talented, and would be an extraordinary asset to the Republican Party—and the nation. I told her she was dynamite—everything wrapped in one package. But she decided against it. Hillary Clinton proved beyond any reasonable doubt in the Democratic primaries in 2008 that a capable woman could run for the highest office and be extremely competitive.

Jock knew Bill Clinton when they both were serving as governors. In fact, they sat next to each other at National Governors Association (NGA) meetings because the states were seated according to the date of their entry into the union. Hillary and I met as members of the NGA's spouses group. After Jock and I got married in Lewiston, Maine, on February 24, 1989, we traveled to New York City and then to an NGA winter meeting in Washington, D.C., two days later.

With my Aunt Mary and a family friend at St. Basil Academy.
(*Courtesy of Olympia Snowe*)

My parents and my older brother John. (*Courtesy of Olympia Snowe*)

Senators Margaret Chase Smith and Nancy Kassebaum
attended a luncheon for me in 1992. (*Courtesy of the
Bangor Daily News*)

Women senators and congresswomen in the Old Senate Chamber in
1983. (*Photograph by Rhoda Baer*)

With Secretary of State
Edmund Muskie. (*Courtesy
of Olympia Snowe*)

With President Jimmy Carter in 1979. (*Courtesy of the Jimmy Carter
Presidential Library*)

President Ronald Reagan and the Whip organization at the White House in 1985. (*Courtesy of the Ronald Reagan Presidential Library*)

President George H.W. Bush (Vice President at the time), my husband, Jock, and I walked in the parade at the Fryeburg Fair in 1987. (*Courtesy of William Haynes*)

Congresswoman Patricia Schroeder and me with President Bill Clinton in 1993. (*Official White House Photograph*)

Greeting First Lady Hillary Clinton in Maine in 1994.
(*Official White House Photograph*)

Celebrating Moxie soft drinks with President George W. Bush at a rally in Bangor in 2002. (*Eric Draper, courtesy of the George W. Bush Presidential Library & Museum*)

Meeting with President Barack Obama in the Oval Office in 2009. (*White House Photo / Pete Souza*)

Majority Leader Trent Lott and Minority Leader Tom Daschle met with the Senate Centrist Coalition in 2001. (*AP Photo/Kenneth Lambert*)

The health care "Gang of Six" in one of its numerous meetings in the spring of 2009. (*Stephen Crowley*/New York Times/*Redux*)

Women senators before a dinner with Supreme Court Justices Sandra Day O'Connor and Ruth Bader Ginsburg in 2007. (*Courtesy of the Senate Photographic Studio*)

With my husband at my first press conference in Maine announcing that I would not seek a fourth term in the US Senate. (*AP Photo / Robert F. Bukaty*)

Governor Clinton, Hillary, and I were on the program for a women's event at Union Station, which is just down the street from the Capitol, where we got a chance to talk. Jock suggested I ask Hillary how she divided her time between the incredible demands of her law practice and being First Lady of Arkansas. Later, when I was sworn in for my second term in the Senate and Hillary for her first, Jock said to former President Clinton, "Now we're the spouses!"

When she ran for the Democratic nomination, Hillary conducted herself in exemplary fashion. I think the voters are ready for a woman President. The fact of being a woman is no impediment to holding any office, nor should it be.

And yet despite our gains, the Republican Party's increased focus on single-issue social questions has harmed its standing with women in the country. President Obama won 55 percent of American women's votes in 2012, and his margin of victory over women with challenger Mitt Romney was ten percentage points, higher than Ronald Reagan's own gender gap. While in polls, women agreed with men that the economy was the most important issue in the election, Governor Romney's promise to eliminate funding for Planned Parenthood was unpopular with many women.

The debate over contraception coverage felt like a retro 1950s debate and something I thought we had settled in the 1970s. The excoriation of a Georgetown law student by some Republicans for her testimony before Congress supporting access to birth control was appalling, and she should have been commended, not condemned for her courage in expressing her opinions. Nor was the party well served by the presence of candidates like Todd Akin in Missouri, who used the indefensible term "legitimate rape," or Richard Mourdock in Indiana, who posited that if a woman became pregnant as the result of rape, it was "something that God intended to happen."

Some of the Women's Caucus's hard-won gains will be threatened if ideological rectitude is promoted above common sense. The nation's commitment to reducing violence in the home, if measured in dollars, grew from the $65 million for domestic violence services and shelters we approved in 1983 to the $1.6 billion under the Violence Against Women Act, signed by President Clinton in 1994. The legislation has historically garnered bipartisan support. Joe Biden as Democratic senator from Delaware spearheaded the legislation in the Senate and it was shepherded through the House by passionate women's advocate Congresswoman Connie Morella, and it was readily reauthorized with broad support in 2000 and 2005.

This watershed legislation established the Office on Violence Against Women at the Department of Justice, helped improve law enforcement and prosecution of violent offenders, and funded shelters at the local level. The act has had a profound impact. The reporting of violence increased by 51 percent and the incidence of domestic violence fell by 50 percent from 1994 to 2012.

When the Violence Against Women Act was scheduled again for reauthorization by the Senate in 2012 in a measure that included a number of improvements to the law, the Senate vote was 68-31 in favor of reauthorization, with all seventeen women senators in the affirmative. When the bill reached the House, however, there was strong opposition from Republicans because the bill added protection to three groups: Native Americans, undocumented aliens, and the lesbian and gay community. Vice President Biden worked hard to secure the bill's passing but the House passed a version without the new provisions and the bill was never reconciled in conference, where it languished.

The fact that this bill was then ignored at the end of the session was an unfathomable insensitivity to women who find themselves in heinous situations of domestic abuse. Vulnerable women depend on programs like the ones funded by the Violence Against Women Act, and without them, many wouldn't be able to extricate themselves from harm. I have visited shelters and spoken with women who embody the tremendous courage it takes to leave an abusive situation. Their resolve can only be reinforced by the reassurance that there is a support system waiting to assist them and a safe harbor outside their home. Otherwise it is infinitely harder to walk away. We must not allow these vital advances to wither away through inaction or neglect.

It was heartening that the Senate voted in February 2013 to reauthorize the Violence Against Women Act by a vote of 78-22, including twenty-three Republicans in support. After seventeen House Republicans wrote Speaker Boehner and Majority Leader Eric Cantor (R-VA), the House followed suit at the end of the month.

I am confident women in Congress will continue to offer a model for how bipartisanship can produce good and necessary legislation. Despite the loss of formal caucus memberships, women senators have long provided support for each other. Following the system of mentorships that's been established for incoming senators, when Senator Amy Klobuchar (D-MN) was first elected, not only was it a pleasure to get to know her as another woman senator, but also I was delighted to be her mentor—although in full disclosure, Amy was already well prepared to hit the ground running! These bipartisan and, in this case, woman-to-woman partnerships are yet another way to foster relations across the aisle, and Amy and I have teamed up on a number of initiatives over the years.

Throughout my time in the Senate, I joined the monthly ritual that was established among women senators of gathering for dinner. These occasions were originally organized by the senior Democratic and Republican women, Senator Barbara Mikulski and Senator Kay Bailey Hutchison (R-TX), and senators continue to meet in an ornate room in the Capitol.

The beauty of these dinners is that we keep it light; they are informal and off the record, with no set agenda or planned strategy sessions. Instead, we share our thoughts on everything from our families to issues we're working on to what might be happening in our respective states. It is always a free-flowing discussion in an environment of mutual respect, evidenced by the fact that there has never been a breach of disclosure.

After the last election, the standing senators invited the newly elected women senators to join us and work with the group in the years ahead. Beginning in 1999, we also held the same dinners with women Supreme Court justices—Sandra Day O'Connor and Ruth Bader Ginsburg, and more recently Sonia Sotomayor and Elena Kagan—sometimes with the justices hosting the senators at the Supreme Court.

Senators rarely share the most basic of social experiences anymore. But that does not hold true for the women of the institution, as was the case in December of my last year, when my long-time friend Senator Mikulski, who is the "Dean of the Women" in the Senate, hosted along with all of the women senators a reception for retiring Senator Kay Bailey Hutchison and me. Barbara has always been a mentor for the women of the Senate and a coalition-builder. She has often spoken of nurturing what she calls a "zone of civility" in the Senate. And Kay has been a treasured friend, as well as a stellar example in living by her own credo, "Never give up. If a door closes, open a window." As the first and only female senator from Texas, she transcended partisan differences on an array of issues from defense to homeland security to transportation to driving critical cancer research—and in so doing created a legacy of achievement.

The reception was held in Barbara's "hideaway." (Hideaways are rooms in the Capitol provided for senators to use for various purposes including conducting meetings or other work in a location closer to the Senate floor than senators' more expansive offices, which are housed in three buildings across from the Capitol.) Hideaways are apportioned on the basis of seniority. As she is in her fifth term, Senator Mikulski has a spacious and beautifully appointed one, but in keeping with her personality, it is not ostentatious. I inherited my own hideaway from Barbara when she moved to her present, larger quarters. Access to this little-seen area of the building is by a very small, narrow elevator that I've been told was constructed to fit inside an old chimney flue.

We always enjoyed each other's company in the spirit of bipartisan camaraderie, and I will forever cherish the gift presented to both Kay and me of a framed photo of us as a group; it was personally and thoughtfully inscribed by each of the women senators. On this occasion, we had to keep things brief, because Senator Hutchison and I had to depart since we were attending a farewell dinner for retiring Republican senators. The Democrats held their equivalent event the night before. It was customary at one time that these dinners were held jointly in the Rotunda of the Capitol. I couldn't help but think of our conversations and the irony that despite how well the women get along, the Senate couldn't maintain the traditional dinner, where we wished each other well across the aisle even as we departed the Senate. Knowing these women as I do, however, I doubt they will allow these bifurcated retirement dinners again.

When I think of the fight for women's issues during my career in Congress, I'm often reminded of the women's suffrage sculpture created in 1921 by Adelaide Johnson, officially called *Portrait Monument*. It is a representation of three women, Susan B. Anthony, Lucretia Mott, and Elizabeth Cady Stanton, who led the battle for the right to vote, which women first exercised in 1920. The fight for women's suffrage took seventy-one years, from the petition signed at the Seneca Falls Convention in 1848 to the passage of the Nineteenth Amendment in 1919. But the fight to publicly acknowledge the work of these three women in the Capitol took even longer, seventy-six years. The statue was originally placed in the Rotunda in 1921 but was removed by the (all-male) Congress; it languished down in the Crypt, which was originally designed as Washington's burial place, even as the personification of our democracy—Lady Freedom—stood atop the Capitol dome.

According to the Architect of the Capitol, the Rotunda is "the symbolic and physical heart of the United States Capitol." In 1997, I spoke at the rededication ceremony for the suffrage statue after it had been restored to its rightful place there. As I told those gathered, "In 1995, when a number of us sought the relocation of the statue to its originally intended spot—the Rotunda—we thought that it was a little thing to ask. We never could have imagined that this request, which on its merits seemed so straightforward, would become so problematic."We had been told it was too costly, that the statue was too unattractive, that we shouldn't use public funds to move it, all raising the question, how did those other statues get there?

Finally, we were told it weighed too much. As I noted at the ceremony, "The bottom line is, the debate should not have been about the weight of the statue, but the weight of an argument . . . and the worth of a just cause. When Susan B. Anthony said, 'What is this little thing we are asking for? It seems so little, yet it is every-thing,' she was talking about a woman's right to vote, but she could have been speaking about the moving of her own statue. The difficult and circuitous journey these ladies have had from Crypt to Rotunda is in many ways emblematic of women's struggles for justice and equality throughout our history. For too long, women in this country had to endure the myth of what—or where—a 'woman's place' should be. According to the out-of-date stereotype, a woman's place used to be only in the parlor, the kitchen, and, I suppose, the Crypt. Since then, much has changed. Today, a woman's place is in the House, the Senate, and yes, in the Rotunda."

Recently I had my picture taken with the only marble monument in the Rotunda that features women. In the photograph you can almost imagine a twinkle in their eyes, reflecting the pleasure they must have felt in making it back upstairs, nearer the seats of power!

Chapter 7

Life in the Senate

In MARCH 1994, the Maine congressional delegation held a meeting in the office of Senate Majority Leader George Mitchell. At one point, George excused himself to go to the Senate floor to move some proceedings along. After a while, he returned to the meeting. He apologized for taking so long and confessed that even the smallest thing can take the longest amount of time in the U.S. Senate. He was smiling as he said it, and I thought that despite what must have been frustrating delays, he seemed very relaxed. A couple of days later, George announced that he was leaving the Senate. That explained everything— no wonder he had looked so relaxed during our meeting.

At the time, George's decision not to seek reelection surprised all of us, but today I can empathize with what he must have been going through as he weighed his options. When I learned George was not going to run again, it seemed natural to me that I would run for his seat in the Senate, having served sixteen years in the House. I had contemplated running for the Senate as far back as 1982, after George had been appointed to the Senate in 1980 by Governor Joseph Brennan when Senator Ed Muskie resigned to become President Jimmy Carter's secretary of state.

I also was aware that my colleague, Republican Congressman Dave Emery, had expressed a desire to run, and he was the more senior member of the delegation between the two of us. Dave and I remain good friends; he's continued to provide his advice and counsel to me. Coincidentally, just a couple of months before the end of my tenure in the Senate, I was standing outside on the stairs of the Capitol and Dave happened to walk by. So I took what was one of my last photos at that location with him, and I thought, what a remarkable instance of symmetry, given that I'd begun my years in Washington serving alongside Dave in the U.S. House of Representatives.

There was also a question in Republicans' minds as to whether he should be the rightful heir in 1982, and therefore the Republican nominee on the ballot for the general election. As a result there were concerns about the ramifications of having a major Republican primary between the two current House members. I tested the waters but decided not to enter the primary, which George went on to win.

When George made his announcement in 1994, Jock was down in South America on a gubernatorial trade mission, and there was some speculation that as governor, he might want to run himself. He called me thousands of miles from the action and said, "I have no interest in running—you should run, and I can have my statewide team gather signatures for you." I had been gearing up for my House race, but I decided to jump at the opportunity. It was March already, so the campaign would be relatively short. My opponent was the Democratic congressman from Maine's 1st District, Tom Andrews, and I was heartened when I went on to win every county and prevailed by 60-36 percent. I would learn for myself whether George's lighthearted comment about the glacial pace of the Senate was true.

I was well aware from my experience in the House that the Senate is a very different institution. Many representatives think senators believe they are superior, and some senators probably agree! What is inarguable is that, by design, senators represent their entire state, which in almost all instances means they cover a larger geographic territory and population (sometimes exponentially, depending on the state). The same committee jurisdictional territory is divided among just 100 senators as opposed to 435 House members and there is a commensurate rise in workload. It was only after I had joined the

Senate that I realized why senators have staff members swarming around them whenever they leave the office. With nearly impossible time constraints and the array of meetings, events, and hearings on the schedule, it's wise to use the opportunity to talk with multiple staff on the way to a vote. It's not an entourage for show, it's a practical necessity.

The Senate Chamber is a much more intimate place than the House. Most visitors comment on how small it is. In the House, representatives sit on benches while in the Senate each of us has his or her own desk, and by tradition we sign or scratch our name into the desk drawer. Mine—officially Desk XXVII—had an orderly column of names of senators scratched into the drawer, including Robert Taft, Henry Cabot Lodge, and Elihu Root. Bill Cohen signed his name off to the side.

In the House, speeches are often made from the well of the chamber, and a representative addresses his or her colleagues directly, while in the Senate, you speak from your desk and face the President Pro Tem of the Senate. In either case, rarely are there many other colleagues in the chamber listening, unless there is some debate of vital importance. Because of the sheer size of the institution, in the House speeches are usually limited to a minute or two even on issues of great consequence. That forces the speaker to hone his message for maximum impact in a minimal amount of time.

The Senate is intended to be the more contemplative chamber, operating at a slower, more deliberate pace than the sometimes clamorous House. In the Senate, political fires are tempered rather than stoked. Historically, more routine measures would simply pass by unanimous consent agreements, and floor time would be reserved for major matters of significance. An individual senator has significantly more power than a colleague in the House, potentially at least. In the House the proceedings are managed by the powerful Rules Committee, at the direction of the Speaker, and this system controls debate on every measure. In order to keep business moving quickly, few debates are today held under "open" rules—the least restricted conditions; most are at or near the "closed" rule status, whereby amendments are practically prohibited.

Whereas the House rules are targeted toward empowering the majority and moving legislative business expeditiously, Senate rules are focused on allowing all senators to have a voice, requiring a greater necessity for consensus-building, and providing opportunity to the minority. In a sense, it's a contrast between expediency and deliberation. The rules are designed to allow a senator to take more time to speak—he or she can ask for unanimous consent to extend debate. She might be asked to yield to a question but is under no obligation to accept. She can also hold up proceedings on a particular piece of legislation she objects to. For the most part, senators have unlimited time to speak, which is not to say you are going to make your points any better than if you have two minutes; you just have more time to do it. Often, there are ongoing quorum calls, in which members are asked to come to the floor, but a call itself can serve as a delaying tactic. These quorum calls can continue until a senator decides to come to the floor to speak on a question or offer an amendment.

Such, at least, is the theory. But the trend in recent years has been less and less debate. For my entire tenure in the House, Republicans were in the minority, and measures with which there were concerns were routinely and vehemently objected to, even if they were considered under modified closed rules, which prescribed a limited, specific list of amendments. But now up-and-down votes in the House under closed rules are the norm.

In the Senate, the overuse (or abuse) of both cloture motions and threats of filibusters ultimately undermines the vital principle of an individual senator's rights. When the Majority Leader curtails debate and denies a senator the opportunity to offer an amendment by filling of the amendment tree, he ensures that greater power is exercised by the majority party. The Senate has come to resemble the House, where tactics like utilizing rules or prerogatives to maximum political advantage or to make a point are more common. Some commentators have argued that the many House members making the transition to the Senate (there are 51 today compared to 31 in 1979) have brought House tactics with them. In a story in the *New York Times* in November 2012, Jonathan Weisman wrote that "Republicans and Democrats alike point to a moment in the 1990s when Rick Santorum, then a Republican senator from Pennsylvania and a former House warrior, refused to yield the floor to a colleague when asked, a refusal almost unheard of in the Senate."

The exalted notion of one senator standing on principle and putting a hold on legislation must be balanced against the consequences of inertia and inactivity. A President will want to bring forward his own legislative agenda—this is what is often outlined in the State of the Union message. Ultimately, in order for government to operate effectively, it is necessary for there to be broad agreement between the President and Congress in determining the crucial issues that must be addressed.

The most essential piece of legislation for a functioning government is a budget. The process of drafting a budget has not been consistent since the Budget Act was passed in 1974, but by 2009 the Senate had racked up an unprecedented three consecutive years without passing a budget, coinciding with three of our highest deficits in history. The 2011 debt ceiling agreement and subsequent "fiscal cliff" in 2012 also superseded normal procedure and completed a trifecta of failure that resulted in a downgrade of America's credit rating. They did nothing to address our deficits and debt and only further undermined business and consumer confidence at a moment of economic peril.

The Senate's smaller size and its procedures are specifically designed to facilitate consensus-building, particularly with a sixty-vote threshold to avoid filibusters. It is possible to get to know a good proportion of your fellow members from both sides of the aisle with whom you work closely on committees, providing an opportunity to forge consensus on measures before they go to the floor. Proposing an amendment can act as a bridge in a similar way, because senators have to construct a coalition across party lines to give it a greater chance of success. I did this on many occasions.

However, when the amendment process is degraded, when a cooperative atmosphere is lacking, when little work is accomplished in committee, and when debate is curtailed on the Senate floor, any collaboration is a tremendous challenge. Congress has devolved to a three-day work week—Tuesday to Thursday—with constant travel between home and Washington. There is little time, and few unofficial gatherings like the women's dinners to bring people together informally. If we don't work together, or socialize or get acquainted with each other at all, the chances of one hundred relative strangers agreeing on even the smallest of issues are slight.

January 4, 1995, was the opening day of the new Congress, which as a whole intended to enact meaningful legislation. Just within the first few weeks, we passed a series of important legislation, and our effective work stands in contrast to the opening days of the 112th Congress.

After the election, I had convened the first meeting of the eleven new Republican senators in my office. Before being sworn in, Jock and I went to Williamsburg, Virginia, for what would be his last National Governors Association event, and I came back for a meeting with the Republican conference to learn about procedures and begin the process of receiving our committee assignments. The election of 1994 was one of historic victories for the Republicans. We secured a net gain of nine seats in the Senate. In addition to myself, the other members of my Republican Senate class were Jon Kyl (AZ), Spence Abraham (MI), Craig Thomas (WY), Rod Grams (MN), Mike DeWine (OH), Fred Thompson (TN), Bill Frist (TN), Rick Santorum, John Ashcroft (MO), and Jim Inhofe (OK). The House results were even more dramatic, with a 54-seat swing that resulted in

Republicans controlling both houses of Congress for the first time since 1954.

Republican Senate committee assignments are essentially determined according to seniority, and thanks to my sixteen years of service in the House of Representatives, which counted, I was able to secure seats on the Foreign Relations and Small Business committees, following my experience on similar panels in the House. In addition, I became a member of what was the Commerce, Transportation and Science Committee, a post that was very much in demand since it was anticipated that the committee would rewrite the key Telecommunications Act for the first time since the early 1930s.

It is the prerogative of the leaders to select senators for the Budget Committee, and I was fortunate that Bob Dole, who was about to become Majority Leader, appointed me to a coveted seat on this key panel. Previously I had served two years on the House Budget Committee—where then-Representative and now Governor John Kasich (R-OH), a hardworking and committed fiscal conservative, was the Republicans' ranking member—so I had the experience. I also wanted to work with Senator Pete Domenici (R-NM), who had done yeoman's service in his leadership capacity on the committee. Since Republicans had captured the majority in the Senate, Pete was once again about to assume the chairmanship.

Bob Dole was a true legislator and I was excited by the prospect of working under his leadership. Beginning in 1984, I served on the board of Bob's Dole Foundation for Employment of Persons with Disabilities. In the Senate, I found Bob to be very pragmatic and approachable; his door was always open. He had a commanding knowledge of the institution he had served since 1969, and a deep and abiding determination to make the Senate function as the Founders intended by hewing to its traditions and practices.

Bob Dole was a uniquely effective legislative leader. His passion for service and reverence for the institution was reflected in his leadership, which had a profound impact on virtually every realm of public policy. When there was a major issue—like the State Children's Health Insurance Program, or S-CHIP—Bob would customarily instruct us to meet in his conference room at eight-thirty in the morning and tell us in his familiar refrain to "work it out" if we had been unable to move past a specific point. He would often be seen around the Senate deep in conversation with different members, assiduously trying to assemble a solution to a problem. At one point in 1996, when it was clear we'd have to address the imperative of access to safe and affordable child care before passing any meaningful welfare reform, Senator Dole shuttled between the Democrat and Republican cloakrooms attempting to reach a deal on increased child care funding. And by putting in the legwork, he was ultimately successful.

When Senator Dole resigned from the Senate in 1996 to run for President, Senator Trent Lott was elected Majority Leader and continued his predecessor's problem-solving approach. Trent and I continued our close and friendly relationship, literally, as he was my next-door neighbor for a time on the fourth floor of the Russell Senate Office Building. He used to knock on the door and walk into the room where my executive assistant, Karen Gleason, sat, just to chat. Another lighthearted way he would communicate was to randomly knock on the wall that separated my personal office from his—it was just an additional means of getting my attention!

When Republicans won control of the legislative branch in 1994, Bob Dole spurred the Senate Republican conference to rise to a new level of responsibility and accountability. Newt Gingrich's Contract with America dictated the House agenda, and the Senate considered measures from the Contract as well.

The Unfunded Mandate Reform Act was introduced in the Senate on January 4, 1995, the opening day of the new Congress. In the House, I had introduced one of the first two bills ever to ban unfunded mandates, which were requirements the federal government imposed on states and municipalities without providing the funding. In employing this practice, Congress was having its cake (telling states, cities, and towns what to do) and eating it, too (not having to spend the money). Senator Dole designated the Senate's version of legislation to end unfunded mandates as "S. 1"—literally and symbolically, the number-one Senate bill. That was an indication we were determined to fulfill the commitments we'd made. That same day, several hours after being sworn in, I made my maiden speech, which was unusual for a new senator.

The Budget and Governmental Affairs committees debated the unfunded mandates bill on the second day of session, with both reporting the measure out of committee on January 9. Floor consideration began on January 12 (228 amendments were introduced and 44 voted on over two weeks of debate, incidentally). I spoke on the issue on January 12, saying how pleased I was that the Majority Leader had made this legislation a priority. Maine, I was happy to note, had eliminated unfunded mandates, and trust in state government and partnership between it and county and local governments was being reestablished. Maine's motto is *Dirigo*—I lead, and we should follow my state's example. "My philosophy is simple," I said. "No money, no mandate." The Senate approved the legislation on January 27 by an overwhelming bipartisan vote of 86-10.

On my second day in the Senate, I addressed my colleagues on another key legislative priority, S. 2, the Congressional Accountability Act, which was designed to ensure that the laws of the land would apply equally to Congress as they did to every American citizen. Ten years previously, I had argued before the House's Post Office and Civil Service Committee that Congress should treat its employees in the same way we require private businesses to treat theirs. In both of the last two Congresses, I introduced legislation to extend coverage for congressional employees under the Civil Rights Act and the Age Discrimination Act, as well as the Occupational Safety and Health Administration. This was the aim of the Senate bill I was supporting in 1995. (In a speech in 1998, I noted that "[t]he U.S. Congress has shown great skill over the past twenty years in passing laws barring discrimination of various forms. Unfortunately, the Congress has shown even greater skill in avoiding these same laws.")

The issue was simple: one of fairness. Why should Congress be exempt from the Americans with Disabilities Act, and eleven other important legislative safeguards, when they applied to everyone else in the country? The Senate concurred, and this became the second major law that was passed early in the session.

For more than a month, we debated a Balanced Budget Amendment, a third part of our drive to enact meaningful legislation at the very beginning of the session. The amendment passed the House and received a good deal of bipartisan support in the Senate, until it was defeated, albeit very narrowly, on March 2.

We can contrast this level of legislative activity with the opening days of the 112th Congress. We had to avert a government shutdown because we had failed to complete our work in the previous session. We extended the debt ceiling and spent half our time in quorum calls and morning business, according to the Congressional Research Service, and as far as new business was concerned, the Senate was almost completely inactive.

We were granted time to discuss the Balanced Budget Amendment in 1995, in contrast to 2011, and I spoke in its favor on the floor of the Senate. My words in 1995 could equally have applied in 2011:

> We in Congress are at a precipice—a crossroads—in our relationship with the American people. We can either rise to the occasion and meet their expectations, or, we can merely do nothing and uphold the economic status quo.

The difference was, in 1995 there was the motivation and spirit in the Senate to attempt to take positive action to rectify the situation.

I was very excited to be able to work on the Telecommunications Act of 1996, the first overhaul since 1934 of the legislation overseeing this major sector of American life, and the first time that the Internet was being included in major legislation.

The 1934 law mandated the establishment of a "universal service" system for national telephone coverage, meaning that remote and poor rural areas would have the same access to this vital technology as towns and cities. Under the law, phone providers had to offer service at an affordable rate. I believed it was time for a different kind of universal service, one that would help merge education with technology in the twenty-first century—specifically, the Internet. I wanted a child in Machias, Maine, to be able to browse the shelves of the Library of Congress just as easily as a child in the wealthiest school in Manhattan. It was vital that we leverage the Internet to better prepare our students for the ever-evolving and increasingly competitive digital global economy.

Recognizing that cost was the biggest barrier, I drafted a provision designed to ensure that every school and library could be wired to the Internet through deep discounts for advanced telecommunications services. Jay Rockefeller, also a member of the Commerce Committee, had authored his own provision to make the burgeoning field of telemedicine more affordable and accessible to health care professionals. At eight o'clock one morning in March 1995, prior to the continuation of the Commerce Committee markup of the Telecommunications Act, he called me to suggest we combine our two amendments. I said, "Jay, that's a great idea, let's do it!" So along with Senators James Exon and Bob Kerrey, both Democrats from Nebraska, we offered our Snowe-Rockefeller amendment.

Our provision passed by just one vote, and subsequently we were forced to fight off an effort to have the measure stricken from the bill. The implementation stage at the FCC was no less precarious, but ultimately the final rules for the Snowe-Rockefeller provision, which ultimately came to be known as the "E-Rate" (or Education rate), were adopted by a unanimous vote of the FCC commissioners. There was a separate commission set up to make recommendations to the FCC on the implementation of the program, and during that process in 1996, Jay was running for reelection. He called me just days before the election to discuss how that commission was going to be voting. "Jay," I said, "don't you have more pressing matters right now?" But he responded that this was more important to him.

The E-Rate is significant because we had been instructed by the chairman, Larry Pressler (R-SD), that the leadership, anxious to get the bill completed, was discouraging Republicans from offering any amendments to the bill at the Commerce Committee markup. The reauthorization of the Telecommunications Act had proven contentious in previous attempts in the House and Senate, and the leadership was concerned that a prolonged markup would undercut the momentum and support for the bill. But in my view deferring our amendment for floor consideration lessened the possibility of its success. If no amendments had been allowed, the E-Rate program would not have come to fruition. I had reached an agreement with Senator Rockefeller and I indicated my intentions were to move forward. But Jay was still nervous because he knew there was considerable pressure to forgo amendments. In fact, he kept coming over to me during the markup and asking, "You're still going to do this, right?" "Don't worry, Jay," I assured him, "I'm planning on it."

Before the E-Rate, just 14 percent of schools were wired to the Internet. Today that level has reached nearly 100 percent, including 94 percent of individual classrooms and 98 percent of libraries. At an event celebrating the E-Rate, attended by Vice President Al Gore, an avid supporter, Gordon Ambach, executive director of the Council of Chief State School Officers, stated that "[h]istory will record this Act as the most important federal initiative to advance education into the information age of the twenty-first century." In 2005, computer scientist Seymour Papert and his wife, the Russia expert Suzanne Massie, who lived in Maine, came to my office and gave me a copy of *Technology & Learning* magazine, which ranked Senator Rockefeller and me fourth in a list of people who had shaped the landscape of education technology in the past generation. We were in excellent company: ahead of us were the likes of Steve Jobs and

Steve Wozniak of Apple, Bill Gates of Microsoft, and Papert, who had created the Logo computer programming language for children.

The E-Rate program exemplifies the rich and fertile ground of the open amendment process. It demonstrates how the germ of an idea can flourish into a powerful act of law, and that we can't even imagine what we're missing when amendments are not considered or permitted.

Another issue arose in my first year in the Senate that further illustrates the power of the amendment process. In early 1995, reductions in student loan funding were proposed that threatened to lock out countless students from our nation's colleges and universities. I knew how vital student loans had been to my ability to pay for my tuition at the University of Maine.

When I was in high school, I worked in a drugstore called Anderson & Briggs several afternoons a week during the school year. The summer before my junior year I worked in a restaurant called Callahan's, whose owner, Bert, rented from my uncle and aunt. We all lived in the same building, and my uncle convinced him to hire me even though I had no prior experience in waitressing, which became immediately apparent. When I started working, he told me, "You're as green as grass, Olympia," and I said, "I know, I'll learn." I was shy and I'm sure it was painful for him to watch me, but he said I should make an effort to engage in conversation with the customers. And then I talked to them too much! But at Callahan's, I discovered my affinity for meeting the public. I developed an ease in approaching people I didn't know, whether they were car dealers, lawyers, or police officers.

I especially remember Mrs. Brody. She and her husband owned Cancellation Shoes, a discount store next to the restaurant. The elegantly dressed Mrs. Brody would come in every afternoon and order the same thing—a cup of hot water with a tea bag and a slice of lemon on the side. Many years later, when he was governor, Jock appointed the Brodys' son, Mort, to the Maine Supreme Judicial Court and I described for Mort my warm memories of waiting on his parents.

Our father had left my brother and me a small amount of money in a savings account, and along with grants and scholarships as well as loans under the National Defense Education Program and also what later came to be called Stafford Loans, I was able to cobble together enough money to go to the University of Maine.

So I was alarmed when, in 1995, the original Senate budget resolution included more than $13 billion in cuts in student loan funding. The House version included a reduction of $18.66 billion. As a result, I and fellow Budget Committee member Senator Spence Abraham and others offered an amendment providing offsets in order to restore $6.3 billion to the program. We thought our amendment was in keeping with the twin goals of fighting for higher education and for fiscal responsibility, yet it lost on the Senate floor by a vote of 39-60.

But I refused to believe it couldn't be done. So two days later, Democrat and fellow Budget Committee member Paul Simon and I sought to restore an even larger amount, $9.4 billion. After just two days, we passed our amendment by an overwhelming vote of 67-32. Today it would be difficult to reach consensus on an issue—never mind returning with a higher number. We were successful because of an open amendment process and an atmosphere of legislative possibility.

In my early years in the Senate, there was a formal effort to bring together potentially like-minded legislators from both parties. The Senate Centrist Coalition, which I joined after arriving in the Senate, was formed by Senators John Chafee (R-RI) and John Breaux during the 1994 health reform debate to bridge the political divide. The coalition lapsed for a time after the government shutdowns of 1995 and 1996. After President Clinton's impeachment trial in the Senate, and after Senator Chafee passed away in 1999, Senator

Breaux and I thought it was imperative that we revive the coalition to help foster the spirit of bipartisanship.

After the government shutdowns, President Clinton, Speaker Gingrich, and Majority leader Trent Lott came together to forge bipartisan coalitions on important legislation in the Clinton years. They played a key role in the 1995 attempt to overhaul the welfare system and managed to make changes in the Senate to the House's more stringent proposals, paving a middle road between conservative Republicans and liberal Democrats. Ultimately, twenty Republicans joined Democrats to excise the "family cap" from the House bill, a provision that would stop welfare payments to children whose parents were themselves on welfare. We increased both child care funding and the level at which the states should continue their existing level of welfare spending (called "Maintenance of Effort," it was meant to prevent a "race to the bottom," in which some states would stop providing their current share of welfare costs).

A *Congressional Quarterly* piece on the welfare bill identified seven moderate Republicans who were instrumental in putting together a piece of legislation that the Senate as a whole could agree on. The seven were John Chafee, Jim Jeffords (R-VT), Bill Cohen, and myself (four New Englanders), and Nancy Kassebaum, Pete Domenici, and Arlen Specter. As I said, "We knew we could be the counterweight on the floor" between Democrats and our more conservative fellow Republicans. The seven of us didn't agree on everything. Some wanted more money for child care and more continued funding at the state level. Of course, many Republicans wanted deeper cuts in welfare and many Democrats no cuts at all. Describing the outcome, Pete Domenici said, "Everyone's going to have something in this bill that they don't like."

This is a key tenet in bipartisan consensus-building. In order to get a lot of what you want, you may have to accept a little of what you don't want. Welfare reform was another example of how the Senate can address issues at the forefront of our national agenda, either by informally identifying willing partners both within the party and across partisan lines, or in other instances with groups specifically formed to facilitate bipartisan cooperation.

Following the landmark Supreme Court ruling *Bush v. Gore,* and Al Gore's concession in the presidential election vote count in Florida in 2000 which cemented George W. Bush's victory, and amid an evenly split Senate, Senate leaders Lott and Daschle joined with nearly one-third of the Senate at a meeting of the coalition to explore how to move forward in a bipartisan fashion. The Centrist Coalition never had official membership. At the first meeting after we reconvened in 1999, almost a quarter of the Senate were present. In 2005, a core group of fifteen or so of us met every week. After Senator Breaux retired, in 2006 I, along with Senator Mary Landrieu, who was a key ally in the battle for bipartisanship in the Congress, re-formed the group as the Common Ground Coalition. We met for a while, but under the weight of partisanship, even semi-official groups like this have fallen by the wayside.

By 2003 one of my colleagues suggested I might be more at home in *Jurassic Park* than on the floor of the United States Senate! We lost people willing to "cross the lines," like Alan Simpson, Warren Rudman, Nancy Kassebaum, Bill Cohen, Sam Nunn, and John Chafee, who in 1995 had started the tradition of a weekly lunch for Republican moderates every Wednesday. We always looked forward to those lunches; they were enjoyable times and we had some vigorous discussions over the years. But with Senator Jim Jeffords's decision to caucus with the Democrats, giving them the majority in the Senate, our numbers dwindled to just four.

Where there was once a large coalition in the center, we now have a Gang of 14 or 8 or 6 that forms around a particular issue. These gangs have a tendency to devolve into their constituent units, and dissenting voices are likely to find themselves in a Gang of 1, as I did on health care reform. Few legislators like to be exposed to that degree; it can get lonely out there and increase your susceptibility to attacks. Some senators will privately express their reservations about a vote, but they don't want to deviate from the norm.

It was always hard work to effect a consensus, even when there was a large enough pool of senators who occupied the theoretical middle ground. Anytime you have comprehensive or controversial legislation, there will be multiple opinions and senators will come to the debate from different places, so building consensus is naturally and rightfully difficult. I don't think anyone underestimates that reality—least of all me. Laying the groundwork for identifying common ground is a challenging, grinding effort. Unfortunately, it's also been made infinitely more difficult by the fact that moderates, particularly in the Republican Party, have come under increasing pressure to conform to the more conservative positions.

A major factor in the decline in the moderate ranks of the Republican Party has been the increased power and influence of social conservatives. I have always contended that the party is an umbrella that can accommodate a broad array of opinions, especially on social issues, as long as there is general agreement on basic fiscal principles like low taxes and debt reduction. But for years since the 1990s the party's ideological battles have played out at the national conventions.

Social conservatives have traditionally had greater influence at conventions than their numbers in the party as a whole would suggest, meaning that the party platform decided at the convention has been to the right of the average Republican voter. A single-issue activist is always likely to be more committed to organize, to take the time and spend the money to attend a convention, than more centrist supporters. More recently, the number of ideologically motivated Republicans, as represented by self-identified Tea Party members, has grown substantially, narrowing the gap between convention platforms and the views of the party's national base as a whole. The rightward drift was already evident in the southern states before the advent of the Tea Party.

I have attended every national convention since 1972, except 1980, when I was running for my first reelection. In 1972, in Miami, my husband Peter and I walked to the convention center past crowds of thousands of antiwar demonstrators and the National Guard; the event was marked by nights of sit-ins and protest marches about Vietnam and hundreds of arrests on streets filled with tear gas.

The 1980 platform was conservative, but conciliatory in tone, "recognizing differing views" on abortion while supporting a constitutional amendment to protect the life of the unborn child. It acknowledged that neither Hispanics, nor any other group, should lose education or employment opportunities because English is not their first language (in 2012, English was described as "the nation's official first language").

In 1992, in Houston, the official Republican Party platform called for a complete ban on abortion, which became a litmus test in the party. Television evangelist Pat Robertson spoke at the convention in prime time. In a conversation with Mary Matalin, deputy campaign manager for the Bush reelection campaign, I advised against Robertson's involvement because I didn't think it was helpful to have Robertson define the party. I argued that the convention and the party as a whole should be as inclusive, not exclusive, as possible. It was here also that President George H. W. Bush's primary opponent Pat Buchanan gave his famous "culture war" speech. Yet, in sharp contrast to today, the times were such that, even as a moderate Republican, I was asked to make remarks before the convention on the night of the President's nomination. I said that President Bush "cares about service, patriotism, and freedom. These values are found on every Main Street in the country, and no one represents them better than our President. . . ."

When Bob Dole ran for President in 1996 there was some speculation that he would look to me as a potential running mate. But my pro-choice stance was anathema to elements in the party who insisted on applying that litmus test to a candidate. Repeated attempts have been made to overturn *Roe v. Wade*—by 1999, there had been more than three hundred roll call votes in Congress over abortion rights.

In 1996, Bob Dole took a somewhat softer stance on abortion than some activists liked when he used the word *tolerance* to describe his views. I remain one of Bob Dole's biggest supporters for what he was able to achieve in his career in Congress, and I was a champion of his candidacy in 1996.

I spoke during, but not at, the Republican National Convention in San Diego in 1996, along with Governors Pete Wilson (California) and William Weld (Massachusetts), and anti-abortion activists tried to shout us down. The convention had adopted a constitutional ban on abortion, but as I tried to tell the disrupted news conference, the majority of Republicans and the majority of Americans were opposed to the abortion ban plank.

The changes in the platform were incremental. Beginning in 2004, the party has officially said the unborn child "has a fundamental individual right to life that cannot be infringed." Now, the kind of tolerance Bob Dole espoused is literally and metaphorically nowhere in sight on the official Republican Party platform on abortion—as of 2012, it allows for no exceptions for the life of the mother or any other reason in its abortion policy. Now the base is catching up to the platform; the increased polarization in Congress reflects a more conservative mood of the Republican primary base since 2010.

In the years after I joined the Senate, Republican candidates for office became more ideologically defined and more for their social than economic views. Even when we had a larger number of centrist-minded senators on both sides of the aisle, crafting consensus-building legislation was never easy. But on economic matters, it became even harder as each party took on a more entrenched position, trending toward the no tax increase/no spending cut dichotomy that describes the current situation on Capitol Hill. I would argue that our failure to take decisive action on fiscal policy continues to bedevil the Congress today, when consensus is needed more than at any time for almost four decades.

Chapter 8

Fiscal Responsibility

Fiscal responsibility used to be the quintessential Republican belief. Since I first arrived in Congress, and even during my election bid in 1978, I have been a strong advocate of a Balanced Budget Amendment to the Constitution, because I believe it is the only guarantor of sound and forward-thinking government policy and the only way we can ensure that a balanced budget will be the rule rather than the exception. In the last fifty years our government has managed to balance its budget only five times, and I know of few realms in which a one-in-ten ratio is considered a success.

Since the current recession started in 2008, we have suffered the consequences of high unemployment and the low growth that are exacerbated by the historic size of our national debt. The debt affects our competitive advantage and handcuffs future generations who have to pay for our profligacy. In 2011, the Congressional Budget Office estimated that in 2035 we could be paying a higher proportion of gross domestic product (GDP) to service our debt than we currently spend on Social Security or Medicare.

Congress did vote on balanced budget amendments on many occasions. In October 1982, I voted for the Jenkins-Conable amendment. In the Senate, we came close to passing a Balanced Budget Amendment (BBA) to the Constitution in 1995 and 1997. It lost by just one vote, then remarkably, we failed to vote on the measure for another fourteen years. In the mid-1990s, a BBA had support from members of both parties, and even "liberals" like Senator Paul Simon voted for it. Since then we have squandered budget surpluses as entitlement and discretionary spending has skyrocketed, and our debt has risen alarmingly. Finally, in 2011, the debt ceiling accord incorporated a requirement that both chambers vote on a resolution proposing a Balanced Budget Amendment by the end of the year. The first scheduled vote occurred in the House, where regrettably it failed—the Senate followed suit with the same result.

The Senate action seemed entirely pro forma, as it had been deferred for consideration until the final, hurried moments of the session on December 14, just three days before our final vote of the year. The manner in which we considered the BBA was also telling. It was a marked departure from how the Senate had debated similar measures on the five occasions since 1982. We had two separate votes on two separate resolutions, one Democratic and one Republican, creating a parallel legislative universe with two distinct balanced budget amendments and zero opportunity to reconcile our differences. In the past, the Senate typically voted on a single resolution and amendments were permitted. As I said on the Senate floor during the 2011 deliberations (such as they were), "we know what the strategy is. It is called lip service."

Where we had more than a month's debate in 1995, and a month in 1997, in 2011 a scant eight hours were allotted to the subject, at a moment, remember, when we were making history for the wrong reason—as for the first time ever our debt was equal to the entire size of our economy. In all, I cosponsored eighteen balanced budget amendments and spoke in support of their passage and ratification thirty-five times.

Today, however, debates in Congress mostly center on how much or how little we increase our overall level of debt, rather than on developing constructive ways of reducing it. In 2012, 95 percent of Republicans in Congress signed the "Taxpayer Protection Pledge" of Grover Norquist's Americans for Tax Reform. The problem is, if one side pledges not to raise taxes while the other side starts from a position that they won't address the growth in entitlement spending, it's likely to take a very long time to reach any agreement, let alone balance the budget.

Only through the ultimate authority of the Constitution can we compel Congress to return to the regimentation and discipline of the budget and appropriations processes, and force the government to establish priorities and abide by them. The point is *balance,* and a constitutional requirement curtailing both uncontrolled spending and unaffordable tax cuts is, to my mind, consistent with my record and views as a Republican.

This was one area where my colleague Jim DeMint and I agreed, so we coauthored an op-ed in the *Wall Street Journal* in July 2011, restating the case for a Balanced Budget Amendment. Especially given the debt ceiling debate, we thought it was an ideal time to discuss how we might avoid ever again reaching the heights (or depths) of fiscal recklessness, recognizing that we couldn't reconcile spending and deficits overnight given the historic levels of our deficits and debt. The Balanced Budget Amendment was an issue that Republicans had largely abandoned. Even during the periods in which Republicans controlled both the executive and legislative branches of the government following the 1997 BBA vote, the issue never came to the floor. It was hardly ever mentioned, and certainly not advocated, but we were spending $200 billion per year in interest alone, restricting our growth, which was running at a puny 1.9 percent, and exacerbating an unemployment rate that in 2011 stood at between 8.7 and 9.4 percent.

People have called the BBA a "gimmick," but as I've stated many times to my colleagues, if it really were a gimmick Congress would have passed it long ago! To the contrary, an amendment would be an enforceable mechanism, enshrining in the Constitution the idea that we cannot spend more than we take in (with contingency provisions for emergencies and states of war). That's why I believe many of my colleagues over the years have objected to the BBA; they simply don't want their hands tied when it comes to spending.

Almost every state has a constitutional or statutory provision to balance the budget and some state governors and legislators cannot leave their capitols if their budgets aren't balanced. The United States Congress should be no different. In the early 1990s, my good friend Tom Carper (D-DE), who later joined me in the Senate, and I co-sponsored the BBA during the period when Jock was governor. I observed that flying back and forth between Washington and Maine was like shuttling between fiscal fantasyland and the real world of Augusta, Maine—the capital—where they were wrestling with the monumental task of meeting a balanced bottom line.

The fact is, if we had established a constitutional requirement to balance our federal budgets years ago, we wouldn't have experienced an explosion in our deficits from $32 billion in 1978 to $1.2 trillion in 2012—making the current fiscal landscape much worse than anything I could possibly have imagined.

How did we get so far off track?

When I was first elected to national office, it was a time of great challenges. We were still grappling with the aftermath of the oil embargo; high taxes were a burden—the top rate was 70 percent—and deficits, though small by comparison with now, were rising quickly. The main enemy of U.S. economic growth was inflation. President Gerald Ford declared war with his "Whip Inflation Now" (WIN) campaign, and in 1978, Jimmy Carter said inflation, then running at 7.6 percent and spiking to 11.2 percent in 1979, was "our most serious domestic problem."

Among other insidious factors, individual tax rates weren't indexed to inflation meaning that taxpayers were driven into higher income tax brackets (individual tax rates had skyrocketed by 144 percent over the previous ten years!). At the same time, Americans' purchasing power was seriously eroded by high prices for goods and services. Therefore, one of the issues dominating the national political landscape in 1978 was the notion of reducing individual federal income taxes. As a result, a focal point of elections across the country that year, and again in 1980, was the so-called Kemp-Roth tax cuts.

Named for Republican Congressman Jack Kemp of New York and Republican Senator Bill Roth from Delaware, the legislation, which lowered rates on individual and corporate taxes, had failed to pass the Senate in 1978 but remained a topic of fierce debate.

In my campaign, I drew the distinction that I staunchly supported tax cuts. By contrast, in general, Democrats were arguing that lowering taxes would be inflationary, as Americans would have more money to spend, which would drive up demand and in turn increase prices further. I have never taken a "scorched earth" approach to government (as opposed to those who would drastically slash taxes in order to "starve" the government), but I have always believed that our first instinct as elected officials should be to allow people to keep more rather than less money in their pocket to spend as they see fit. Moreover, my view was that allowing tax revenues to continue to soar would not only take more of Americans' hard-earned paychecks, but, given the government's track record of profligacy, also result in increased spending and, in turn, spur higher inflation.

While I supported the overall goals of Kemp-Roth, I also sounded a theme that I would repeat throughout my tenure in the U.S. House and Senate: responsible and balanced deficit reduction. We ought to ensure that any action the Congress takes, whether on the revenue or the spending side of the federal ledger, sets us on a path to balanced budgets and decreasing our debt. Regardless of whether one believes that lower taxes ultimately result in higher revenues (with a reduced tax burden producing a more robust economy and subsequently more taxes paid in the aggregate), at least in the short term, revenue decreases add to the budget deficit. In 1978, I believed we should have moved on a simultaneous track of spending cuts and offsetting any new spending with commensurate reductions in federal outlays, to help mitigate any potential inflationary effects if Kemp-Roth were enacted. The offsets concept distinguished me from many other Republicans then, and it would do so again, dramatically, when I was in the Senate.

High levels of deficits continued into 1982, when President Ronald Reagan negotiated an agreement with Democrats that for every dollar in taxes raised, spending would be cut by three dollars. So what happened? You guessed it: taxes were hiked immediately; the spending reductions were never realized. Then, in 1985, Reagan signed into law the bipartisan Balanced Budget and Emergency Deficit Control Act, requiring the incremental reduction and eventual elimination of budget deficits by 1991. All Republicans and almost half the Democrats in each chamber supported the measure. Better known by the names of its creators: Senators Gramm, Rudman, and Ernest "Fritz" Hollings (D-SC), it established a mechanism to drive down spending on defense and discretionary budgets (not including Social Security) by a "Sword of Damocles" of automatic cuts known as "sequestration" if the law's mandated annual deficit spending limits were exceeded. Ideally, this "meat ax," as it was described, would compel both sides to work together and produce results without ever having to be used, and in fact, it never was. As Senator Rudman later acknowledged, the threat of sequestration was meant to intimidate lawmakers. I would have preferred a Balanced Budget Amendment, of course, but absent that, I believed this approach was necessary because there was no other means of enforcement. Rudman himself described it as "a bad idea whose time has come."

In 1986 the Supreme Court ruled the sequestration provision of Gramm-Rudman unconstitutional, and when a revised version of Gramm-Rudman was passed with a new mechanism for implementing automatic cuts, the date for balancing the budget was deferred to 1993. Budget deficits were reduced between 1986 and 1989, but budget gimmicks were increasingly employed to reach the target numbers for deficit reduction. When eventually those targets weren't attained even with fiscal trickery, the impending threat of Gramm-Rudman's automatic cuts prompted the President and congressional leaders to initiate a summit at Andrews Air Force Base in Washington, D.C.

An agreement was reached on a package of spending cuts together with tax increases, and the Budget Enforcement Act was the result. I didn't support it, because, among other things, it violated my long-standing belief in balanced deficit reduction. We'd been down this road before—yet again, the Budget Enforcement Act represented a legislative approach that relied more heavily on tax increases than on spending reductions, even as the congressional Joint Economic Committee had found that for every dollar increase in taxes, Congress spent 1.59 dollars. The net effect would be no long-term restraint in the growth of the federal budget.

On the positive side, however, the act instituted a concept I'd embraced since I first ran for Congress, called "PAYGO," short for "pay as you go." This meant that any new legislation affecting either taxes or spending that increased our budget deficit would have to be offset by a corresponding amount through adjustments in other areas of federal revenue or expenditures. PAYGO was combined with caps on discretionary spending (that is, areas of the budget other than programs like Social Security and Medicare), and if these measures had been consistently adhered to over the ensuing years, we might have avoided the fiscal showdowns of 2011 and 2012.

Throughout my tenure in the U.S. House, I'd worked on budgets with various Republican ad hoc groups like the Gypsy Moths, and as cochair of the 92 Group. I'd wanted a seat on the Budget Committee, but that only became reality in the last of my eight terms. Collaborating with colleagues like Nancy Johnson (R-CT), Tom Tauke, Stewart McKinney (R-CT), Sherry Boehlert (R-NY), Steve Gunderson (R-WI), and others, we crafted our own initiatives and alternatives to Democratic budgets for the leadership to consider when resolutions came to the floor. And remarkably, we did it without the vast resources accorded the formal Budget Committee. None of this is to say we had all the answers; simply that we had our own perspectives on budget cuts with a special focus on the implications for the debt and regional fairness in spending allocations.

There was always a sense that we could somehow "get there from here" by reconciling differences of opinion to reach the common goal of imposing a greater level of fiscal responsibility on the Congress. That's what held us together.

I had fought for sixteen years in the House of Representatives for Republicans to become the majority, and in 1995, I finally got my wish, and not only in the House, but in the Senate, to which I'd just been elected. The historic shift to Republican control on Capitol Hill opened myriad possibilities for restoring fiscal sanity, and I felt like a kid in a proverbial candy store. Not long after the elections, our Republican freshman class issued a transition agenda that included a raft of measures to restore fiscal responsibility.

Just a day after being sworn into the Senate in 1995, I testified before the Judiciary Committee in support of a Balanced Budget Amendment to the Constitution, which was at the forefront of the Republican majority's agenda. Speaker Gingrich led the effort in the House, where it passed 300 votes to 132, but in the Senate, where it required the two-thirds supermajority for a constitutional amendment, regrettably it lost by two votes. Fourteen Democrats voted for it, with Republican Senator Mark Hatfield of Oregon voting against it. (Majority Leader Dole switched his vote to "no" solely for parliamentary reasons; he staunchly supported the amendment.) Senator Dole said on *Face the Nation,* "[Mark] told me he would resign before the vote if that would make it possible to win with 66 votes instead of 67. I said, 'That's not an option, Mark; that's not an option.'" Senator Hatfield was indisputably a person of conviction.

Even with the loss of the BBA, however, efforts to attack the deficits and debt very much persisted. In 1996, the Senate Centrist Coalition, which I had joined, met weekly for months to craft an alternative plan to balance the federal budget. And while it didn't ultimately pass, people were shocked at how close we came, and it served as a prelude to passing a balanced budget in 1997 that produced four consecutive years of budget surpluses for the first time since 1930.

Beginning with the 107th Congress in 2001, Republicans controlled both branches of government for parts of six years under President Bush. Initially, the Senate was split 50-50 (Vice President Cheney broke any ties as President Pro Tem). Beginning in June of that year, there was a period of Democrat majority when Jim Jeffords left the Republican Party to become an Independent who caucused with Democrats. In retrospect, I cannot understand why there was no attempt by Republicans to take any action on a Balanced Budget Amendment during those periods when we were in the majority.

In the absence of a BBA, as a member of the Senate Budget Committee I focused attention on a new idea. In January 2001, Federal Reserve Chairman Alan Greenspan's testimony to the Budget Committee included a proposal to use the surpluses that we were projecting over the next ten years to pay down the debt. Chairman Greenspan's concept was that any new tax plan or spending initiative could only be followed if it did not imperil the surplus or debt reduction policies.

Projections for surpluses were just that: projections. We often collected less revenue than anticipated, and had no way to forecast unforeseen events that would have a budgetary impact. Therefore, Greenspan's idea struck me as an effective mechanism to preserve the surpluses we had accumulated, or any that might materialize in the future. So in 2001, which ended up being the last year of federal surpluses to date, I, along with Senator Evan Bayh (D-IN), developed and proposed a kind of legislative "trigger" based on Chairman

Greenspan's idea. This trigger would link the phase-in of any new budgetary changes, including new spending, to specific targets in preserving our surpluses and reducing our federal debt, which at that time was $3.6 trillion. As I argued at the time, this was also our window of opportunity to strengthen Social Security and Medicare with the surpluses.

So we introduced a resolution in Congress with the bipartisan support of like-minded senators Lincoln Chafee (R-RI), Landrieu, Collins, Feinstein, Jeffords, Robert Torricelli (D-NJ), Specter (R-PA), Tom Carper, and Debbie Stabenow (D-MI). It was a great opportunity to get ahead of the curve, and the President was a prominent supporter of the idea. I equated the purpose of the trigger to preparing for bad weather in Maine: just because the calendar shows it's spring, we don't put our shovels away, because it very well might snow again. We didn't want to fritter the surpluses away because you never know when emergencies might arise. I thought, surely the trigger would attract at least broad Republican support, but I was wrong: my effort was met with opposition from a majority of my colleagues, including Republicans. In fact, one Republican colleague said to me, derisively, "Trigger? You mean like the horse?"

As of early 2013, the debt totals more than $16 trillion—nearly four and a half times what it was when my plan was equated to Roy Rogers's horse.

In the aftermath of the terrorist attacks of September 11, 2001, it was clear that despite the fact that we had recently enacted two significant tax cuts—the largest in history in 2001 and an additional round in 2002 as part of an economic stimulus effort—the faltering economy required an additional jump-start. As a result, later in 2002, Larry Lindsey, President Bush's chief economic adviser, solicited views on a potential stimulus package. I told Larry I concurred with the prevailing wisdom that some kind of additional fiscal measures were essential to continue priming the economy. At that juncture, the general sentiment was centered on a range of $300–350 billion in tax reductions.

So when the administration promoted a package of $674 billion in January 2003, I was shocked. I continued to express my support for a robust short-term growth package, but I shared my deep concern that the proposed stimulus contained too many measures that might have merit but weren't fast-acting, and therefore shouldn't be paid for with additional deficit spending. I thought, what could be a more fundamentally Republican position than that?

After all, in 2003 we were already facing a confluence of realities conspiring to bolster our deficits: lingering economic uncertainties, our global war on terrorism, and Afghanistan. And while we could not yet have known the true cost of our engagement in Iraq, it didn't take a soothsayer to predict it would be well beyond substantial, as we discovered. Given that, as the President said at the time, many challenges at home and abroad had arrived in a single season, and given the gathering clouds over Social Security and Medicare, how could we countenance a cycle of burgeoning deficits in perpetuity? By various accounts, the actual stimulus bill would be between $800 billion and $1 trillion. With 77 million baby boomers soon beginning to retire and the true, cumulative deficit through 2011 forecast to be nearly $4 trillion at the time we debated the package, we simply couldn't afford to endorse deficits as far as the eye could see.

So in March, a week before the invasion of Iraq, I, along with Senators George Voinovich (R-OH), John Breaux, and Max Baucus, wrote to Majority Leader Frist and Minority Leader Daschle arguing that we should offset the tax cuts beyond the $350 billion that was critical to stimulating the economy. The $350 billion still would have represented the third-largest tax cut in twenty-five years and I stated I could not support any measures that would contribute to the deficit above that figure.

Senator Voinovich and I traveled down to the White House to meet with President Bush, speculating on our way about the course of the coming discussion. The Oval Office is inspiring; no matter how many times I've had the occasion to find myself there, it's a tangible reminder of the power of the presidency and the tremendous history that's been made within its rounded walls. When I walked into the room, I encountered some very familiar faces: the President himself I had known since 1988; Vice President Cheney was in my House class; Bill Frist, our Majority Leader; I served in the House with Speaker Dennis Hastert (R-IL); and I was a longtime friend of Chief of Staff Andy Card. The conversation was cordial and collegial—because of the President's easy manner I have always enjoyed spending time with President Bush, even when we have disagreed. And this was one of those occasions.

I did tell the President I agreed with his proposal to stimulate the economy, and spoke about the significance as well of fiscal responsibility and paying for non stimulus-related tax cuts that were also in the plan. I also relayed the history of deficit reduction since the Reagan years. "I thought we were committed to balanced budgets," I said to the room rhetorically. "We're supposed to believe in all that. We don't anymore?" I said to Vice President Cheney, "You remember, we were in the same congressional class, and we always talked about balanced budgets and what our party stood for."

President Bush said he was prepared to sit there as long as it took for him to secure our support but I said I didn't think that was going to happen. We did talk for an hour, at which point Senator Voinovich said, "Mr. President, we don't want to keep you; we know you have other things to do." President Bush, who was hosting very few if any outside meetings because he was embroiled in the Iraq War, said, with a smile, "No, I'm rather enjoying this." The meeting ended shortly thereafter. We shook hands, differing in views—but still friends.

The leadership scheduled the markup of the bill in the Finance Committee for the following Thursday. In the meantime, on Monday night I had a conversation with Majority Leader Frist and Chairman Chuck Grassley (R-IA). I'd already conveyed my position to Chuck, who had discussed it with the Majority Leader. Now they were asking me if I was still opposed and I said that I was. I couldn't vote for cuts over $350 billion without offsets. I explained that a stimulus package was necessary, but given that we'd had two consecutive years of tax cuts, we'd just commenced the war in Iraq, and the package had grown considerably, I was deeply concerned that we were adding to the deficit for measures that wouldn't have an immediate effect on the economy.

The Majority Leader asked Senator Grassley to schedule the markup despite my opposition and the fact that my vote was likely required for passage in the committee. The Finance Committee markup was to begin at ten, and the chairman requested that the Republican members convene a half hour earlier in the anteroom. Any time there is consideration of a major tax initiative you can expect a packed committee room, with hordes of lobbyists and press, and that day was no different. I was amazed: I was well aware that my side didn't have the majority votes to report the bill out of committee. With tax cuts central to President Bush's plans to, in his words, "speed up economic recovery and the pace of job creation," the Majority Leader was anxious to prevail. I reiterated my opposition to the bill and the chairman postponed the markup.

It is never easy to oppose the leaders of your own party on legislation they deem important; but I analyzed the issue in great depth, heard numerous viewpoints, and measured them against my own. I love a contest of ideas that forces the exploration of an issue in greater depth. I am intrigued by others' perspectives because examining them can make your own sturdier. Give-and-take is essential for the health of our democracy.

Nonetheless, it is even more difficult when you find youself in direct opposition to a President of your own party, especially President Bush, who was and is a good friend, but it was my obligation to fulfill the Founding Fathers' notion of checks and balances. One vote can and does make a difference. My conviction was to seek to use my voice and my vote in that fashion, to influence the process.

In response to the concerns that George and I expressed, when the bill reached the Senate floor, offsets were included, enabling me to vote for the legislation. However, once the bill emerged from the Senate/House conference, where differences between the two versions were reconciled, I could no longer support it, as it artificially "sunset" the tax relief measures, which masked the true cost of the package and could only lead to larger federal deficits. Even proponents acknowledged they didn't expect the tax cuts to expire as anticipated. "At its heart, this is a trillion-dollar tax cut masquerading as a $350 billion tax cut," I said. "And in keeping with the principles I have outlined from the outset of this debate, I cannot support it."

The Club for Growth attacked me, running ads against me in Maine even though I wasn't even a candidate that year for office. The ads denounced me as a "Franco-Republican," hoping to hurt me by linking me with France, which was unpopular at the time, having resisted President Bush's entreaties to join the Iraq invasion. I had just returned to Maine from Washington when my communications director, Dave Lackey, told me that they were scheduled to air.

During the period the ads were running I went to visit my aunt, and she said, "Everybody is talking about them in church. Do you have the people with you?" I said, "I don't know, but I'm about to find out. . . ." But something else was at play that the Club for Growth folks didn't consider or anticipate: for me, being labeled a "Franco-Republican" was a great badge of honor and a point of pride. There are many hardworking Franco-American communities in Maine. I'd grown up in them, and their heritage is integral to our state. Franco-Americans comprise approximately 25 percent of Maine's population. Columnist Bill Nemitz wrote in the *Portland Press Herald,* "Did they stop to think that calling Snowe a 'Franco-Republican' . . . might actually help her in a state where more households speak French than anywhere else in the nation? Apparently not."

Another reason for my stance on the 2003 tax package stems from my belief then, and which continues today, that we have failed to effect any changes in our bloated and creaking tax code, which is far too complex and onerous. The individual income tax form has more than tripled in length from 52 pages for 1980 to more than 174 pages. American taxpayers spend 7.6 billion hours and shell out $140 billion—or one percent of GDP—just struggling to comply with tax filing requirements. But then what would one expect, given that there have been 15,000 changes to the tax code since the last overhaul in 1986! Yet, regrettably, the Taxpayer Protection Pledge complicates any discussion of taxation, including tax reform, and reverberates across issues far beyond marginal rates. It's hard to discuss tax policy when legislators are worried that even closing tax loopholes will be viewed as raising taxes, and therefore as violating their pledge. A lot of policy is revenue neutral (taxes neither go up nor down); some have multiple effects. But when members of Congress sign a pledge before they have reached Washington, it inhibits their ability to get anything done when they arrive there.

The 1986 tax reforms were a Herculean effort. When Reagan announced at the 1984 State of the Union address that one of his goals was tax reform, there was laughter in the chamber. Reagan stopped and said, "Did I say something funny?" But the President wasn't deterred, and he found a collegial partner in Democratic Congressman Dan Rostenkowski of Chicago, longtime chairman of the House Ways and Means Committee. Rostenkowski demonstrated once again that building relationships and trust is essential in lawmaking. And the President was actively engaged in the passage of this bill, even calling me as a member of the House within two hours of the vote to address some of the concerns I had raised on the legislation.

But we have not seen that type of joint executive-legislative effort in recent years on tax reform. Although Chairman Baucus deserves credit for holding a series of hearings on various aspects of the tax code; the missing ingredient is the essential presidential leadership to execute a major overhaul. I understand the difficulty of this endeavor cannot be underestimated. Thousands of groups will want to lobby Congress to make certain their interests are reflected in any new law. Bob Dole used to describe the hearing room when they were marking up a tax bill as "Gucci Gulch," for the array of expensively attired lobbyists in attendance. There are tremendous ramifications resulting from every change in the code. What happens if, for example, you reduce deductions for mortgage interest, charitable contributions, and employers' contributed medical benefits? And there is untold conflict over the rates.

The last tax reform was so long ago that we have to educate a whole new generation of legislators on how to make it happen. It is yet another economic issue that has been repeatedly deferred. I spent more time fighting rearguard actions to prevent us from falling further and further into debt while battling at the same time to safeguard some of the vital safety net provisions that protected vulnerable Americans of limited means.

In 2001, when the first round of Bush tax cuts was discussed, I moved heaven and earth along with my great bipartisan partner on the Finance Committee, Senator Blanche Lincoln (D-AR), to make the Child Tax Credit refundable. Amid all the tax cuts, I wanted to make certain that Americans at the lower end of the income scale would benefit. The Earned Income Tax Credit is unique in being refundable (meaning that, even if a person's income is too small to incur any tax liability, the government still pays the full credit or the difference if the credit reduces the liability to zero, so that low-income earners will receive the full amount in all circumstances). Republicans opposed my approach, but I believed it was a matter of fairness that we extend the Child Tax Credit to an additional 37 million families—and refundability was the only means of achieving that end.

Senators Baucus and Breaux took me aside to ask if I would vote against the 2001 tax package if the refundable Child Tax Credit wasn't included. They were both members of the House-Senate conference committee and my vote could prove pivotal to the bill's final passage, so they would have to transmit my answer back to the committee. "I'm afraid I'm going to have to," I responded. As it turned out, President Bush also supported the provision, and as the conferees met late into the night before the vote on the following day, the

President called them to urge them to retain my measure. As a result, the refundable credit, with increases built in over ten years, was included in the $1.35 trillion tax cut package.

In so doing, we extended a consequential tax credit to an additional 37 million American families and 55 million children nationwide. As I've expressed to President Bush, I will be eternally grateful for that call—because I know how families struggle, and this refundable credit has made a tremendous difference in the lives of millions of America's less fortunate families.

"Saving" Social Security had also been a consistent position of mine. In 2012, the Social Security Administration Trustees reported that the trust fund will be exhausted by 2033, when only three-quarters of benefits can be fulfilled. Frequent efforts have been made to ensure its solvency. Proposals had come before the Senate that included the idea of "personal savings accounts," or PSAs, through which an individual could invest some or all of their Social Security tax in the stock market, where, it was hoped, long-term gains would ensure a longer life for Social Security. President Clinton introduced a plan whereby the government rather than individuals would invest some of their Social Security trust fund in the market but it was resoundingly defeated, 99-0, in the Senate.

In 2000, then-Governor Bush of Texas outlined six principles for saving Social Security, including the introduction of PSAs. But after President Bush won a second term and introduced his proposal to allow a partial diversion of contributions to the Social Security program to fund private accounts, I couldn't support it. My experiences in and out of the workplace as a young woman informed many of my actions in Congress, and I knew how vital Social Security was in the lives of millions of Americans. I couldn't sanction turning over money to the vagaries of private investments, where it would be subject to the unpredictable swings of the stock market and, in so doing, undermine the value of the defined-benefit plan, which I consider the strength of the Social Security program.

After my uncle died, my aunt received Social Security to help support herself and her children. I also received Social Security benefits as an orphan. Then, fortuitously, around the time I began to think about attending college, in 1965 Congress passed a law extending benefits to those ages 18–21 if they were attending college or a university. This was a blessing and a real lifesaver for me.

Ours was a working family. After my aunt was widowed she became an assistant to a tailor in a men's shop in Auburn on a part-time basis. When I was nineteen, I worked in a glass factory, standing on the assembly line putting Christmas tree ornaments in boxes. One day, I squeezed one of the bulbs too hard, it shattered, and glass shot up into my face and a piece lodged in my eye. I had to take several buses from Lewiston to get home, and the pain was searing. My aunt washed my eye but she couldn't see anything, nor could the eye doctor. The next morning I looked in the mirror and I made out a large but fine sliver of green glass that had somehow worked its way to the side of my eye. I nearly passed out.

When the Occupational Safety and Health Administration was created in 1970, it instilled fear into the hearts of business owners across America. I attended a conference with my husband Peter, who was a small businessman, and I heard the stories and deep concerns about the government's heavy-handed and adversarial enforcement measures. That was precisely the wrong approach for government to take—at the same time, I understood firsthand how important workplace safety was. If I had been wearing safety glasses in the factory, my eyesight wouldn't have been imperiled.

At the plant, I was stationed at ovens blowing up the glass. It was about 135 degrees around the open oven, and I burned my arms when the glass stuck to my skin. All I did that summer was sweat and drink Tab, and lose a lot of weight. The women I met in the factory, such as the uncompromising but fair forewoman on the first shift, taught me many life lessons. That certainly was the case when one of them said, "Let's have Olympia guess our ages." When you are nineteen, everyone looks older, but in some cases, I missed by about twenty years—which made me feel terrible. The women were mortified, and I felt awful. I have never guessed anyone's age again.

I witnessed firsthand how difficult it was for people to work hard for not much money, and I could identify with them because I was in similar straits—and Social Security was a crucial safety net for me. So when I learned about the proposal to divert a portion of FICA taxes from Social Security into the stock market in the form of personal savings accounts, I was unequivocally opposed. It was important, and in our national interest, to make certain that in retirement, people have at least some guaranteed income—which is what Social Security represents. I also recognized that if the stock market took a dive, government would be on the hook to address the calamitous consequences for millions of Americans.

I couldn't help but recall October 19, 1987, when the market fell by 508 points—or 23 percent—on a single day. It was the equivalent of a 3,000-point drop today. I remember that day clearly because I had been following the trends on Wall Street, and developed a sense of foreboding; I thought we were in for a correction. So I placed a call to my broker to convince her to get me out of the market, but she talked me out of it. The following Monday, I was addressing a child care conference that Jock sponsored as governor. I had no idea what was happening until I flew back to Washington and arrived at my office and my chief of staff, Kirk Walder, informed me the market had dropped 500 points. I was at least twenty-five years away from any possible retirement, but imagine if someone had just retired and had their Social Security money invested in the stock market? Furthermore, this event wasn't an isolated occurrence: when markets opened after 9/11 they fell 684 points in a day and 1,370 points in a week.

The appearance of the PSA idea early in President George W. Bush's second term was surprising to me. However, in 2007, Joshua Green wrote a piece in the *Atlantic* that offered some explanation, stating that after the 2004 election, Karl Rove believed an electoral "realignment" could be prompted by a series of major government policy initiatives. A realignment that swung power to one party for a substantial period had last taken place in 1896 with the election of President McKinley and 1932 with FDR, and Rove saw a historic opportunity to create a long-lasting Republican majority. By means of five policy initiatives, he would attract enough Democrats to forge the same Republican dominance that followed McKinley's election. According to Green, the five components were education standards; the "faith-based initiative"; privatization of Social Security; private health care accounts; and partial immigration reform.

The education plank of the platform, "No Child Left Behind," was passed with overwhelming bipartisan support and the invaluable contribution of Ted Kennedy, but Congress ultimately wasn't willing to embrace a partial privatization of Social Security. I attended a Republican Finance Committee meeting that Chuck Grassley convened, and I sensed there could be fireworks, as the PSA idea was very divisive. As I was walking over to the Finance Committee hearing room, I was accompanied by a new member of my staff. I thought I should forewarn her what might occur, so I said, "I don't want you to be alarmed, but when Chairman Grassley turns to me for my views, particularly on Social Security, and if he doesn't agree with them, don't be surprised if he raises his voice. Don't worry about it; it doesn't mean anything."

The Republican committee members met informally in an anteroom primarily to discuss the Social Security issue with White House liaison officials, and eventually Chuck turned to me and said, "Mrs. Snowe, what do you have to say on this issue?" I said I was totally opposed. It's not anything I could ever support because it could jeopardize people's retirement. As I predicted, Chairman Grassley did raise his voice, asking why I couldn't support the idea. After he had finished, I said, "Chuck, I just told my new staff person not to become alarmed if, when I expressed my view on this issue, you began to yell," and he broke out into laughter. It was nothing personal!

It was another example of how I'd made Chuck Grassley's life more difficult but he took it in stride. I've always held Chuck in the highest regard since I served with him in my first term in the House of Representatives. Several years ago, when he was the ranking member on the Finance Committee, he approached me, opened the palm of his hand, and showed me some pills. He said, "Olympia, *you're* the reason I take these pills!" Later, when Senator Grassley was no longer ranking member of the Finance Committee and Senator Orrin Hatch had assumed that position, I asked Chuck what happened to those pills. He replied, "I gave them to Orrin!"

In my view, it wasn't just the role of the market that was problematic; there were also estimates that we would have to pay out up to $2 trillion in "transitional costs" while the personal savings accounts were being established. Even when it was proposed that less money be put in the accounts, or a "reserve fund" be set up to protect Social Security surpluses, as Senator Jim DeMint proposed in 2006 and 2007, I didn't shift, because there was no doubt that once this particular gate was opened, it couldn't be closed.

I've tried to look as far down the road as possible in anticipating and averting problems. Too much of what we have done in Congress in recent years has been so desperately shortsighted that deferring a disaster for a couple of months as we did over the fiscal cliff is now perceived as an achievement. It's clear what is required: electing the kind of legislators who can see past ideology to the core beliefs that unite us and which I tried to promote in my thirty-four years in Congress.

If Congress as a whole had been serious about our deficits and debt, the country would be in a different place today. And if the two parties continue to sacrifice the long-term interests of this country for short-term political gains, then we will have failed the American people by forfeiting our economic future—and we will find that strict adherence to ideology is very expensive.

Chapter 9

Rising to the Occasion

THE CORNERSTONE OF the U.S. Capitol Building was laid by George Washington in 1793 and the great edifice has been built and rebuilt almost constantly ever since. The building houses statues of great Americans, two from each state, in the Statuary Hall, the Rotunda, the Visitors Center, the Crypt, and in corridors throughout the building. On the second floor is a statue of William King, the first governor of Maine, presented in 1878, and in the hall stands Hannibal Hamlin, Lincoln's first vice president. As national legislators we are surrounded by history, yet rarely in our day-to-day operations do we seem inspired by it. But there were times over the course of my Senate service when the institution found itself able to rise above partisanship and ideological differences and meet the demands of the occasion in a way that honors the history of the Capitol.

These are instances and events that had the potential to tear the country apart but instead came to illustrate the inherent strength in our institutions as enshrined in the Constitution. They embody how the power of conciliation and compromise, combined with the instrumental authority of Presidents and congressional leaders, has guided us through some of the most momentous crises a nation could face.

One of the two most historic events during my tenure was the impeachment and trial of President Clinton in 1999, superseded only by the attacks on September 11, 2001. The last impeachment of a sitting President was in 1868, when Andrew Johnson escaped conviction by one vote. President Nixon resigned after the House Judiciary Committee had drafted articles of impeachment, but before the full House voted on them. As a result, the Senate was devoid of any firsthand experience in how to act in this situation.

The Constitution gives the Senate "the sole power to try all impeachments" but does not offer examples for the method, manner, or process of the trial. Therefore, after the House impeached President Clinton, the Senate had to decide on trial procedures—how long each side was going to have to present its case, whether there would be witnesses, and so on. If we had been unable to forge a bipartisan agreement over the rules governing the procedures and what kind of proceeding to have, the resulting divisions and arguments could have been disastrous for the country. A partisan trial would have eroded the integrity of the process and public confidence in it. The process, which was difficult enough to begin with, would have been biased from the outset.

President Clinton's impeachment was an enormous undertaking and consumed much of our time for more than a year. The events were set in motion in 1994, when Paula Jones filed her sexual harassment suit against the President. It was during that investigation that Linda Tripp's tape of Monica Lewinsky talking about her relationship with President Clinton surfaced. Independent Counsel Kenneth Starr's report on his investigation led the House to charge President Clinton with perjury for lying to the Jones grand jury and with obstruction of justice for coaching witnesses who were going to appear before the grand jury.

The year before the matter reached the House, the movie *Wag the Dog* was released. Robert De Niro starred as a spin doctor who, with film producer Dustin Hoffman, conjured up a fake war in Albania to save the President from losing an election because of fallout from a sex scandal. Jock and I along with our friends, the Millers, have a New Year's tradition of dinner and a movie—this year, it happened to be this particular film. I didn't think much of the movie; it just didn't keep my attention, and I actually fell asleep! The whole premise was preposterous to me, as I told Jock and our friends on the way out.

Little did I know at the time that life would largely imitate art, as less than two weeks later Linda Tripp would contact the office of Independent Counsel Kenneth Starr to talk about former White House aide Monica Lewinsky and the tapes Tripp had made of their conversations about Lewinsky's relations with the President.

Throughout the spring and summer, media coverage of Monica Lewinsky and the possible impeachment of President Clinton saturated the capital. You literally could not get away from the topic in any conversation, and what a small town Washington is was also brought home in June 1998. When Jock and I were sitting at our table at the Bombay Club, one of our favorite Washington restaurants, a large party came into the restaurant, and the first person we saw was Monica Lewinsky. She arrived with her mother and stepfather, her father and his fiancée, and her lawyer. We watched Lewinsky walk over to the piano player and ask for a song. On her way back to her seat she stopped by a couple's table. She recognized the man, who I knew was a reporter from *Time* magazine. He introduced Lewinsky to his dinner companion—I couldn't make out who it was, but Monica became very engaged in conversation with the woman.

I thought little more about the incident until a couple of days later, when I read Maureen Dowd's column in the *New York Times*. The encounter we had witnessed was the subject of the column, and I realized it was Maureen Dowd that Monica Lewinsky had been talking to so closely.

Dowd wrote that she had recognized Monica Lewinsky; when her friend introduced the two of them, Dowd wrote, "Her smile went cold." She put her hands on her knees and bent down so their eyes were level and said, "Do you mind if I ask you something? Why do you write such scathing articles about me?" According to Dowd, that was the first time such a thing had happened to her. In her very amusing column she wrote about all the things she might have said in response, but in the restaurant she had only managed to utter, "I don't know." I couldn't help thinking what a unique city Washington is—there in the same restaurant was the woman who was a part of the episode that started the impeachment of a president, two members of the press, and a senator who would be voting in the trial.

Six months later, on December 19, 1998, the House drew up its charges against President Clinton and the Senate was empowered to act as his jury. In the Constitution it states:

> When the President of the United States is tried, the Chief Justice shall preside. And no person shall be convicted without the concurrence of two thirds of the members present. The President . . . shall be removed from office on impeachment for, and conviction of, treason, bribery, or other high crimes and misdemeanors.

The most immediate and urgent question confronting the Senate was how to conduct the trial. Between the two extremes—summary dismissal of the charges or summary conviction of the accused—lay a middle ground in which we had to devise a means to move forward. That necessitated trying to find a bipartisan agreement that was likely to hold the most promise.

My abiding concern at this momentous time in our history was that we not fall prey to party politics. Obviously, some Republicans were anxious to haul the Democratic President over the coals whatever the merits of the case may have been. And by the same token, some Democrats insisted that Kenneth Starr's concerted investigation and the entire trial were politically motivated despite the uncomfortable facts that Starr asserted he had uncovered.

The only way for us to avoid a rancorous and divisive partisan spectacle was, in my opinion, to find a fair and meaningful process that best served the needs of the nation at this unfortunate moment. If we couldn't agree on the rules governing the conduct of the trial, its legitimacy would be open to question and any verdict would similarly be compromised. In the House, votes had largely fallen along partisan lines (with thirty-one Democrats voting to impeach and one Republican voting against), and two further articles—another count of perjury and a charge of abuse of power—had failed. The proceedings had already taken on a very partisan tenor, which, if allowed to persist at the same level in the Senate, would trivialize the trial and encourage politically motivated impeachments in the future.

Indeed, when the issue is the removal from office of a duly elected President of the United States, and the process by which the Senate operates is essentially like the Supreme Court, whose ruling cannot be appealed, the undertaking must transcend politics.

My overriding concern was that we not initiate proceedings without being adequately prepared. I conveyed my reservations in a letter to Majority Leader Trent Lott on January 4, 1999, differentiating the role we senators would be playing in the impeachment trial compared to the normal legislative one. I wrote that as legislators we listened to testimony to become informed about an issue but our task in the trial was to sit essentially as jurors hearing legal arguments and facts that were in dispute.

Trent is a lawyer, so I knew he would understand the importance of the distinction I was making, especially when the extensive publicity surrounding the case might lead to what I called "a false sense of accurate knowledge." I suggested that the Senate ask each party to submit written materials to every senator before they presented their cases. House managers should, by January 11, submit evidence they deemed material; the President should by January 15 supply a brief of not more than twenty-five pages admitting to or denying the House managers' submissions; and both sides should offer briefs as to whether or not the facts constituted "treason, bribery or other high crimes and misdemeanors." I further wrote that, once the senators had the opportunity to review this evidence and to determine whether or not more evidence was necessary, we could decide on a framework for governing the trial. Trent responded on January 6, agreeing that this preparation was essential.

Events were moving quickly. A major point of contention was whether the Senate was going to call witnesses. On one side was Henry Hyde (R-IL), the chairman of the House Judiciary Committee, who had led the proceedings in that chamber. I'd served with Henry in the House, where I thoroughly enjoyed sitting beside him on the Foreign Affairs Committee for more than a decade—he had a great sense of humor and unquestionably he was a forceful and eloquent orator. Henry wanted the freedom to call witnesses, from perhaps five to as many as fifteen. The White House believed that none were necessary. Senator Pat Leahy (D-VT), ranking member of the Senate Judiciary Committee, argued, "It'd be a prescription for a never-ending saga if we go to witnesses. The House didn't have witnesses." Senator Bob Kerrey was quoted in the *New York Times* as saying, "The Senate's supposed to write the rules. Henry Hyde's a fine human being, but frankly I don't give a damn what he thinks about what our rules are going to be. He doesn't have a vote here."

The trial opened on January 7 without an agreement as to when and how we would hear arguments or whether we would call witnesses. Ninety-six year-old Senate President Pro Tem Strom Thurmond (D-NC) called the Senate to order and Henry Hyde, accompanied by his thirteen House managers, read the articles of impeachment to the Senate with House members present.

In the early afternoon of that day, I was appointed by Majority Leader Lott as one of the six senators—three Republicans and three Democrats—to escort Chief Justice William Rehnquist, who would preside over the trial, into the Senate. Each senator was then sworn in and we had to sign a book affirming that we would be impartial. I'm not sure what it signaled that the pens we were given to use and keep were misprinted with the words Untied States Senate, but we subsequently recessed, still absent an agreement on how to proceed.

Peter Baker, then the *Washington Post* reporter on the story, described the scene in his book *The Breach.* At the conclusion of the swearing-in, senators first began gathering together on the floor of the Senate around their respective leaders, Trent Lott and Tom Daschle, and then senators from both parties began to approach one another to seek a means of breaking the stalemate. Nancy Gibbs of *Time* magazine described what she viewed as the initial awkwardness of the situation: "It looked like a junior high dance, when the boys and girls finally tiptoe into the center of the gym."

These first exchanges appeared to bear fruit. Senators discussed the idea of convening in the Old Senate Chamber, a location that could be secured without television cameras and reporters parsing every utterance and piece of body language. Subsequently, there was confusion that such a meeting had been canceled by the Democrats, but as it turned out, that wasn't the case. In the meantime, however, a Republican conference was scheduled in the Mansfield Room in the Capitol to discuss the way forward.

On my way to the meeting, I was stopped by a reporter from Maine who asked me what I thought about the plan that, unbeknownst to me, had been announced: that there would be two party-line votes at 5 P.M.——one on a Republican proposal that would have opening statements by the House and White House followed by a vote on whether to call witnesses, and one on a Democratic plan that called for opening statements followed by a vote on conviction. I said, "You've got to be kidding me. I have to get in there." At this defining moment for the Senate, rancor and divisiveness would only serve to cast a shadow over the integrity of the entire trial and the legitimacy of its result, while a bipartisan agreement between

Republicans and Democrats might allow the Senate to accord the process the dignity and solemnity it deserved.

Having spoken with the reporter, I arrived a little late to the Republican conference in the Mansfield Room, but the discussion rapidly confirmed what the press had told me. I couldn't believe we would have two separate votes with no agreement from the other side. Sitting down behind Senator Jim Jeffords (R-VT) and my Maine colleague, Senator Susan Collins, I tapped Susan on the shoulder and said, "I have to say something." I didn't want to be the skunk at the lawn party, but it wasn't the first time and it wouldn't be the last. Silence wasn't an option—we had to do this right.

I stood up and made a plea to the Majority Leader and the conference not to proceed under these circumstances, but instead to delay the vote and propose once again that a bipartisan meeting be convened to forge an agreement. Trent agreed.

In *Time,* Nancy Gibbs described the scene when I spoke: "They had just taken a historic oath, she reminded her colleagues—some of them still fingering the souvenir pens with which they signed the impeachment book. Did they really want to start the process with such a partisan move? She appealed to a sense of personal trust that has not dissolved completely; Senators still shake hands across the aisles." Gibbs continued: "The mood in the room swept behind her as Republicans rose in agreement. Said Larry Craig of Idaho, a conservative: 'If there's any chance of not having this be a partisan vote, let's go for it.'" We were jurors, not legislators, and we had to act differently than if we were discussing a regular bill. Others joined in supporting this position: Arlen Specter, Susan Collins, John Chafee, and Ted Stevens (AK). In *The Breach*, Peter Baker wrote that it was "Olympia Snowe's over-my-dead-body speech."

The conference adjourned. Trent Lott subsequently went to the floor to speak with Minority Leader Daschle, who was about to make a statement that Democrats had not, in fact, canceled the joint meeting. Their relationship was such that the two men talked every day and were used to working together; in fact, Trent had said he and

Daschle had a direct phone line to each other to discuss any issue. They quickly agreed to the bipartisan meeting and held a joint news conference to announce it. Trent reported that he'd offered a proposal to restart the suggested bipartisan meeting in the Old Senate Chamber and that he'd spoken with Senator Daschle. "We think that the best way to keep calm and cool and dignified is to look at each other and talk to each other," Lott said. "Senator Daschle and I are not dictators. . . . We have to bring along ninety-eight other senators. We are struggling very hard to do that."

As a January 10 piece in the *Washington Post* reported, "The spur-of-the-moment decision to appear together in a show of solidarity proved to be the turning point in the Senate's marathon effort last week to forge an agreement between Republicans and Democrats on how to conduct the impeachment trial. . . ."

The following day, one of my Republican colleagues wrote me a note saying, "Olympia: Many thanks for your stand in delaying the 5:00 pm vote." The next day, all one hundred senators duly met in the Old Senate Chamber, where congressional business had last been conducted in 1859. The chamber remained the ideal location because it would provide an atmosphere commensurate with the gravity of the situation we were obliged to address. Since there were fewer states in 1859 and the room consisted of only sixty-eight desks, additional chairs were set up to accommodate every senator. The chamber is surprisingly small and dark; at the front and center of the room is the ornate vice president's chair, which is elevated and canopied by opulent red drapery, capped off by a great eagle with spread wings. Most of what's considered the "Golden Era of the Senate" transpired in the Old Senate Chamber, from Senator Daniel Webster's speech in defense of the Union to the censure of President Andrew Jackson, led by Henry Clay.

We agreed that we would hear arguments and questions according to a predetermined schedule and then decide which, if any, witnesses we wanted to hear from at the conclusion of the presentations. It was a truly bipartisan plan—100-0 was the final vote tally.

The trial took place between January 9 and February 11. As members of a hundred-strong jury, we read the briefs and listened to the oral arguments from both sides. What we heard in our closed-door sessions was sensitive and discomforting. The atmosphere was very solemn. We decided more evidence was required, but the Senate wanted to avoid the spectacle of live testimony on the Senate floor, so the Senate requested depositions from three witnesses: the President's friend Vernon Jordan, senior Clinton adviser Sidney Blumenthal, and Clinton's assistant, Betty Currie. We would review the deposition transcripts and then decide if live testimony was required.

The question I had to answer finally was, what were "high crimes and misdemeanors"? I researched the issue thoroughly. Before the trial, I hired Derek Langhauser, a lawyer from Portland who was well versed in constitutional law. Derek took a leave of absence from his job and commuted to Washington for six months. Our team worked day and night in the office, going through the Starr Report, briefs, reply briefs, and depositions. We examined the whole question and the role of the Senate, and traced the roots of the concept of impeachment back to English law in 1386 and how it was used in Parliament on approximately fifty occasions between 1621 and 1725. The Framers of our Constitution adopted a different model, and we investigated American cases for precedent.

I found that "high crimes and misdemeanors" spoke to offenses that go to the heart of matters of governance, social authority, and institutional power—offenses that, in Alexander Hamilton's words, "relate chiefly to injuries done immediately to the society itself." These crimes must be of such magnitude that the American people require protection, not by the traditional means of civil or criminal law, but by the extraordinary act of removing a sitting President. In other words, removal was intended by the Framers to be the only remedy by which the people, when their core interests are meaningfully threatened by the President's conduct, could be effectively protected.

The final vote on impeachment came on February 12. Article One, the perjury charge, failed by 45-55, with ten Republicans, myself included, voting "not guilty." Article Two, obstruction, resulted in a 50-50 tie, and therefore didn't begin to approach the two-thirds majority that was constitutionally required to remove the President. On the second charge I also voted "not guilty." As I described in my statement to the closed Senate, I did not believe the standard necessary for his removal had been met, even as I also said at the time that the Senate's decision didn't absolve the President's responsibility for the harm he had inflicted. In another break with tradition, senators made their statements from the floor of the Senate and we addressed our fellow members, instead of speaking to the President Pro Tem (or in this instance the Chief Justice).

I concluded my statement to the Senate by saying:

> In my mind and in my heart, I believe to a moral certainty that my verdict is just. As men and women of honor, that is the highest aspiration to which we can aspire. For we are writing history with indelible ink, but imperfect pens.
>
> In the end, when future generations dust off the record of what we have done here may they say we validated the Framers' faith in the Senate. May they say we reached within ourselves to discover our most noble intentions. And may they say we achieved a conclusion worthy not just of our time, but of all time.

The *Marquette Law Review* later awarded me ten-out-of-ten for my rhetorical performance, and I was one of only seven senators who spoke to get that rating. But I was much more gratified knowing that our long deliberations regarding the conduct of the trial were ultimately vindicated.

How the institutions of government are viewed by its citizens should be of paramount concern to elected officials, but in crisis, this is all the more critical. On September 11, 2001, we had a duty to demonstrate that we, as members of Congress, were in command of the circumstances; as with impeachment, however, it became immediately apparent there was no existing blueprint for doing so.

That morning, I was due to meet with the author Bob Woodward for his latest book project, in my office in the Russell Office Building. As I was turning the TV off on the way out of my condo, Matt Lauer of NBC's *Today* show interrupted an interview to say they had a breaking story about the World Trade Center. After the show came back from a commercial, Katie Couric said that "apparently a plane has just crashed into the World Trade Center," and she interviewed an eyewitness. I thought, could it be a commuter plane as was mentioned? But it was such a strange thing to happen on such a beautifully clear day that I had a sense something was wrong, so I hurried out the door. I went to my office and the second plane hit. When Flight 77 crashed into the Pentagon at 9:37, initial reports said it was the Old Executive Office Building. It was clear that America was under attack.

I was going to get Bob Woodward and his assistant to bring them from the reception room into my office when I ran into Congressman Dana Rohrabacher (R-CA), who had been in Senator Mike DeWine's office across the hall from me. "Dana," I said, "who do you think is behind this?" He'd obviously seen the attacks and he referenced events that had occurred over the previous weekend, in which Ahmad Shah Massoud, the Afghan leader of guerrilla forces that fought the Taliban, had been assassinated by suicide bombers masquerading as journalists.

The call came to evacuate the building (in what the *Washington Post* reported was the first ever mandatory and complete evacuation of the House and Senate complexes) and my chief of staff, Jane Calderwood, entered my office to say that we should leave immediately—but I instructed her to first ensure that everyone on staff had gotten the message and had exited the building. A short while after that was accomplished, Woodward, his assistant, and I left the building.

Just outside, we ran into Senator John Warner (R-VA), who said we should get away from the doorway. When I asked why, he responded that the building didn't have any vertical supports and would simply collapse if it were hit. So we moved to the sidewalk, where we continued to discuss the horrific events that had descended on America. At that point, there was a roar of a plane overhead, and the hundreds of people we saw standing on the street and in the park next to the building turned en masse to move in the same direction, away from Capitol complex. I'm certain we all had at least a fleeting thought that this was another hijacked plane, and the air was thick with rumors that more were on their way. Later, when I wanted to go back into the building to get my briefcase (as I discovered, reasonably enough, no one was being allowed in), I coincidentally bumped into a reporter covering the Maine congressional delegation, Bart Jansen—and we talked about the enormous dimensions of what had occurred.

On my way back to my condo, which is near the Senate office buildings, I drove by my assistant press secretary, Lucas Caron, who was standing on a traffic island. He was trying to find Holly Miller, a friend of his and the daughter of our friends Dan and Sharon. Holly worked at the White House and when he'd last spoken with her, she said she'd told her mother, "They've told us to run for our lives," and Sharon had said, "Well then, run for your life!" But now Lucas couldn't find her. I gave him a ride over to her apartment; she wasn't there, but we later learned she was in an office building downtown with other coworkers. Driving over, I had to stop for gas—usually a mundane chore, but that day it seemed like a ridiculous act. I pulled into my usual gas station on Pennsylvania Avenue, and it was like a movie with bumper-to-bumper traffic in every direction in a massive exodus from the city.

My chief of staff, along with my communications director, Dave Lackey, and I gathered at my condo where we fielded press calls, disseminated press releases, and of course kept an eye glued to the television the entire time. At that point, I learned from Senator Jeff Sessions and his wife, Mary, who are my neighbors, that a group of senators was gathering at the Capitol Police Headquarters. The news had to travel by word of mouth because there was no cell phone service—the system was overwhelmed. (This situation resulted in senators and senior staffers being equipped with BlackBerrys shortly thereafter.)

As I recall, more than two dozen of us met in a room in the police headquarters, which is located very near the Senate complex. After an initial period of confusion—there was no plan for an eventuality such as this—the congressional leadership was moved to a secure and undisclosed location outside of Washington. Along with the obvious sense of indescribable loss that had been inflicted on our country by the horrific acts of violence and terror, we talked about next steps given there was no template for how to proceed under these circumstances. We discussed the importance of showing America and the world that the United States government was continuing to function, and I evoked King George VI and Queen Elizabeth stalwartly refusing to leave London during the Blitz in World War II. It was noted that it would be important to communicate with leadership as soon as possible, and staff arranged a conference call to occur during a subsequent meeting at headquarters later that day.

We were also informed that leaders were planning to hold a bipartisan, bicameral leadership press conference that evening on the Capitol steps. All of us agreed that was a great idea, but we wanted to stand with them. I conveyed my view that it would be essential to demonstrate that no one was hiding under their beds, and that we present a united front to our nation while sending an unmistakable message to our enemies that they would never prevail.

That evening, about 150 representatives and senators assembled for a press conference on the stairs of the Capitol. House Speaker Dennis Hastert said that "senators and House members, Democrats and Republicans will stand shoulder to shoulder to fight this evil that has perpetrated on this nation," and Senate Majority Leader Tom Daschle concurred. "We, Republicans and Democrats, House and Senate, stand strongly united behind the President. . . ." He also announced that Congress would convene the next day. Together we sang "God Bless America."

Compared to the rescue and recovery work going on at the World Trade Center in Manhattan, at the Pentagon, and in the field in Shanksville, Pennsylvania, where Flight 93 went down, and to the security efforts taking place all over the world, convening members of Congress on the steps of the Capitol was simple, but I believe it was symbolically crucial to demonstrate that Congress was united and going back to work. We couldn't be expected to do less than to press on, of course, but it was vital that we were seen doing it.

I have never been more proud of the way our President and our legislative leaders conducted themselves than on and after 9/11. In fact, one of the most reassuring expressions of bipartisanship in a time of great consequence came after President Bush spoke to the nation before a joint session of Congress on September 20, 2011. At the conclusion of his speech, as he was leaving the chamber, he shook Majority Leader Tom Daschle's hand, and then they embraced. The country had unified quickly, with the Senate having voted on September 14 to authorize the use of our military in Afghanistan.

In October 2002, the Iraq War Resolution was passed. Before that vote, we reviewed evidence that Saddam Hussein had weapons of mass destruction—evidence we now know was false. These decisions have such enormous implications that trust is essential. The American people must be confident that we are putting the country first and basing our decision on the best information available.

Any vote authorizing a war is the gravest decision we can make as senators. To prepare for the vote on the Persian Gulf War, which had begun with Iraq's invasion of Kuwait in August 1990, President George H. W. Bush had held briefings for members of Congress in late summer. And I'll never forget a bipartisan meeting the President convened in the Cabinet Room with my colleagues in January 1991, the day before we were to begin debate on a resolution giving the President the authority to go to war, to discuss with him the use of force in the Persian Gulf. During the meeting, President Bush excused himself to take a call from Secretary of State James Baker on the progress of his talks with the Iraqi foreign minister. When Bush returned, the look of determination on his face told me the talks had failed. Force would have to be used. His face also reflected the years of solid experience and the judgment that marked him as a leader. I thought to myself, "Thank God we have George Bush as our commander in chief."

We understand the terrible truth that once we send Americans into danger, there will be casualties. Two of the eighteen Americans killed in the Battle of Mogadishu in Somalia in 1993 were from Maine. Master Sergeant Gary Gordon from Lincoln, Maine, volunteered to try to rescue comrades injured when their Black Hawk helicopter crashed, as portrayed later in the book and movie *Black Hawk Down*. He and a fellow sniper rescued the pilot, Mike Durant, but were killed by the overwhelming Somali forces. Sergeant Gordon posthumously received the Medal of Honor at a ceremony I was honored to attend at the White House—one of the most poignant moments of my public service. Among the men on the ground Gordon fought alongside and who also died was Staff Sergeant Thomas Field of Lisbon, Maine.

Every time I go past Arlington National Cemetery I think of the heroic and supreme sacrifice that is represented by every tombstone. The willingness to defend our country has made our nation exceptional. In October 2012, I attended the funeral of Sgt. First Class Aaron Henderson of Houlton, Maine, a Green Beret who was killed in Helmand Province on his first deployment in Afghanistan after three tours of Iraq. One soldier told the 1,200 mourners in the Houlton High School gymnasium that Sergeant Henderson had volunteered to go to Afghanistan because the men on his team were young and he thought they could benefit from his experience. Then his commander spoke about Henderson's extraordinary skill and professionalism. As an elected official with the power and responsibility to vote to send the country to war, I think it is difficult to convey the nation's profound gratitude to the families of people who are willing to serve the country knowing they are putting their lives in peril.

––––––⦓⦓⦔––––––

In the last fifteen years we have been roiled by foreign and domestic crises, each of which has been epic in its own right: impeachment; *Bush v. Gore;* 9/11; the wars in Afghanistan and Iraq; and more recently, the fiscal crisis of 2008–2009. Often those of us in government have proved able to provide the leadership that our country has required. I believe we all abide by the notion that our country comes first, but too often of late we have failed to follow that credo in addressing our country's challenges.

We certainly scrap for positions in the day-to-day business of Congress, but we should not forget the standard that we have applied at times of national crisis: that our problems are not insurmountable if we refuse to be intractable. It can be messy and time-consuming, but we should always recall our illustrious forebears and act accordingly. Because it's not about what's in the best interests of a single political party, but what's in the best interests of our country.

On December 19, 2012, Harry Reid and Mitch McConnell jointly invited all senators with spouses and senior staff to a screening of Steven Spielberg's movie *Lincoln* in the National Visitors Center Auditorium. The movie dramatizes events surrounding the extraordinary efforts of our most remarkable President to pass the Thirteenth Amendment, abolishing slavery in 1865. It was a treat for us to mingle beforehand with Spielberg and the star of the film, Daniel Day-Lewis, together with screenwriter Tony Kushner and Doris Kearns Goodwin, upon whose book *Team of Rivals* the movie is based.

The event was dripping with symbolism, of course. Here we were in the midst of the then-failing fiscal cliff negotiations watching a movie about one of our greatest Presidents in his finest hour. Lincoln's Herculean efforts to pass the amendment at a time when Confederate leaders were on their way to negotiate a peace settlement were stirringly re-created. A movie about the 112th Congress would be somewhat less inspiring. There was accord when Majority Leader Harry Reid managed to get a dispensation allowing popcorn to be served in the auditorium, but it took the Senate until 2 A.M. on New Year's Day to pass legislation to avoid the fiscal cliff.

The movie showing had a purpose: to inspire us in the moment. But it shouldn't take a movie to inspire Congress when we work in some of the very same chambers as Lincoln had, where so many have shaped so much of our history. We should acknowledge the awesome responsibilities of our offices and elevate our aspirations each and every day for producing results. As the record demonstrates, it *can* be done.

Chapter 10

Health Care and Partisanship

THE PRESIDENTIAL INAUGURATION of 2009 took place at the intersection of optimism and anxiety. America had plunged into recession in late 2007. In 2008, the 158-year-old finance industry giant Lehman Brothers, which was in operation during the Civil War, went bankrupt, wiping out twenty-six thousand jobs and billions of dollars in customers' savings. The federal government took over American International Group and financed JPMorgan Chase's purchase of Bear Stearns; Fannie Mae and Freddie Mac imploded and entered into federal conservatorship; we witnessed $557 billion in losses and write-downs on subprime investments worldwide; and we experienced the largest single bank failure in the history of the United States with Washington Mutual. All of these catastrophic events illustrated the unconscionable and unchecked dimensions of greed in our financial systems, which imperiled the very underpinnings of our economy.

At stake were future economic growth, jobs for hardworking families, retirement savings for seniors, and the ability of Americans from all walks of life to access credit to attend college, purchase a house or automobile, or start a small business. People were rightfully panicked, and were asking how nearly $3 trillion worth of toxic financial securities could have been swapped like casino wagers with no transparency, no oversight, and no questions asked by those in business and government who had legal obligations to do so.

At the same time, in 2008, more young people were becoming part of the electoral process as presidential candidate Barack Obama sounded themes that spoke to hopefulness and change at a time of tremendous cynicism about our future. Obama also made the concept of "post-partisanship" a centerpiece of his campaign, and many believe this was a critical component to his success. Many voters were persuaded there was at least a significant potential for shifting the political environment toward unification and away from serial disharmony. With a new congress and President, government might finally draw together to meet the challenges of our economic and financial catastrophes. Indeed, in the very first days preceding and following the new administration, some seeds of bipartisanship held the promise of germination. But they were not to take root.

The book and movie *The Perfect Storm* document how, in October 1991, the elements of Hurricane Grace and a low-pressure system that formed over Canada collided with a strong high-pressure system that extended from the Gulf of Mexico to Greenland, creating what became a monstrous maelstrom. In similar fashion, political phenomena were unfolding at the beginning of 2009 that would produce the monumental level of partisanship that we are still grappling with today. In short, circumstances conspired that crystallized for many the fact that government was stepping far beyond its bounds, while others were convinced it was still doing too little as Americans continued to suffer under the worst recession since the Great Depression.

In 2008, when the housing boom went bust, the enormous holdings of mortgage-backed securities throughout the financial sector collapsed in value. The vast amounts of these "toxic assets" caused a rapid and catastrophic loss of liquidity in the financial markets, and in swift succession sank many of our financial institutions and paralyzed the credit markets.

The question was, is government intervention justified? For me, given what we experienced—that regular investors had pulled $335 billion out of money-market funds; that the cost of overnight lending between banks had jumped 50 percent; that capital had evaporated; that major banks had failed; and that small firms as well as large were suddenly being denied access even to existing credit lines, never mind new loans—it was difficult to conclude there wouldn't be serious and systemic consequences for the economy in the near term if we didn't act. In a statement on September 19, Treasury Secretary Hank Paulson said that "illiquid assets are clogging up our financial system, and undermining the strength of our otherwise sound financial institutions. As a result, Americans' personal savings are threatened, and the ability of consumers and businesses to borrow and finance spending, investment, and job creation has been disrupted." Federal Reserve Chairman Ben Bernanke warned, "This is the most significant financial crisis of the postwar period."

As a senator I was faced with a single choice—either rescue the country from a depression or allow our economy to free-fall into the precipice. I didn't have the luxury of equivocation; I had the responsibility of casting a vote. So on October 1, 2008, I voted for the Troubled Asset Relief Program (TARP), authorizing the Treasury to spend up to $700 billion to buy the troubled, or "toxic," assets from banks to get the credit markets moving again. The widespread recognition of the severity of the crisis was reflected in the broad bipartisan support for the proposal, because our financial system was on the verge of collapse.

It was infuriating that the country had been placed in this position and imperiled to the extent that it required action of this magnitude. The dimensions of failure and fraud were breathtaking. Before any prospective vote I would measure the ramifications and reflect on whether I could stand by those consequences. I decided I would much rather explain why I voted for TARP than explain why I allowed a run on every bank in America. That was the risk I could not live with. Small businesses were suffering nationwide. My home state of Maine failed to sell an important AA-rated transportation bond because the market had disappeared. The signs of calamity were unmistakable The measure passed the Senate by an overwhelming vote of 74-25, with 34 Republicans voting in support.

⸙⸙⸙

On December 8, 2008, five weeks after being elected and six weeks before his inauguration, President-elect Barack Obama called me. TARP had been in place for a month at this point, and with the economy in tatters it was essential that we focus on lighting a legislative fire under the economy. There was a common understanding among Republicans, Democrats, and economists across the political spectrum that the current crisis warranted congressional enactment of a stimulus plan, which the President-elect was already assembling as a matter of urgency in preparation for taking office in January.

Following up on our call, two days later, on December 10, I sent Obama a note congratulating him again on his historic victory and reiterating that I shared his sentiment that this was a critical time in our nation's history, and that we must work together closely, across party lines, for the good of the country. I went on to suggest priorities that would have the maximum stimulative effect, including extending unemployment benefits, increasing food stamps, assisting small businesses in getting credit and allowing them to expense rather than depreciate investments, boosting the New Markets Tax Credit Program, which helps spur investment in low-income communities, and investing in health information technology.

Two days after I wrote to the President-elect, I received a phone call just after I stepped off a plane in Florida. It was from my former Senate colleague Joe Biden, now Vice President–elect, and he had some questions for me. Joe was contacting Republicans and also soliciting input on an economic stimulus package. I thought Biden's early outreach was another promising sign. He said, "I want to give you time to consider it all, of course," so I think he was a bit surprised when I told him I had a number of ideas already! We discussed a few and he said, "Olympia, that's great, and could you write up your ideas and send them to me?" Later that day I sent over a package of proposals and suggestions that included those I had shared with President-elect Obama.

The context for my rationale about a stimulus had been dictated by the recession that had commenced a year earlier, in December 2007—and all indications were that the economic situation was worsening. In the fourth quarter of 2008, gross domestic product contracted and 1.5 million jobs were lost, with the year as a whole being the worst for job losses since World War II. In time, we would understand that the recession was the gravest the United States had experienced since the Great Depression. Economists of all political stripes testified in Senate Finance Committee hearings that without economic stimulus, the prospects of an even steeper decline would intensify.

Early in January 2009, it appeared promising that bipartisan progress toward a stimulus package was possible. The President-elect urged that any House proposal include Republican input, and in turn Republican leadership expressed optimism their voices would be heard. As reported by *Congressional Quarterly* on January 8, "[Mitch] McConnell said he thought Obama was listening to Republican ideas but that the true test will be what makes it into the final piece of legislation. 'I don't have any complaints about the communication so far,' he said." "I'm hopeful," minority whip Eric Cantor said on January 14. "I take the President-elect at his word that he wants Washington to start working in different ways."

That same day, 40 House Republicans voted with 249 Democrats to expand the State Children's Health Insurance Program (S-CHIP). Analyst Larry Sabato said that roughly the same number of Republicans might back an Obama stimulus package. Yet on January 15, House Democrats, aware they had enough votes to pass their own plan, unveiled a draft proposal that had no Republican input for an $825 billion stimulus, which prompted then-Minority Leader

John Boehner to exclaim, "I just can't tell you how shocked I am at what I'm seeing."

Barack Obama continued to reach out to Republicans to solicit ideas. I had received a phone call from the President-elect on January 13, and we discussed the necessity of a stimulus. The inauguration took place on January 20. On January 23, I spoke by phone again with Vice President Joe Biden. A week into his presidency, on January 27, the President met with House Republicans on the same day that chamber began floor consideration of its stimulus proposal, and he later spoke before the Senate Republican Conference policy lunch. At that meeting, he described the unprecedented situation and expressed that time was of the essence, as every economist was indicating to him that the situation was worse than people thought, and deteriorating. President Obama laid out his plan but indicated there was still time to "work this out," that he wanted to hear the best ideas and had no pride of authorship.

However, that very same day, both the Senate Finance and Appropriations committees marked up stimulus bills that had already been written—and the ranking member of the Senate Finance Committee, Chuck Grassley, noted that "[w]e were never at the negotiating table." Meanwhile, then-Speaker of the House Nancy Pelosi, referencing the process in the House, said: "Yes, we wrote the bill. Yes, we won the election."

I thought the President would have accrued far more benefit to himself, and to the country, if at the outset he had brought people on both sides together, rather than allowing the House to move so precipitously. Without bipartisan input, the version of the stimulus bill that Speaker Pelosi crafted behind closed doors sent all the wrong signals.

The Senate Finance Committee staged a ten-hour markup of our version of the stimulus and passed the relevant legislation by a vote of 14-9. That day, I was the only Republican to vote in favor, and in my remarks to the committee, I noted the extreme urgency of the situation—we had lost 600,000 jobs in January alone, and over the prior thirteen months, 3.6 million jobs. Stimulus was required, but it had to be "timely, targeted and temporary," as similar measures had always been, and we had to "deliver job creation and assistance to people in need."

Among other measures, the Finance Committee package secured $90 billion in funding for Medicaid programs and reduced the earnings threshold for the Refundable Child Tax Credit. It also included providing tax relief for working Americans and tax incentives to small businesses, an extension of unemployment insurance, and the addition of a payroll tax credit. The Finance Committee shaped a significant portion of the stimulus bill on the Senate side with its tax initiatives—it was ultimately responsible for 61 percent of the provisions of the final American Recovery and Reinvestment Act of 2009.

In the House Appropriations Committee, the Democrats constructed a bill that incorporated at least $100 billion for programs, money included just to circumvent the regular budget process. Republicans expressed their grave concern over the size and scope of the stimulus package, but on January 28, 2009, the Democratic-controlled House passed their economic stimulus package, including that extra $100 billion, without a single Republican vote.

The President invited me to the Oval Office on February 4 to further discuss the stimulus package then pending in the Senate. The proposal would cost nearly $900 billion. Whether any particular item was a tax cut or a spending increase, the only question was whether it created jobs. As I'd expressed, the question wasn't whether stimulus was called for, or how much we labeled as "tax relief" and how much we labeled as "spending." In the final analysis, it was about the merits of the individual measures in the legislation, and whether the totality of the package could create jobs and deliver assistance to those who had been displaced.

I presented the President with a list of reasonable measures, many drawn from Republican Policy Conference proposals, that would reduce the cost of the package by $100 billion. President

Obama and I met alone, and I found him receptive. The times and the weight of the initiatives he was advancing were also reminiscent of the challenges President Reagan had confronted, so I encouraged the President to adopt what I've described as the "Reagan model" and engage in the process to work hand in glove with members of Congress to shape the package, working from the middle to draw bipartisan support.

As I told Carl Hulse of the *New York Times,* "Once you relegate it to someone else, you lose control. The [administration] really needed to guide it and nurture it." And when the White House did begin to push through passage of the stimulus by lobbying members of both parties in the House and Senate, they did so with an eye to future strategic considerations. "Mr. Obama directed his staff members to set a respectful tone," the *Times* reported on February 13, "keeping in mind that Republicans would be needed on future issues like energy and health care."

The Senate had begun to consider the stimulus on the floor on February 2. I was concerned there were appropriations measures on the spending side of the bill that didn't meet the criteria we had set in the Finance Committee. "We must not confuse stimulus with omnibus," I said in a statement on the floor. Working vigorously to improve the bill, I wanted to make it as stimulative as possible—too many of the appropriations were discretionary and would not boost the economy—and as quickly as possible, since half of the spend-out was coming in the next two years. I also filed amendments requiring that the specific job-creation numbers be provided by each department or agency, an issue that was a priority for me. I had raised it in my meeting with President Obama and my conversations with Vice President Biden.

In the meantime, my Republican colleagues Senators Arlen Specter and Susan Collins, along with Democratic Senator Ben Nelson of Nebraska, were also engaged in addressing those appropriations measures that simply weren't designed to be stimulative. All four of us had meetings with White House Chief of Staff Rahm

Emanuel and Office of Management and Budget Director Peter Orszag in the Majority Leader's office to pare back the package to below $800 billion. Ultimately, we were the only three Republicans who voted for the package. To the consternation of House Democrats, the cost of the measure was reduced in the Senate to $787 billion. Although I didn't agree with every provision, I believed it was important to be part of a legislative process that yielded a consensus-based solution—and inaction simply wasn't an option.

Nonetheless, the January vote in the House on a purely partisan stimulus bill didn't bode well for the prospects of bipartisanship when it came to health care, a key component of Barack Obama's agenda. President Obama addressed a joint session of Congress on February 24 and said "we can no longer afford to put health care reform on hold." I'd long identified health care as a legislative priority of my own throughout my tenure in Washington. In my first campaign for the House in 1978, I raised the imperative of addressing the subject of America's uninsured, whose numbers were growing by leaps and bounds. It was also a perennial challenge for small businesses that were unable to offer benefits at affordable rates, which threatened both their bottom line and their competitiveness in attracting the more skilled members of the workforce. It remained a major problem into 2009, especially in Maine, where rates were astronomical and many people could only afford catastrophic coverage, since deductibles were as high as $15,000 and there was no access to preventive services. In the first decade of the 2000s, premiums soared by 131 percent nationally, and in Maine, a small market dominated by two companies, they skyrocketed 271 percent between 2001 and 2009. During my reelection campaign in 2006, I conducted a Main Street tour in Houlton, Maine. On my first stop, I walked into a store and the owner dropped his Blue Cross Blue Shield bill onto the counter and asked, "What are you going to do about this?"

Still, President Obama's decision to pursue health care reform while the economy was struggling in the wake of the financial crisis was puzzling. The stimulus should have been a bridge to additional, concentrated efforts that would contribute to the regeneration of the private sector. What was necessary was to pivot to address issues such as tax and regulatory reform, which was integral in encouraging employers to take risks, grow their businesses, and create new jobs at a time when unemployment was over 10 percent.

I urged the President to tackle comprehensive tax reform when I participated in a White House Fiscal Responsibility Summit he convened on February 23. I sat on the tax panel that day, which assembled in the Eisenhower Executive Office Building, just across a narrow, closed-off street from the White House. Our breakout session was chaired by Treasury Secretary Geithner and Christina Romer, chair of the Council of Economic Advisers. When it was my turn to speak, I stated that "we have a window that we must take advantage of, to determine how we can ensure our tax system is right for the nation as we emerge from recession and face a staggering budget deficit," and that the current economic crisis should be the impetus for setting up a collaborative process for fundamental tax reform, as was the case prior to the Tax Reform Act of 1986. But that was not to be.

Obviously, it was the President's prerogative to bring up health care reform as his party controlled both Houses of Congress, but concentrating on that subject exclusively wasn't going to benefit a economy that was in dire straits in the short to mid-term. Moreover, it was an extraordinarily complex subject that would consume a disproportionate amount of time and attention when our economy deserved our undiluted effort.

Consider this scenario: what if the President and the Congress had instead focused like a laser on job creation measures, which were desperately required for millions of Americans who were now struggling—and which at least might have engendered a degree of bipartisanship? We could have built on the stimulus by further undergirding an environment for private sector growth as well as potentially establishing cooperation between the two parties to build on for future debates on initiatives such as health care reform. Instead, we took a path that produced greater uncertainty and widened the political gulf.

In the President's address to the joint session of Congress on February 24, he pledged to take action on health care within a year. In the Senate, as chair of the Health, Education, Labor and Pensions Committee (HELP), which would share jurisdiction, and legendary in his zeal for health reform, Senator Ted Kennedy would have been a titan in driving the issue in the Senate—but his illness didn't make that possible. The other obvious figure was Senator Max Baucus as chair of the Senate Finance Committee, which also has jurisdiction over health care.

Indeed, as early as February 2007, Chairman Baucus announced his intention to make health care a priority in the Finance Committee by commencing a series of roundtable discussions over the following two years, hearings and forums in which, he said, "[w]e will plant the seeds of an informed dialogue." The committee was an ideal environment in which to build a record for drafting legislation to address the 75 million under- or uninsured Americans.

To Chairman Baucus's great credit, when the President focused his attention on health care reform in 2009, he established a promising template: assembling the bipartisan group of senators on the Finance Committee that became known as the Gang of Six. At the time, multiple approaches to reform were being discussed and introduced as legislation in both the House and Senate, and the Gang of Six was formed in an attempt to develop consensus among an array of approaches. Senator Baucus asked me to participate, and I agreed.

The Senate's Gang of Six included Chuck Grassley, the ranking Republican on Finance; Mike Enzi, ranking Republican on the HELP Committee, which had marked up its own version of health reform legislation; and Chairman Baucus; Kent Conrad (D-ND), chairman of the Budget Committee; and Jeff Bingaman (D-NM), chairman of the Energy and Natural Resources Committee. Mike Enzi has a true appreciation and love for legislating; Kent, who departed the Senate at the same time as me, was relentless in using his leadership capacity at the Budget Committee to underscore the perils of deficits and the failure to act upon them; and Jeff Bingaman cared about policy. I worked with him on a number of energy initiatives. It was a compatible group, composed of senators who were all committed to upholding the integrity of the legislative process.

The Gang of Six met more than thirty-one times over a four-month period as the only bipartisan health reform effort in any committee in either the House or Senate. Following a blueprint for how the Senate should function, we debated policy, not politics, in attempting to reach common ground. And to those supporters of health reform who were critical that our process was taking too long, I countered that it took a year and a half to pass Medicare to cover 20 million Americans—so we could not put one-sixth of our economy and a matter of such personal and financial significance to every American on a legislative fast track.

We met in the chairman's conference room in the Hart Senate Office Building, which is a much more contemporary space than the Russell Building, with its fireplaces and ornate sconces. The perimeter of the room became crowded with health care staffers, and often snacks were brought in—when they were cookies and potato chips, it made us all laugh given that the topic of discussion was health!

Our discussions were intense and substantive, using the chairman's draft of the health care legislation as a starting point. Each gathering had an assigned topic, at which the staff would make their presentations on the issue; on other occasions we would hear from various experts, such as Doug Elmendorf, director of the Congressional Budget Office, or speak by conference call with a bipartisan group of governors to solicit their views on how to approach expanding Medicaid coverage or health insurance exchanges, for example. Or we might follow up on information that staff had gathered to answer our inquiries from a previous meeting. In between our staffs held their own separate meetings. We systematically focused on and examined every area that was incorporated in the overall, base proposal—and made determinations on what we could (or could not) accept. At this point there was an issue that continued to be a major point of contention—on including a public option, a government-run health plan that all Republicans opposed.

President Obama was pressing to complete health care reform in both the House and Senate by the August recess, but the Gang of Six meetings, in my view, continued to be fruitful. Each day we would make progress. After Congress adjourned for the August recess, however, the bottom fell out of the health care debate. As full-scale, congressional town-hall meetings across the country stoked antigovernment antipathy, House and Senate offices were flooded with emails and phone calls from citizens vocally opposing the notion of a comprehensive solution. The Tea Party drove the opposition; the public tenor changed, and the debate grew more angry, hostile, and partisan.

The issue of so-called death panels became a lightning rod for the anti-reform forces and their fury overwhelmed the national debate. There were multiple versions of a "health care reform bill," creating tremendous confusion, and one House iteration included a provision on "Advanced Care Planning" to pay for a Medicare recipient's discussions about "end of life" services like hospice care. At a town-hall meeting in Iowa, Senator Grassley said that "[i]n the House bill, there is counseling for end of life" and that we "should not have a government-run plan to decide when to pull the plug on grandma." The opposition seized on the House proposal and all the reform bills came to be painted with the same brush—even though the Senate version didn't contain any reference to end-of-life issues.

Those of us in the Gang of Six continued discussions individually and by conference calls over the August break, and the President called me on August 19 to discuss my current thinking. As it happened, that call came through on my BlackBerry as Jock and I were driving down what's known as the Mud Creek Road in Hancock, Maine. It's a narrow, winding country lane—a few miles from where a scene from the movie of Stephen King's novel *Pet Sematary* was filmed—with notoriously spotty cell reception. Since we had reception when the President called, Jock pulled to the side of the road just as a farmer who had been haying his field came up behind us on his tractor. Jock had to keep inching along the side of the road to stay ahead of the tractor. I was certain we'd enter another dead zone at any moment and the call would drop. I thought, "If only this man knew that the person in the car in front of him is on the phone with the President of the United States!" But I completed the call without incident, and Jock and I laugh about it every time we take that road.

When we returned after August recess, the President requested that I meet with him once again in the Oval Office, on Labor Day afternoon. As the President was preparing to address the nation two days later in another joint session of Congress, he was calibrating his role in developing the legislation. Presidential speeches to a joint session of Congress were relatively rare—excluding President Obama's State of the Union-like address in February 2009, this was only the first since President Bush spoke in the aftermath of 9/11. As Robert Pear of the *New York Times* reported at the time, "In scheduling a prime-time speech . . . before members of the House and Senate and a national television audience, Mr. Obama chose to put his political standing on the line more directly and dramatically than he has so far on health care, his signature domestic issue." In his Oval Office meeting with me, he wanted to discuss the path to enactment and search for areas of common ground.

In our conversation, I emphasized that the Gang of Six had tackled a long list of issues, and that continuing the Finance Committee's proceedings that would result in a markup of the bill was the only route to a bipartisan solution. I also expressed my appreciation that the President was open to alternatives on the issue of a so-called public plan option. The concern I had expressed was that simply inserting a government-sponsored plan into the dysfunctional insurance marketplace wasn't the panacea for the problems of obtaining health coverage. Depending on the requirements imposed on a public plan, its introduction could inhibit the ability of other plans to compete, and could have a variety of adverse effects, such as discouraging the entry of insurers into smaller state markets. At the same time, it would be critical to ensure that private health plans would offer affordable coverage.

That's why I proposed a carefully designed measure that could play a critical role if private plans failed to provide competitive pricing. Under my health security safety-net plan, insurance plan pricing would be reviewed as much as a year in advance to determine whether a state's residents had affordable options available to them. If there were states where insurance companies were failing to offer plans that met the standards of affordability, my proposal would then bring a federally sponsored public option to that state immediately with no gap in affordable coverage. This was what I called the so-called trigger mechanism. This mechanism would ensure that the health insurance industry delivered affordability and put in place a safety net to ensure that affordable coverage would be available from day one.

In his joint address to Congress, the President stated he would "continue to seek common ground in the weeks ahead." He also said he would "not waste time with those who have made the calculation that it's better politics to kill this plan than improve it." By mid-September, however, the Democratic leadership set a deadline for a markup in the Finance Committee, which would ultimately commence on September 22 with or without a bipartisan consensus from the Gang of Six. Senator Grassley expressed his disappointment, but said that he would continue to "work with [Senator Baucus] and . . . any other members interested in real bipartisan reforms as the process moves forward." I had participated in the Gang of Six deliberations for months and felt a responsibility to continue the process we'd begun. I couldn't tell my constituents that I had walked away from the table—they simply wouldn't countenance a refusal to participate in a constructive, collaborative process until the very last moment.

Frankly, I didn't know myself where the legislation and my vote in the Finance Committee would end up. One evening, after a particularly long and arduous day, John Richter, my chief of staff, came into my office and asked, very matter-of-factly, "Do you really know where this is all going?" I replied, "No. I honestly don't. I'm just still following the road and seeing where the proposals lead—since health care has always been a critical issue for me so it's a road worth taking."

So I was deeply disappointed when our Group of Six deliberations were concluded prematurely without agreement. However, after the chairman laid down the language of the bill we would be debating in Finance, I stated my full intention to keep moving forward and working with him during the committee process toward crafting a bill that hopefully at least a number of Republican members of the Finance Committee could support. As I noted in my opening statement at the markup, the reality that crafting the right approach is arduous in no way obviated our responsibility to make it happen. And to Chairman Baucus's credit, we had a seven-day bipartisan markup, the longest in twenty-two years. There were extensive amendments from both sides: out of 564 amendments submitted, 135 were considered and an additional 122 had already been included by the chairman in the base bill that was before the committee. He was committed to the integrity and legitimacy of the process and maintained the transparency and credibility of the markup.

The morning of the vote on reporting the legislation out of committee was thick with anticipation and suspense. By that point, it seemed clear that, from the Republican side, only my vote remained in question. I entered the large, high-ceilinged hearing room—the largest in which a hearing can be held on the Senate side of Capitol Hill—and took my seat at the dais, facing a swarm of reporters and camera flashes. I knew at that moment how I would vote, but other than a few of my staffers, no one else did, except for the

Minority Leader, Mitch McConnell. That morning, I called Mitch because it is important not to surprise your leader on a matter of this magnitude. Mitch said he appreciated the call. He was obviously extremely disappointed, and sorry that I felt compelled to reach that decision.

As the markup commenced, all eyes were on me. I began my statement before the vote praising the conduct of the markup. It wasn't until near the end that I began to signal the direction in which I was headed.

"So is this bill all that I want? Far from it. Is it all it can be? No, it is not. But when history calls, history calls. And I believe the consequences of inaction dictate the urgency of allowing for every opportunity to demonstrate our capacity to solve this monumental issue." I continued: "I would have preferred to continue to work within the committee to further modify this bill before a final vote. But it is clear the majority has the votes today to report this legislation. Therefore, I will collaborate with other centrists . . . to advance improvements. So there should be no mistake—my vote today is my vote today. And it in no way forecasts my vote in the future."

I shared concerns that we could not create vast new bureaucracies, and that there must be a propensity to earn broader support in the Senate and resist the impulse to retreat into partisanship— because "policies that will affect more than 300 million people should not be decided by partisan, one-vote-margin strategies." I concluded: "Ultimately, the credibility of the process will determine the credibility of the outcome. Mr. Chairman, in the first meetings of this committee to discuss health reform as your foremost priority, you expressed your desire for legislation that would garner significant bipartisan support in the Senate. That is my goal, it should be the goal for all of us, and I look forward to working with my colleagues to make it happen in the days and weeks ahead."

And when the roll was called, I voted "aye."

In spite of the fact there was a clear public record of the markup, Tea Party activists have repeatedly insisted that I was the "deciding vote" on passing health care reform legislation out of the Finance Committee. That was never the case. There were 10 Republicans and 13 Democrats on the committee. It was obvious that our panel would approve the bill since the Democrats had the majority; the only question was whether it would be by a vote of 13-10 without my vote or 14-9 with it.

At one point during the markup, I swiveled around in my chair with a coffee cup in one hand and my BlackBerry in the other, and stood up to walk back to the anteroom behind the dais. I moved past Senator Kyl but there was a staff person kneeling on the floor talking to the senator. I didn't see the staffer's leg; I tripped and went flying headfirst—landing hard on the floor. I could see all of the staff seated against the wall as I was falling, so I focused on holding onto the cup to avoid scalding anyone. Somehow I managed to spill barely a drop. The whole room heard my landing and the collective gasp was audible. To me it all seemed like it happened in slow motion; I could have broken my jaw, my wrist, my elbow—but miraculously, I was only bruised and sore.

The fall was so hard, however, that it prompted Chairman Baucus and also Senators Jay Rockefeller and Blanche Lincoln to follow me back to the anteroom to ask if I was all right. Several weeks later, I was speaking to Bill Nemitz, a reporter from Maine, who had traveled down for the week to cover the proceedings, and he asked me if people approached me after my fall to ask if I was okay. I said, "Yes, they did." He then asked me, "Were any of them Republicans?" I thought for a second and had to laugh. "Now that you ask, no!"

In actuality, both sides were unhappy with me, but for opposite reasons. On October 8 on the House floor, Representative Alan Grayson (D-FL) said, "We as a party have spent the last six months, the greatest minds in our party, dwelling on the question, the unbelievably consuming question of how to get Olympia Snowe to vote on health care reform. I want to remind us all that Olympia Snowe was not elected President last year. Olympia Snowe has no veto power in the Senate. Olympia Snowe represents a state with one-half of one percent of America's population." Representative Lynn Woolsey (D-CA) said, "This is the United States of America. This is not the United States of Maine. I mean that one senator cannot hold the entire nation's health care plan hostage." I agree, and it's not the United States of California, either. The genius of the Constitution resides in its protection of the rights of the smallest of states. Moreover, it wasn't an issue of time or holding anything hostage—it was a matter of substance on a bill with monumental ramifications.

The President also called me after the conclusion of the markup. He began by telling me, "A great statesperson once said, 'When history calls, history calls,'" and said I could make history by supporting health care reform when it's considered on the Senate floor. "You could be a modern day Joan of Arc," he offered. I laughed and replied, "Yes, but she was burned at the stake!" I added, "I don't mind taking the heat, but I have to believe it's the right policy for America." The President responded, "Don't worry, I'll be there with a fire hose!"

Regrettably, however, after the Finance Committee passed its bill, the wheels came off the process in the full Senate.

Long gone was the transparency of the Finance Committee debate. The melding of the Finance bill and the Senate HELP committee legislation was conducted in the shadows, and in a back room rife with partisanship. What resulted was a bloated 2,700-page bill—1,200 pages longer than the Finance Committee bill. This package imposed a new mandate on businesses with more than fifty employees to offer health insurance or face penalties, an $86 billion Medicare payroll tax increase that would disproportionately hurt small businesses (which concerned me all the more as ranking member of the Small Business Committee), and an expensive new long-term-care program that would go into the red just five years after paying benefits, and which in fact was later rescinded by executive order.

At the same time, the American people were voicing a sharp and legitimate note of caution as we pursued health reform, especially during challenging economic times. Americans were expressing apprehension about Congress's ability to reform the system, with Gallup finding that 66 percent of Americans believed their member of Congress didn't have a "good understanding" of the issues involved in the current debate.

On October 19, Senator Reid invited Senator Ben Nelson and me to meet with him personally, as both of our votes would be instrumental in the final passage of health care reform and neither of us had reached any conclusions on how we would vote. At the outset of that meeting, Senator Reid turned to me and said, very directly, "We will have an open amendment process." I responded, "That's great." Unfortunately, however, that open amendment process never materialized.

We also discussed a specific list of remaining concerns I believed were important to address. No guarantees were made, and I wouldn't have expected any. Nor did I believe that my proposals on how to address the concerns would all be accepted. The problem, however, is that I would repeatedly submit my list of issues to various principals in the health reform debate, but nothing ever resulted.

One of my central objections was that the legislation included a mandate for individuals to buy health insurance or incur a penalty. I didn't support this concept, so during the Finance Committee markup, Senator Chuck Schumer (D-NY) and I teamed up on an amendment, which passed 22-1, to reduce the penalties and introduce them more gradually. As one indication of how Democrats had been approaching me at that point, Chairman Baucus announced that the next amendment the committee would consider was a "Schumer amendment," whereupon Chuck responded, "It's now a Schumer-Snowe amendment." Whereupon the chairman replied, laughing, "A Schumer-Snowe amendment. Oh, are you not good! Are you sure it's not Snowe-Schumer?"

With respect to the mandate, I was surprised that we would have high-level punitive measures on the average American when, in fact, no one could demonstrate that health insurance plans would be affordable enough under the new law. I thought, shouldn't the burden of that proof rest with the government? We didn't have answers to the most basic questions: What will the premiums, copayments, and deductibles cost? What is the lowest-cost plan for a small business? That's why I posed these questions and others in a letter to the Congressional Budget Office asking for a state-by-state analysis on the affordability of plans in the exchanges, but I didn't receive a response. In fact, CBO Director Elmendorf later apologized that they weren't able to provide answers during the period of the health reform debate.

Democratic centrist senators and I also met numerous times in an attempt to determine a consensus on a package we could all support. Senator Nelson was involved in these discussions—a December 7 article in *Roll Call* noted that he "has said it would be easier for him to support the bill if it had some support from Republicans." In the end, however, we couldn't shape any concrete alternatives since there was disagreement within the overall Senate Democratic ranks with respect to what their conference could accept for changes. In September the Majority Leader called my concept of a trigger mechanism for a fallback safety net plan "a pretty doggone good idea." So when he was merging the Finance and HELP bills, I suggested it be included—but ultimately he chose a public option from which states could opt out. That was his prerogative, of course, but I was surprised when at an October 27 press conference he described me as "frightened" of the public option. I wasn't frightened of anything—I simply didn't believe it was good policy, and the Majority Leader later apologized for his comment, which I appreciated.

In the course of the health care debate, I met with the President at least eight times in addition to more than a dozen phone calls. He had made this rigorous outreach effort because he was seeking a bipartisan partner who he recognized cared about the issue as well. The last of these meetings took place on the Saturday before Christmas, five days before the Senate vote on the final health care bill on Christmas Eve day.

There was a snowstorm in Washington that day (fortunately, since I'm from Maine, that wasn't a hindrance!). Jock and one of our neighbors shoveled out our car, and my longtime staff member Pat Doak—who is from the far-northern city of Caribou, Maine, and therefore undeterred by the weather—rocked it back and forth, changing gears from drive into reverse, to get it over a mound of snow into the narrow lane that had been plowed through my condo's parking lot. When I arrived at the White House and was ushered into the Oval Office I could not help but think it was like a scene from a Norman Rockwell painting. The Obamas' children, Sasha and Malia, were playing in the snow outside the Oval Office, along with their dog, Bo, while the White House photographer was capturing the moment. In fact, I mentioned to the President it reminded me of the famous photos of Jackie Kennedy, Caroline, and John Jr. riding in a horse-drawn sleigh on the White House lawn.

Later the dog bounded inside, encrusted in snow, and the President introduced me to Malia, who was also covered in snow. He had a fire roaring in the fireplace, and he was in a very good mood.

The President continued to urge me to support the legislation in the impending final vote the following week, scheduled for Christmas Eve morning. The difficulty, I explained, was that as much as I had met with his staff and with Democratic leadership in the Senate, there had been no headway on any of the issues I had been discussing with him for the last six months, like it was "all windup and no pitch." And so, regrettably, I wasn't going to be able to vote for the bill on the floor.

At that point, he summoned his staff and mine into the Oval Office to determine where the breakdown had occurred. My aide described the specific items we had continually raised that hadn't translated into action. The President was somewhat surprised—but he was eager to proceed with the bill, offering that these issues could be worked out in a House-Senate conference as he'd indicated in the past, and stating he would have me right by his side with other negotiators during the conference to help shape the final product.

Throughout the health reform debate, the President worked with me in good faith, and I believed he was doing so now. By this point, however, I realized the legislation had essentially been pre-ordained and the majority leaderships in the House and Senate were not going to deviate from their comprehensive packages. "Mr. President," I responded, "I sincerely appreciate your offer. But if I couldn't secure changes in the bill now, it's not going to happen when I'm the only Republican in that conference with all the Democratic leaders." I did suggest that the President call for a kind of legislative "time-out" and reconvene in January, to allow both sides a "cooling-off period" over the upcoming three-week holiday recess and one final opportunity to convene a bipartisan working group. Ultimately, the President wasn't convinced that would be a fruitful course.

Though disappointed, the President wished me well and thanked me for all the work and time my staff and I had spent on the legislation. Later, he wrote me a very thoughtful letter of appreciation for my involvement.

Almost a month had passed between the completion of the Finance Committee's efforts and the bill being called up on the Senate floor—a month in which progress might have been made toward building greater consensus on some of the most critical and contentious matters in the health care debate. But that opportunity was regrettably forsaken. David Broder captured the ramifications of this lost moment perfectly when he wrote in the *Washington Post*, "Scholars will also make the point that when . . . complex legislation is being shaped, the substance is likely to be improved when both sides of the aisle contribute."

For a total of just under three weeks, the full Senate considered legislation addressing one of the most complex issues in our history, and we considered fewer than two dozen amendments out of more than 450 filed. Just days before the vote on final passage, the Senate received a nearly four-hundred-page amendment that could not be changed or altered. Instead, the Senate majority leadership held votes at 7 A.M., then 1 A.M., then 7 A.M. on December 24 to pass the bill before the self-imposed Christmas deadline—without a single Republican vote. Not one single member in Congress—Republican or Democrat—could answer whether the newly created health insurance plans would be affordable, yet we hurtled headlong toward a final vote on a monumental bill affecting every American. At a moment when I hoped the Senate would step up to its responsibility as the world's greatest deliberative body, it failed to meet that test.

As I said on the Senate floor, just consider whether Social Security, the Civil Rights Act, or Medicare would have been as strongly woven into the fabric of our nation had they passed on purely partisan lines—it would have been unthinkable. Social Security was supported by 64 percent of Republicans and 87 percent of Democrats in the Senate, and 79 percent of Republicans and 89 percent of Democrats in the House. In the Senate, 82 percent of Republicans and 69 percent of Democrats voted for the Civil Rights Act, with 80 and 61 percent, respectively, supporting it in the House. And for Medicare, in the Senate, 41 percent of Republicans and 84 percent of Democrats voted in favor of the bill, with 50 percent of Republicans and 81 percent of Democrats doing so in the House.

Whether President Obama could have had a bipartisan vote in favor of health care legislation is still up for debate. Regardless, he and the Democratic leadership in the Congress chose to solidify the Democratic majority behind a Democratic bill, as was their right given that they were in control of both the presidency and Congress.

However, significant ramifications would result from that approach. The Democrats' utilization of their supermajority to pass health care reform placed Republicans in the position of the "loyal opposition" and defined their role as one of simply challenging the President's initiatives without engaging in the process. It also gave the President's critics a focal point for their dissatisfaction—an unpopular health care law that stirred the passions of conservatives across the country.

Presidential-legislative relations are a difficult balancing act. The Founding Fathers designed the two branches as coequal, so there is a natural tension even when the two branches are controlled by the same party. Ironically, the large Democratic majorities in both houses of Congress in 2009–2010—a filibuster-proof Senate majority in particular—proved to be both a blessing and a curse for the President. Just because you have the ability to pass something in the Senate with sixty partisan votes doesn't mean it's a good idea to do so, even though those in the Senate will usually want to pursue that course; and it's no way to engender bipartisan entreaties from the opposite side on other issues.

When Republican Scott Brown was elected in January 2010 to the Massachusetts U.S. Senate seat previously held by Ted Kennedy, who had died in August 2009, the Democrats lost their sixty-vote margin even though Scott turned out to be one of the most bipartisan senators in the 112th Congress. By then we were also in an election cycle, and any pretense of cooperation, even of collegiality, was gone. Democrats and Republicans were bitterly divided in that campaign realm of winners and losers, and when that is transferred to Congress's relationship with the President, everyone loses. The entire health care effort spanned a year and consumed all the political oxygen in Washington, and in the view of many had done so at the expense of addressing the economic issues crucial to rejuvenating job growth at a time of historically high unemployment. It certainly played out at the expense of both bipartisanship and the economy.

The relationship between a President and the legislative branch depends on both sides making a concerted effort. If strong overtures to the leadership and members of the minority party on Capitol Hill had been made by President Obama at the outset of his term, perhaps they could have survived other encumbrances from the respective caucuses.

However, once the President deferred to Speaker Pelosi on the stimulus legislation and then turned his focus to such a massive government spending program as health care, it was unlikely he could have built a rapport with many Republicans. The Republicans read their congressional victories in 2010 as confirmation that President

Obama had lost the support of the electorate, and the GOP set out to build on their victories further in 2012.

The President and the Democrats, on the other hand, looked to reelect the President and maintain their majority in the Senate—so the die was pretty much cast, and little was accomplished in the 112th Congress.

Chapter 11

Why We Are
So Divided

Wᴇɴ ᴘʀᴇꜱɪᴅᴇɴᴛ ᴏʙᴀᴍᴀ's health care legislation passed the Senate without any Republican support, it highlighted and deepened the political divisions in the country. Health care followed stimulus and TARP, and the enormous financial commitment represented by yet another expensive government program, dubbed "Obamacare," troubled a significant proportion of the Republican Party. But more significantly, it inflamed the far right and became the focus of a loud and insistent rallying cry for the loosely affiliated groups under the umbrella of the Tea Party. It also was the main reason Democrats were trounced in the 2010 midterm election, where they lost six Senate seats and control of the House of Representatives, which led to a 63-seat majority for Republicans. In addition, more candidates on the right were encouraged to seek elective office.

Under what we might consider normal circumstances at other times in our history, we may have been able to paper over the cracks exposed by the Republican Party's opposition to the Obama administration's policies. But the reality is that the policy divide on health care only served to reflect and reinforce what had been erupting across the country. It's now the case that close to a majority of Republicans, or even a majority in some states, have moved much farther to the right, and the increasing polarization in both parties has resulted in the unworkable stalemate we witnessed in Congress in 2011 and 2012. If successful, collaborative government is going to reemerge, we must work our way back as a nation to finding common ground.

Since 1982, the *National Journal* has published an annual survey that locates members of Congress on the political spectrum from most liberal to most conservative based on their vote ratings. In 1982, there were 58 senators arrayed between the most liberal Republican senator and the most conservative Democrat. This meant that there was a significant overlap of political viewpoints between the parties, and that the majority of the Senate could potentially be of a like mind on a given issue, increasing the likelihood of cross-party support for any particular measure. In the House, where the Boll Weevils and Gypsy Moths existed, the common ground was even more crowded, including no fewer than 344 members out of total of 435 (244 Democrats and 191 Republicans). But by 2010 the number of senators occupying that middle ground was zero. Not one member of the Senate had a voting record placing them between that of the most liberal Republican and the most conservative Democrat. The results for 2011 and 2112 were the same.

It has been a similar story in recent years in the House. In 2012, the *Journal*'s vote ratings revealed that 16 members of the House were in the center in 2011, and the number for 2012, reported in 2013, was 13.

Labeling a given congressional vote with a "liberal" or "conservative" ranking is a subjective matter, but the trend couldn't be more clear. However you analyze this information, it makes for grim reading because it diminishes the prospects for legislative consensus-building. In the Senate, every Democrat is more liberal than any Republican; every Republican is more conservative than any Democrat. The number of congressmen and congresswomen whose voting records reflect at least the potential for consensus-building has shrunk until it has almost disappeared, or actually vanished, as it has in the Senate. As an institution, when we vote in the Senate we are both more liberal and more conservative than before, and therefore less likely to be able to reach common ground.

The reasons for this polarization are many and have evolved over a number of years. I will elaborate on those factors as I've seen them emerge, but I think Thomas E. Mann and Norman J. Ornstein delineated many of them in their book *It's Even Worse than It Looks: How the American Constitutional System Collided with the New Politics of Extremism.* They describe the most problematic features of the party system as including

> the vast ideological gulf between the parties, their increasing internal homogeneity, the prevalence of constituencies safe for one party or the other, the news organizations and outside groups' reinforcement of ideological purity and extreme partisanship, and the rough parity between the parties nationally that contributes to the intensity and stakes of conflict. All these factors together produce a hotly contested, never-ending permanent campaign to control the White House and Congress.

It's clear that the increased partisanship ensures that Congress has increasingly taken on an aspect of the British parliamentary system, where members vote only with their own party, except in extraordinary circumstances. It also suggests that the bills are narrowly focused and reflect concerns of the party's political base, not of the American public. When it came time to vote, I was often left with a Hobson's choice on the floor: to side with either the right or the left without the opportunity to craft a more balanced legislative solution that might appeal to members of both parties and be more consistent with my own views.

Voting in the Senate now tends to follow party lines, and rigidly. The percentage of "party unity votes"—that is, members voting for a measure in the way that their party leadership advocates—is at an all-time high. In the House of Representatives, in 2011, 84 percent of Republicans and 81 percent of Democrats voted with their party at least 90 percent of the time.

If each side spends all of its time exclusively advancing segments of their party platforms or agenda, and those positions do not prevail, it's impossible to solve matters of national concern absent a willingness to get beyond the differences.

Legislation that might compel a senator to cross the aisle and vote with the other side is all too frequently regarded as troublesome and likely to be avoided if at all possible. As we observed in the 112th Congress, in many instances, we entirely forgo taking action on key measures.

This polarization has become historic. Research conducted by Keith Poole at the University of Georgia demonstrated that Democrats and Republicans are more divided than at any time since 1879 in terms of who votes together and how often.

Voting blocs in the Senate increasingly resemble presidential votes in the general election. In 1987, 57 senators had a party affiliation that was the *opposite* of the presidential candidate their state supported, but in later years, the numbers dwindled. When I was sworn in to the Senate in 1995, 35 senators fell into this category, including both my colleague from Maine, Senator Bill Cohen, and me. In 2001 the number declined to 29 and, today, only 21 senators would fit this model.

In 1988, when Democratic presidential candidate Michael Dukakis suffered a crushing electoral defeat of 426 to 111 electoral votes, the 40 states that voted for George H. W. Bush were represented by 43 Democratic senators. Twenty-five years earlier, there were a significant number of conservative southern Democrats in the Senate. But shifting the South from Democratic to Republican was part of a successful Republican strategy, and it helped create the red state/blue state division that has fractured the political landscape.

In the 100th Congress (1977–79), states that more consistently return Republicans today had Democratic senators: John Stennis in Mississippi; Fritz Hollings in South Carolina; Sam Nunn in Georgia; Bennett Johnson and John Breaux in Louisiana; Dale Bumpers and David Pryor in Arkansas; and Howell Heflin in Alabama. These legislators found common ground on matters with Senate Republicans.

Even when I joined the Senate in 1995 and into the mid-2000s, it was still a badge of honor, rather than a "scarlet letter," for a legislator to work with the other side. It indicated you were willing to be supportive of fellow lawmakers who first and foremost considered the merits of an individual issue. Independence of thought was considered a virtue and consistent with the legacy of the Senate. But today, for those seventy-nine senators who represent more politically homogeneous red and blue states, there is a consequence: if they attempt to work across the political aisle on issues that run counter to the position of their own party, or show insufficient ideological rigor, they are likely to be punished with a serious primary challenge. The escalating polarization that ensues has become the defining component of the dysfunctional Senate, and the same phenomenon has manifested itself in the House of Representatives—where party-line voting is now rampant.

In a piece in the *New York Times* at the end of December 2012, statistician Nate Silver provided shocking analysis on just how polarized the nation has become. He noted, "In 1992, there were 103 members of the United States House of Representatives elected from what might be called swing districts: those in which the margin in the presidential race was within 5 percentage points of the national result. But based on an analysis of this year's presidential returns, I estimate that there are only 35 such Congressional districts remaining, barely one-third of what there were 20 years ago."

If Silver is correct, these numbers will have severe implications for the House moving forward. With only 35 members out of 435 facing any real electoral threat from the other party, there is no reward for them to forge bipartisan solutions or to reach across the political aisle. A diverse constituency invites electoral competition—which compels a member of Congress to more seriously consider a wider range of views. But if their seats are safe, barring a primary challenge if they step out of line, 400 of 435 congressmen and congresswomen do not have to fully analyze the issues. Rather, they simply vote the party line.

I've been a lifelong Republican in what arguably is now a safe blue state for Democrats in presidential races. Maine hasn't voted for a Republican president since 1988, and Senator Collins and I have been the only Republicans to serve in our state's congressional delegation since Tom Allen, a Democrat in Maine's 1st Congressional District, defeated incumbent Republican Jim Longley in the 1996 election. But Maine is now the national exception. Of the 18 states that have voted for the Democratic candidate for President in every one of the last six presidential elections (of which Maine is one), there are only 4 Republican senators out of the 36 senators representing those states. There is one moderate Republican in the Northeast: my former colleague Susan Collins of Maine—a sharp contrast to when there were so many socially moderate Republicans they had their own label: "Rockefeller Republicans," after former Vice President and New York Governor Nelson Rockefeller.

Moreover, fewer states are now in play in presidential elections. In the fall of 2012, the National Election Pool, the group created in 1990 to conduct exit polls and that produces the returns we all watch on election night, reduced the number of states where they would conduct surveys down to just thirty-one. States such as Texas, Alaska, Hawaii, and Rhode Island were all deemed noncompetitive, and the cost of running the exit polls outweighed the benefit when it was obvious who would win in each state.

But why is there so much polarization now? Why has the electorate aligned itself into two separate camps? Why are nearly all of the states becoming ideologically homogeneous, and what caused these changes? There are myriad answers to these questions, none of which is simple, but we can draw some conclusions.

Over the last century, the United States has seen a considerable shift in its political landscape. The presidential election maps for the country over the last few elections show us that Democrats have created strongholds in the Northeast, the Great Lakes, and West Coast states, while Republicans continue to carry the South and much of the Midwest and the Mountain states. It wasn't always this way, though, and the South has had the most profound political transformation.

In the first half of the twentieth century, the two political parties were essentially split into three distinct ideological centers: the Republican Party, southern Democrats, and northern Democrats, a structure that meant legislative successes required coalitions among the three. President Roosevelt's policies in his second term and during World War II, such as minimum wage and voting rights in the armed forces, helped divide southern Democrats from those in the North. This divide persisted until President Lyndon Johnson signed the Civil Rights Act of 1964, at which point LBJ presciently predicted to his aide Bill Moyers, "We have lost the South for a generation."

According to Ronald Brownstein in his 2007 book, *The Second Civil War,* "For the 1970 midterm election, [President Nixon] centered his election strategy on elevating sharp-edged 'wedge' issues that he thought could divide the culturally conservative silent majority from a Democratic Party dominated in its leadership by social liberals." Brownstein went on to write that "Nixon's embrace of the wedge agenda ignited what would become one of the most powerful engines of polarization over the next quarter century: the rising prominence of issues that divided Americans along cultural rather than economic lines."

At the same time, as Matthew Lassiter has argued in his book *The Silent Majority,* demographic changes in the thirty years after World War II moved political centers to the major cities, and the middle-class suburbanites became swing voters, a trend that predates

Nixon and stretches back to the Eisenhower campaign of 1952. Over time, the southern Democratic strongholds faded and the South and the mostly rural West became solidly Republican.

Today, in the 16 states the United States Census Bureau defines as the South, there are 20 Republican senators compared to 12 Democrats, with 8 of those Democrats located in the upper northeast of the region in the states of Maryland, Delaware, West Virginia, and Virginia. The Republican Party clearly has an advantage in the South, but these changes at the "grassroots" over the last century are indicative of the polarization being experienced across the country.

The country has also become divided in another way, by urban and rural areas, which heavily favor Democrats and Republicans respectively. For example, in the 2012 election, even in states where President Obama lost, he won Dallas County, Texas, with 57.1 percent; Houston's Harris County with 49.4 percent; Atlanta's Fulton County with 64.2 percent; Jackson, Mississippi's Hinds County with 72.2 percent; Memphis's Shelby County with 62.6 percent; and Louisville's Jefferson County with 54.8 percent, to name just a few. Indeed, according to a CBS exit poll, President Obama won 70 percent of voters living in big cities, while Romney won 58 percent of those residing in small cities and rural areas.

This rural-urban political divide has become self-reinforcing. Americans are more mobile than ever and can more easily self-select where they live based on the ideologies of the surrounding community. Many recent articles and publications have noted that Americans want to live around people who share the same political beliefs. As Nate Silver put it, "the differences between the parties have become so strong, and so sharply split across geographic lines, that voters may see their choice of where to live as partly reflecting a political decision."

However, paradoxically, while party identification has obviously become more solidified over the last three decades, Americans haven't changed their opinions on individual issues. According to research by Andrew Gelman at Columbia University, "As a nation, we have become much more polarized in our views of the major political parties, without there being much of a move to the extremes on the issues themselves." The *American Journal of Sociology* found similar results: "Since the parties are now more clearly divided—and on a broader set of issues—it is easier for people to split accordingly, without changing their own views."

Where center-right voters and center-left voters used to be willing to support candidates of either party who were in the center, now primaries are producing candidates for the general election that are "right" or "left," essentially eliminating the option of voting for more centrist candidates.

As the electorate now more strongly identifies itself with either the Republican or Democratic Party, the parties have exploited this polarization. In fact, the momentum increased as party leaders realized they could be more partisan and still win elections each November.

Redistricting has also resulted in the political homogenization of the districts. As Silver highlighted, when party organizations oversaw redistricting efforts after the 2010 elections, each one worked to make certain their own incumbents would be safe by redrawing districts so that more Democrats were put into Democratic areas or more Republicans into Republican areas. When a seat is safe, members only need worry about a primary challenge from the left or right, meaning that the base, where the more extreme activists operate, receives more attention than the center. It doesn't take many individuals to mount a challenge: in 2010 incumbent Senator Bob Bennett of Utah finished third at his party's convention of 3,500 delegates.

These distinct divisions have been exacerbated by some in the media. Long gone are the days when we received the entirety of our news from the morning paper, the evening news broadcasts, and a few local radio programs. The transformation of the news media in the last twenty years has been nothing short of revolutionary.

Cable news networks and radio programming often promote an ideological worldview that is sharply critical of, and sometimes hostile to, opposing viewpoints. This means one side of an issue is presented with rarely any nuance or middle ground, let alone a dispassionate rendering of the opposing viewpoint. Moreover, with the expansion of the Internet, blogs, various social media platforms like Facebook and Twitter, and other sites, a steady stream of news and commentary is being pushed to the public—and not necessarily with the journalistic rigor found at the *New York Times, Wall Street Journal,* or the three network news divisions.

At least in recent times, it is rare for officials to highlight bipartisan accomplishments or how they are collaborating with members from the other side of the aisle. When you turn on your television to any one of the cable news programs during prime time, you're fortunate if you can find one that doesn't feature individuals trying to see who can shout the loudest. People with views opposite those of the hosts are often yelled at or shut down completely. Yes, it's entertaining and brings in ratings, but at what cost?

Well, I would argue that the cost is a Congress that has certainly played into this phenomenon by engaging in a perpetual campaign of winning and losing, and feeding news networks with ample material for their talk shows. In today's political environment, both parties promote amendments or bills that fit their messaging and talking points designed to make their opposition look bad, at the expense of offering more substantive measures that build broader support.

As a result, Congress becomes a place of burned bridges and scorched earth. And yet, given that we have a narrowly divided electorate in America, as evidenced by the popular vote in the 2012 presidential election, and a divided government, where one party holds the House and the other the Senate, isn't that a mandate for cooperation?

Chapter 12

Why Moderates
Matter

It was from this historically polarized political landscape that the Tea Party emerged, ignited by the size of the government's intervention in the economy represented by TARP and the stimulus. Fittingly, perhaps, the dry tinder in the country was lit by a member of the television media.

The first "Tea Party" rally may have taken place before the term had been coined. On February 16, 2009, a young blogger in Seattle named Keri Carender organized a small rally against the stimulus (which she termed the "porkulus"). Three days later, during a live segment of the CNBC show *Squawk Box* at the Chicago Mercantile Exchange, on-air editor Rick Santelli lambasted the Obama administration's recently announced mortgage assistance plan to commit a potential outlay of $275 billion to help up to 9 million people avoid foreclosure. "We're thinking of having a Chicago tea party in July," Santelli said. "We're thinking of dumping some derivatives."

Perhaps a third of the Republican Party, combined with activists who had not participated in the political process up to this point, were galvanized. Tea Party supporters showed up in force at the August 2009 town-hall meetings of members of Congress, and in rallies staged around the country to excoriate the proposed health care plans. In the atmosphere of the rising partisanship, Republican lawmakers, who otherwise might have joined with President Obama on some issues aside from health care, were politically dissuaded from doing so. The movement took on a life of its own, and Americans who felt a deep sense of alienation at not being listened to led the opposition to what they perceived as the overreach of President Obama and the Democratic majority in Congress.

This opposition was manifested in efforts by activists to secure the election of Tea Party proponents in Republican primaries for federal office. The success of this drive in some races, and its failure in others, fueled what I saw as more extreme views within our party. Not only were primary challenges being planned for me in 2012, but also some of my colleagues were confronting unprecedented intraparty contests.

Highly respected three-term Republican Senator Bob Bennett from Utah was ousted by his state Republican convention in 2010, after being heavily targeted for his vote on TARP. He also had the temerity to sponsor a health reform bill with Democratic Senator Ron Wyden. Senator Bennett had earned a lifetime American Conservative Union rating of 84 percent, a U.S. Chamber of Commerce rating of 97 percent, and Americans for Tax Reform rating of 90 percent—but it wasn't enough.

That same year, Senator Lisa Murkowski lost a Republican primary against her Tea Party-backed challenger. I'll never forget hearing the discouraging, disheartening news on a beautiful summer day while I was at home in Maine during Congress's August recess. It was a stunning development, given that Lisa encapsulated Republican ideals and had so vigorously guarded Alaska's best interests, that she was defeated by another Republican. And to what end, other than to benefit a group concentrated at the far end of the political spectrum and to make an ideological statement?

After Lisa returned to Washington in September, she and I huddled in the Senate Lobby; a long, ornate, and serenely lit space running the length of the Senate chamber behind the presiding officer's chair. While the portraits of past Senate majority leaders looked on, Lisa told me how she was wrestling with the idea of pursuing a write-in candidacy. We discussed how incredibly challenging it would be to win not only without the backing of a party, but absent one's name on the ballot. I told her that I was there for her no matter where her heart and her passion led her, and whatever conclusion she reached.

Later that month, Lisa described to me how she had grappled with her decision on the long flight back to Alaska, and had reached a conclusion by the time the plane landed. I'm certain it wasn't easy for her to stand and explain to the weekly luncheon of Republican senators her intention to run as write-in candidate against the official GOP nominee. It struck me, how could we even be in this position as a party? But I admired her fortitude and gumption in mounting a brilliant but difficult and unorthodox campaign. Despite the gargantuan odds, fortunately, she won the general election and became the first candidate in more than fifty years to win a write-in candidacy for the United States Senate.

Others, however, were not so fortunate. Republican Congressman Mike Castle had been an exceptional and widely popular public servant—a two-term governor of Delaware who went on to serve nine terms in the U.S. House of Representatives, the longest-serving representative in Delaware's history. So when he lost the Republican primary for U.S. Senate in September to Christine O'Donnell, an obscure, far-right, Tea Party candidate, it was a stunning personification of the fractures within the GOP and the success of a faction whose goal was to "purify" the party.

Everyone had assumed that the open Senate seat, vacated by Vice President Joe Biden, would be a gain for Republicans. But Tea Party organizers and supporters, largely from outside the state, whose aspirations had virtually nothing to do with the best interests of Delaware and practically everything to do with political self-aggrandizement, invested a staggering amount of money into building a primary opponent virtually from scratch.

My husband, Jock, and I had been friends with Mike and his wife, Jane, since Jock and Mike served together as governors in the 1980s. After the primary, they visited Maine, and we all had lunch together. Jock and I were heartbroken. "I think your loss was a travesty," both of us said to Mike. "You would have made a phenomenal senator, and we need more like you in Washington, not fewer."

Mike described his experience with a faction willing to employ almost any tactic to prevail. O'Donnell won 53 percent of the primary turnout. Only 57,000 Republicans turned out to vote, which means the primary election was decided by just 31 percent of those who were entitled to vote in the Republican primary. With O'Donnell going on to lose the general election, 57-40, her candidacy most likely cost the party one of the seats it was counting on to recapture the majority in the Senate. When a deeply admired figure like Mike Castle could be sideswiped by a relatively small number of people willing to systematically eliminate candidates and officeholders who didn't adhere to a single, narrow set of principles, it was a harsh wake-up call for the rest of us in the Republican Party.

In Indiana, Dick Lugar (R-IN) had built a remarkable record over an illustrious tenure of nearly four decades in the Senate, most especially through his indelible influence on the Senate Foreign Relations Committee, where he was a leader in the disarmament efforts with the former Soviet Union during the 1990s. With his independent spirit, Dick partnered with Democrats when necessary to achieve solutions he believed were in the best interests of Indiana and the country. And that's precisely why conservative organizations fought vigorously against his candidacy in the Republican primary: because he was willing to engage in bipartisan compromise. Here was a senator who was a credit to the institution, the party, and the nation, who had sought the Republican nomination for President of the United States—and yet ultimately lost his primary to Richard Mourdock (who would then lose to Democrat Joe Donnelly in the general election) because he didn't meet the Tea Party litmus test.

Until we reached this state of ideological frenzy, throughout my time in office, activists had always been more conservative than most successful Republican candidates. Elected officials accepted that party activists would have their say within certain limits on the Republican Party platforms, just as the Democratic platform was usually further left than most elected Democrats. Convention platforms reflect the positions of the majority of delegates but they aren't a binding document on candidates, who virtually never agree with them in their entirety. The reality is, candidates don't run on party platforms—but we coexisted as Republicans who believed in the broad principles of limited government, strong defense, lower taxes, and individual freedom and opportunity.

As the Republican Party has become more ideologically rigid, however, a number of rural and southern states have become more conservative. Nominating candidates with more conservative views isn't generally a disadvantage to winning a general election in those states. But when you apply that same standard of ideological purity to nominating Republicans in states that are "purple" or blue, they cannot win and, in recent elections, Republican candidates for the Senate have lost in Nevada, Colorado, Delaware, Indiana, and Missouri. If more moderate or centrist candidates had been nominated in those states, they could well have been successful. Senator John Cornyn (R-TX), chair of the National Republican Senatorial Committee, understood this dichotomy and was extremely supportive of my reelection campaign.

The "Tea Party" is by no means a homogenous group, as I discovered in attending multiple meetings with Tea Party members across Maine beginning in the latter part of 2010, as I was preparing to seek reelection in 2012. As it turned out, a significant number of the people I met were either newcomers to participation in the political process, recent arrivals in Maine, or a combination of both—so in essence, we were getting to know each other. For many, virtually all they'd heard about me had come from online Tea Party newsletters and other media sources that, to say the least, weren't providing the full portrait of my record over three decades. My primary aim was to listen, but I also wanted to apprise them of where I stood philosophically and politically.

It was a critical opportunity for me to elaborate on my votes on those issues of fiscal responsibility that were essential to Tea Party members. I was able to discuss how my record clearly demonstrated I'd been a fiscal hawk throughout my tenure in Congress and that it wasn't necessary for anyone to be looking over my shoulder to remind me what's right and what's wrong on that score—I have my own conscience and my own record, which is replete with examples of attacking deficits and debt. Indeed, I'd tell the Tea Party members I met with, I could have used your voices when I was fighting for a Balanced Budget Amendment for my entire tenure in the U.S. House and Senate, or for a trigger mechanism to preserve our federal surpluses when they existed. Their support truly would have been exceptionally helpful in waging those wars.

By and large, these meetings were productive and mutually beneficial, with most Tea Party members willing to hear my perspective. I'd spend hours with each group, which I think surprised most of those in attendance. There was a free and spirited exchange of questions and ideas, which I welcomed—passionate but respectful discourse is something I've never shied away from; to the contrary, it should be embraced. I explained my responsibility was to represent the entire state, and that Maine's political composition simply wasn't analogous to a more uniformly conservative state like, say, Mississippi. Nevertheless, compared to the alternative in a general election I would be much closer to them on the issues they cared about and would better reflect their libertarian streak; the argument found appeal with some, but by no means all. Often I would ask this simple question: "Do you agree with your husbands or wives one hundred percent of the time?" That always broke any tension and elicited a laugh, even as it made a point: no one ever answered, "Yes."

There were those whom I never could have reached in a month of Sundays, but as we departed these meetings many would tell me that, while they still didn't agree with me on everything, they had a better understanding of where I was coming from. Ultimately, a number of Tea Party activists supported me, thanks in large part to the endorsement I received from Maine's Republican Governor, Paul LePage—who had been elected with significant Tea Party backing in 2010. To this day, I appreciate Paul's early and unequivocal political support, which made all the difference at a time when he could have easily stayed neutral. Likewise, supporter Carter Jones, one of the Tea Party leaders in Maine, was extremely helpful as I planned my campaign strategy. His advice and counsel opened doors to other Tea Party activists in the state. Carter said it best when he commented that "Olympia has been a fiscal hawk since I was a kid."

In October 2010, I spoke at an event held by the Androscoggin County Republican Committee in Poland Spring, Maine. The evening's special guest was Andy Card, who captivated the audience with his stirring account of the events of 9/11, including the moment when he whispered into the President's ear to inform him that "a second plane hit the second tower. America is under attack." A conservative radio talk show host in Maine, Ray Richardson, was the emcee, and he called me afterward to invite me onto his show. While we differed on many issues, Ray was thoughtful in eliciting and listening to my explanations for the positions I'd taken. He came to respect the process I'd gone through to arrive at my decisions, even if he didn't necessarily agree with them, which I found to be exceptionally fair-minded on his part. Frankly, it was an ideal example of how two people coming from divergent perspectives could still engage in civil conversation and appreciate each other's thought processes, and Ray went out of his way to allow me to explain my viewpoints to his audience.

Much of the frustration the Tea Party members I met with were expressing about Congress mirrored what I was experiencing and echoed the legislative fights on fiscal issues I'd engaged in for the past three decades. What these discussions revealed is that there was (and remains) a real and legitimate frustration that government has grown perilously disconnected from the will of the people. Americans have borne witness to an expansionist and more invasive government, yet they've experienced no appreciable improvement in their own daily lives—or on core matters of profound concern such as the economy and jobs, and failing to reduce our exorbitant deficits and debt.

The question for our political system, and for our nation for that matter, is how we can constructively channel this profound disaffection to devise practical and reasonable solutions that can attract the bipartisan support necessary for enactment. Simpson-Bowles, for example, could have served as a vehicle for developing a comprehensive, interparty approach to eliminating deficits and mitigating a debt that's growing faster than our GDP. I didn't agree with everything in Simpson-Bowles—nor, I would suspect, did anyone else on the planet. Regrettably, however, we are at a juncture where something that could serve as a means to a worthy end is instead immediately declared dead on arrival by the ideological judges, juries, and executioners.

An elected official has an obligation to do what she believes is right based on the facts. I don't evaluate an issue based on who's proposing it, but rather on its merits. The Tea Party has characterized and categorized legislators as being insufficiently rigorous ideologically, but if you have an individual or group that measures proposals solely against their own philosophical yardstick and is categorically unwilling to compromise, what then is the process for moving forward? I would ask the Tea Party members I met with, "What if all of you had a different interpretation of a particular section in the Constitution, which I suspect you do; you were presented with a major problem that required resolution, but none of you would budge from your position. What happens next? Do you just let the problem languish without addressing it? Does it just end there?" I never received a response to those questions.

Success comes from following those choices that build coalitions, not burn political bridges. The problem is that Tea Party solutions often go one step too far when it comes to managing an enterprise the size of the United States government—with no opportunity for modulation among those who propound those solutions.

None of this is to say that the Tea Party shouldn't have a place in the Republican Party—it just shouldn't be to the exclusion of every other voice. The disproportionate role the Tea Party would come to play in Maine Republican politics became evident at the 2010 Maine Republican Convention, when Tea Party delegates executed a surprise parliamentary maneuver to adopt their platform. In 2012, those championing Ron Paul's run for the presidency wrested control of the Republican State Convention when they packed the event. While Senator Susan Collins and I were allowed to speak, the Republican candidates for the U.S. Senate seat I was vacating were never given the chance to address the convention. That's unheard-of, especially given that it's one of the primary purposes of the event! The convention received unflattering media coverage as a result, and the entire episode cast a shadow over the entirety of our party as a whole—demoralizing many Republican activists who were embarrassed at the lack of civility.

What I found especially disturbing, having been a lifelong Republican myself, is that I've never thought to question the loyalty of those within my party with whom I disagreed politically or philosophically. I consistently and unhesitatingly campaigned for Republican candidates up and down the ticket for almost forty years. From state-wide tours to events to letters to committee meetings to phone calls, I had made every conceivable effort for the Maine Republican Party. It is my belief that our common philosophy as Republicans unites us even when we have disagreements on the specific implementation of our policies.

The intolerance displayed at our 2012 state convention was a marked departure from the Republican Party I knew so well. I have been to every state convention since 1970, and I had witnessed nothing that compared to this one. It is healthy to have differing viewpoints; in fact it is essential. There are, however, no means by which Republicans can become the majority in both houses of Congress and reclaim the White House unless we are more broadly and regionally represented in all parts of the country. Achieving a governing majority and insisting on ideological purity are mutually exclusive objectives. The fact is, with slightly more flexibility on the implementation of our principles, we could have achieved bipartisan support for many of the issues raised by senators supported by the Tea Party, and tackled subjects like immigration, an issue our party is now recognizing as a huge impediment to increased electoral success.

In April 2009, when the *New York Times* requested that I author an op-ed on the departure of Senator Arlen Specter from the Republican Party, I wrote, "We can't continue to fold our philosophical tent into an umbrella under which only a select few are worthy to stand. Rather, we should view an expansion of diversity within the party as a triumph that will broaden our appeal. That is the political road map we must follow to victory." I am a Republican who is prepared to compromise—and contrary to current misconceptions, compromise is not a capitulation of one's principles. Rather, it is a recognition that *not* getting all that you want may be the only way to acquire enough votes to achieve *most* of what you seek—and to institute policies that will reflect the needs and desires of your constituents. I'm a moderate, prepared to battle to achieve a bipartisan solution to a problem as I have done doggedly and consistently throughout my career in countless budgets, amendments, and major pieces of historic legislation. The process is hard work, but it is essential to good governance.

When I served in Congress, I was prepared to be a legislative lone ranger if necessary. Oftentimes I would remark I was already a minority within a minority within a minority—being a moderate Republican woman from New England, you can't be more of an outlier than that! In a cartoon strip by Brian McFadden in the *New York Times* published soon after I announced I was not running for reelection, I appeared as "an endangered moderate Republican." Where we once "roamed across the nation," now we were hunted down and in danger of ending up on display in a cabinet in a museum with other "extinct things" like the progressive Democrat and the Dodo.

Life is not black-and-white, or strictly red and blue. We live in the areas of gray and purple, and that's where the legislative ground can be the most fertile. Being a moderate certainly doesn't mean you are passive, cleaving to the line of least resistance and hoping to avoid confrontation. Contrary to the views of many in the Republican Party, *moderate* is not a synonym for wishy-washy or anodyne. On the contrary, it is far more arduous to depart from the majority than to follow it doggedly. Bipartisanship at times requires taking positions that may be at odds with your party's political base, and in a polarized atmosphere like the one that exists in Congress today, there is pressure to conform and little tolerance for consensus-building. Demonstrating too much independence makes you a target of the party ideologues and single-issue advocacy groups that can and will single out legislators for casting the "wrong" vote.

As a moderate I believe that political decisions arrived at by consensus make better policy. My philosophy is that nothing is impossible if you follow your principles but refuse to be intractable, reconciling differences that inevitably arise. Trent Lott understood my approach, and when I was about to contest a Republican amendment or position, he would kiddingly say, "I know you're going to oppose me, but please don't be too passionate!" We both knew that powerful arguments in an open amendment process can attract bipartisan support.

There are precious few bills that can't be refined during the legislative process, and it is in the close, intense work in committee room markups, conference and caucus meetings, and debates on the floor where representatives and senators bring their expertise to bear to both represent the interests of their constituents and craft the best policy for the nation that has the capacity to be passed and signed into law. The bottom line is, if legislators have a stake in the legislation, they are more likely to support it in the end—even if all of its provisions don't perfectly reflect their individual point of view.

In the same way that a moderate is misconstrued, there is misconception of what bipartisanship represents. It does not imply capitulating to the other side or simply voting for the opposite party's bill so they can laud the appearance of cross-party support. Nor is it the true spirit of bipartisanship to solicit votes in this manner, or for this reason. Genuine bipartisanship is achieved when members of both parties are involved in making legislation from the beginning, in drafting the law, participating in the amendment process in the committee, and collaborating to ensure its passage.

When you make a stand on an issue, there are significant political risks associated with voting differently than the vast majority of your party, so you have to know why you are stepping out and be confident that you're doing it for the right reasons. In 2010, referring to my role in the health care law, Harry Reid told a *New York Times* reporter, "As I look back it was a waste of time dealing with her because she had no intention of ever working anything out." I'm sorry Harry feels that way, but it's never a waste of time for any legislator who wants to try to achieve a bipartisan approach to this issue, and reaching a compromise on an issue as important as health care was an opportunity worth exploring. Besides, as always, I wanted to make a contribution. And frankly, no one in their right mind would have expended the amount of time and energy that I did if they hadn't been possessed of a serious motivation. I wasn't prepared to accept the Senate bill, but neither was I prepared to stand in mute opposition, so, as I described in chapter 10, I attempted to work with the President on his legislative proposals.

After the election in 2012, David Brooks published a column in the *New York Times* called "What Moderation Means." It is an eloquent articulation of my position. I read it and thought, "Hallelujah."

Brooks wrote,

> The moderate tries to preserve the tradition of conflict, keeping the opposing sides balanced. She understands that most public issues involve trade-offs. In most great arguments, there are two partially true points of view, which sit in tension. The moderate tries to maintain a rough proportion between them, to keep her country along its historic trajectory.

Americans have prospered over the centuries because we've kept a rough balance between things like individual opportunity and social cohesion, local rights and federal power. At any moment, new historical circumstances, like industrialization or globalization, might upset the balance. But the political system gradually finds a new equilibrium.

The moderate creates her policy agenda by looking to her specific circumstances and seeing which things are being driven out of proportion at the current moment. This idea—that you base your agenda on your specific situation—may seem obvious, but immoderate people often know what their solutions are before they define the problems.

. . . The moderate does not believe that there are policies that are permanently right. Situations matter most. Tax cuts might be right one decade but wrong the next. Tighter regulations might be right one decade, but if sclerosis sets in then deregulation might be in order.

I couldn't agree more. It's for this reason that I've never been one to sign pledges. Ruling out any course of action as a legislator—such as swearing you will never raise taxes—inalterably narrows your options, in my opinion. Circumstances can and do change in compelling ways over time. I am certain that members of the public who ask about the lack of bipartisanship in the Senate and who lament the state of politics in our nation would agree, as well. And the truth is that the same goes for much of the country despite the polarization we see in both the electorate and the two parties.

The organization No Labels commissioned a poll in advance of the State of the Union in January 2011 and found that 51 percent of Americans believe the country needs "more bipartisanship and cooperation," with just 23 percent saying partisanship is a "healthy part of the two-party system." The even more striking results of a survey conducted by NORC, an independent research organization at the University of Chicago, in December 2012, found that 79 percent of

Americans want members of Congress to compromise. NORC's executive vice president noted, "We found that a majority of Americans overwhelmingly prefer that their own representatives in D.C. work with others and make compromises, even compromises that include policies that they dislike."

In the debate over the message and takeaway from the 2012 presidential election, some political pundits suggested that it was a "status quo election." Indeed, party control of the White House, Senate, and the House remained the same, but the American people did send an unequivocal message that they are fed up with Washington and voted to end the persistent political quagmire. A poll conducted by the Republican Main Street Partnership and by Frank Luntz the day after the election confirmed precisely that.

When Luntz asked what his respondents thought was most important when fixing Washington, an impressive 65 percent said they wanted "leaders who are willing to compromise and work with the other party to get things done."

Despite the well-documented deepening of polarization in both red states and blue states, Americans understand that members of congress and senators will put forward their own policy prescriptions, but if those measures cannot or do not prevail in the Senate or House, Americans expect their elected officials to forge consensus and find common ground, which is what I have done throughout my career. Most promisingly, Americans express a willingness to live with a compromise, even if it includes policies they disagree with, if it facilitates passage of legislation that ultimately will move the country forward.

In his post-election poll, Luntz asked Republicans what they thought the best way to reduce the deficit was, given the then–$1.2 trillion budget deficit and $16 trillion national debt. A longtime plank of the Republican Party has been its opposition to tax increases, but in the poll Luntz found that 65 percent of Republican respondents were in support of tax increases to help reduce the deficit. Only 36 percent said that reducing the deficit should be achieved entirely with spending cuts.

When we drill down below the surface partisanship, there is a fundamental disconnect between the nation (more centrist and consensus-building) and the people nominated to run for office by the parties (more unyielding and partisan). It's that gap that we have to bridge. I am now working outside of Congress on grassroots efforts to reinvigorate our historic approach to governing. We must act quickly before the culture of dysfunction in Washington becomes permanent. Since 2008, an extraordinary 43 new senators have been sworn in: 20 Republicans, 22 Democrats, and one Independent. These senators have been exposed only to a hyperpartisan environment that produces nothing but gridlock, which results in lurching from crisis to crisis. They have no institutional memory of a cross-party success like the E-Rate or the Genetic Information Nondiscrimination Act or even balanced budgets, and only are familiar with the politics of failure—in which the political winner takes all and yet, in the end, everybody loses.

In the lame-duck session of 2012, however, we saw a glimmer of promise as we avoided tumbling off the fiscal cliff with a bipartisan accord. We can only hope it is a precursor to a larger breakthrough, and I for one intend to speak out to urge our leaders to ensure that eleventh-hour crises that defer decisions and place the nation in turmoil won't be required in the future as a catalyst for bipartisan agreements. A great country like ours can't legislate by brinkmanship and still rise to meet the challenges confronting it.

Part Three

Chapter 13

Civility in America

As a result of the partisanship we are experiencing in Congress and in the country at large, and through the profound dysfunction of our political institutions, we're wreaking serious damage on one of America's magnificent virtues, our greatness. I have seen what government is capable of doing, for better or for worse; our history is replete with acts of compromise that were forged by relentless pursuit of mutual solutions to tackle formidable challenges. Yet, precisely at this moment when our country requires our lawmakers to reach the highest levels of leadership, we are losing the ability to conduct ourselves constructively.

The restoration of civility to our political discourse is not the insignificant or trivial detail it might at first appear to be. Despite the increasingly biting tone of bipartisanship, colleagues in Congress are polite to each other on the floor of the House or Senate, for the most part, even when they are failing, as in the 112th Congress, to cooperatively resolve our nation's problems. We do manage to conform to the narrowest definition of the word *civility*, but I would argue that a broader interpretation, if adopted, would cause a seismic shift in how Washington operates. It would change the culture, rehabilitating the notions of consensus and compromise, and illuminate a path out of the dead end we are stuck in today.

The notion of courtesy that civility connotes is, of course, important, and the seemingly archaic rules of debate on the Senate floor serve a real and valuable purpose. Under the rules of the institution, a senator is required to address the presiding officer and cannot proceed until he or she has been recognized. No senator may interrupt another senator and, "no Senator shall speak more than twice upon any one question in debate on the same legislative day." Another rule states, "No Senator in debate shall refer offensively to any State of the Union," and so on.

The etiquette governing debate on the Senate floor is designed to help senators deliberate rather than argue, in accordance with the upper chamber's role as a deliberative forum. According to an article by Ann Gerhart in the *Washington Post* in 2004, "From its beginning, the United States Senate was so preoccupied with decorum that 10 of its first 20 rules detailed proper behavior. But for the longest time, senators resisted adopting Rule 19—'No Senator in debate shall, directly or indirectly, by any form of words impute to another Senator or to other Senators any conduct or motive unworthy or unbecoming a Senator,' certainly a subjective and imprecise standard."

In the House, where members may address each other directly and there is less control and restraint, there are still rules about what one is allowed to say and how one is allowed to say it. These rules and traditions establish a tone of respect for the institution, and we expect lawmakers to behave accordingly in their public interactions.

On a highly publicized occasion, a lawmaker overstepped the boundaries of common decency. In September 2009, President Obama made a speech on health care to a joint session of Congress in the House. When the President said that the proposed legislation would not extend coverage for illegal immigrants, as had been suggested in some quarters, Joe Wilson, a Republican congressman from South Carolina, shouted out, "You lie!" The President paused momentarily, then continued as an undercurrent of murmuring could be heard throughout the House chamber. Representative Wilson acknowledged his error later, in a statement saying, "I extend sincere apologies to the President for this lack of civility."

The fact is that ideological differences are encroaching on working relationships in Congress. Jennifer Steinhauer wrote an article on the "new discord" in Congress in the *New York Times* in February 2013. She noted examples of recent slights in Congress and ascribed part of the reason for a degradation of the atmosphere around Capitol Hill to a changing of the guard. "Many Senate Republicans are newly elected, deeply conservative members who have less regard for the old rules of comity and respect for elders," she wrote.

History, of course, has revealed that Congress has been the site of worse slights than the purely verbal, the place not having been immune from outbursts of physical violence. In 1858, during a debate on Kansas's proslavery constitution, fifty congressmen brawled on the floor of the House while the Speaker desperately tried to call for order. Two years earlier, Democrat Laurence M. Keitt (D-SC), who was involved in the fight, had drawn his pistol on the floor of the Senate while Representative Preston S. Brooks (D-SC) attacked Senator Charles Sumner (R-MA) with a walking cane and beat him unconscious. So we might console ourselves that even though we were the most partisan Congress in more than a hundred years, we conducted ourselves with more decorum than was demonstrated in these incidents.

Some politicians have a reputation for being blunt and acerbic, and a call for civility is not about diluting that characteristic. But in the political arena, civility means not only presenting our points of view and side of the argument, but also taking into account how the other side is responding.

In short, we need to listen.

It's obvious there is no shortage of people inside and outside the Beltway who are talking; it's less apparent in recent times that much listening is occurring. Even when we were able to remain polite and observe the niceties of the process, the 112th was the least productive Congress since 1947. I believe we are afflicted with what Shakespeare in *Henry IV, Part II* called "the disease of not listening." Civility is in speaking, in listening, and, most vitally, in the commitment by both sides that they respect each other's differing views when there are competing ideas and philosophies. True debate is not an exchange of hot air. If we are to incorporate civility into the political process, we will have to agree to talk through these differences to arrive at solutions.

Civility, then, is about being *willing* to compromise and accepting in advance that trying to find the common ground on important issues can be positive and beneficial. There is legitimacy in deeply held beliefs and disparate views. The question is, if you are an elected member of the United States Congress, and your purpose is to solve the nation's problems, how do you meaningfully reconcile those differences? If there is an unwillingness to try to work together, and if the primary objective is to position yourself in the next election to defeat the other side, the result will inevitably be the politics of failure I have discussed, in which case the country as a whole comes away the loser.

American legislators have the greatest exemplar in our founding national document. The United States Constitution wasn't ratified because fifty-five people with identical viewpoints gathered in a room and rubber-stamped their unanimous thinking. These visionaries determined that the gravity and enormity of their common goal required great courage to make decisions through consensus. It was Thomas Jefferson who wrote rules for how members should comport themselves, and as a teenager, George Washington wrote out his own copy of 110 "Rules of Civility and Decent Behavior," beginning with "Every Action done in Company, ought to be with some Sign of Respect, to those that are Present" and ending with "Labor to keep alive in your breast that little spark of celestial fire called conscience."

At one point during the 1787 Constitutional Convention, divisions arose between the larger and smaller states. Benjamin Franklin was instrumental in securing the representational system we have today through what is called the Connecticut Compromise, by which the House is elected proportionately according to population and the Senate gives equal weight to every state.

Franklin beautifully articulated the spirit of compromise to the convention: "When a broad table is to be made, and the edges of planks do not fit, the artist takes a little from both, and makes a good joint. In like manner, both sides must part with some of their demands."

The Founding Fathers duly made their broad table for the country. They understood that if America as a fledgling nation were to succeed, then lawmakers had to embrace the notion of compromise and this larger definition of civility. Each side must understand they cannot get 100 percent of what they want and concessions must be made for the greater good.

Civility is not simply a lofty ideal. It runs parallel with my ideology of a balanced approach to governing, which has informed my forty years as a legislator. I've experienced how civility fosters a positive, bipartisan, and constructive culture during my first days in the Maine House of Representatives and in the Maine Senate in the 1970s. During my years in Congress, we've also operated under what might be labeled the Rules of Civility. But this spirit must be revived not only on Capitol Hill, but also throughout the nation.

In all realms of social and commercial interaction, there is concern that standards of civility are in the decline. There is a pressing need for all members of our society to be able to gainfully engage with people with whom they might disagree. In 2013, the *Harvard Business Review* reported that in 2011, half of the people they polled said they were treated rudely at work once a week, up from a quarter in 2011.

The lawyers' trade publication the *ABA Journal* discussed the issue with respect to members of the legal profession in a story in the spring of 2012. "Incivility among lawyers is not a new concern. But as the general tone of public discourse in the United States becomes more heated, the issue of civility—or lack thereof—within the legal profession appears to be moving to the front burner." Lawyers often need to work in the adversarial theater of a courtroom, and the article made the point that in court, clients—and lawyers—are influenced by what they have seen on television, where legal shows turn a legal matter into a drama.

It is on television where we can readily observe how public civility has declined. So-called reality shows encourage regular people to behave as intemperately and rudely as they can, in the hopes of attracting higher ratings for the show, especially among the younger demographics that advertisers crave.

In some instances, television news has absorbed the notion that it can succeed by "narrowcasting"—appealing to one ideological standpoint or another and harshly criticizing the other side. When news is broken up by a prism, a viewer only sees a small part of the spectrum. The drive for ratings is inexorable, and much of the universe of television news is devoted to sensationalism, which is one of the most virulent enemies of civility. In a desperate race to the bottom, there is a competition for the loudest and most partisan opinionators. Today's twenty-four-hour news cycle serves only to demonize differing viewpoints and solidify the positions of policymakers and therefore cut off any opportunity for thoughtful debate.

In 2009, a *Time* magazine poll found that Jon Stewart, host of the *Daily Show,* which delivers "fake news," was the most trusted newsman in America. Stewart has made a career out of exposing the bias and hypocrisy of more established news sources. In 2004, Stewart appeared on a show in which two pundits on opposite sides of the political spectrum were pitted against each other, but which often descended into a shouting match. Stewart confronted the hosts, asserting the show was "hurting America" and was encouraging divisiveness. "You're doing theater, when you should be doing debate," said Stewart. The yelling has continued unabated.

During elections, we are bombarded on television, on the radio, in newspapers and magazines, and on billboards with political ads.

The majority, maybe the vast majority, of these political commercials are attack ads that make no effort to put forward a candidate's own platform but attempt to undermine the other side. Billions were spent on advertising in the last election campaign, much of it by third parties like Super PACs that were able to raise limitless funds under current campaign finance laws. The *New York Times* estimated that through November 30, 2012, the pro-Romney Restore Our Future spent $143 million, 90 percent of it on attack ads. The similarly aligned American Crossroads spent $91 million, 93 percent on attacks. Comparatively, the pro-Obama Priorities USA Action spent $66 million attacking Mitt Romney, and the Service Employees International Union spent $5 million, 73 percent on attack ads.

In 1990, just twenty-two years ago, total outside spending in the election was a scant $7.2 million. Fast-forward to today, and in 2012, it was $524 million, 75 times the amount in 1990.

Attack ads take the place of debate, but they are no substitute for it. (I actually thought the 2012 presidential debates were excellent: revealing and informative.) If the majority of a candidate's time and money is spent trying to diminish the opponent, he can avoid having to articulate his own position, and the discourse is doubly diminished. The real problem with attack ads is that they can be extremely effective. Today, a candidate can't ignore a well-crafted assault. An ad not responded to within twenty-four hours is believed to be true, and the quickest and most effective way to rebut an attack is to respond in kind. History is littered with well-intentioned candidates who have attempted to stand above the fray and have ignored attacks to the detriment of their chances of success.

The culture of incivility in political advertising might take decades to shift, if it can be altered at all, but we are not well served by its divisiveness and ill-considered rhetoric. As many Mainers have told me, they've simply turned off their TVs or switched the channel when these ads appear.

While the Internet has revolutionized the way we communicate and interact, the standard of public discourse has been in many ways degraded. It is very difficult to stand out being positive on the World Wide Web; similarly, it easier to make a name for yourself with a blog if you are outrageous than if you are quiet and contemplative. It is easy to hide on the Internet and use the technology to anonymously belittle and humiliate another person. Even when a comment is made on the record and with attribution on Twitter, it seems to be part of our culture that the instantaneous gratification of the tweet and its necessary brevity leads users to act as if they were anonymous, and as if there were no consequences to their actions.

We need to embrace areas of society that reduce confrontation and embrace compromise. Since the late 1970s the Maine judiciary has taught students about conflict resolution. And the judiciary has offered Alternative Dispute Resolution as a cheaper and less onerous option than going to court, including in divorce and medical malpractice cases. The two sides can sit down and resolve their differences in a less adversarial environment. It has had a high rate of success.

Many Americans share my concerns about civility. Prominent among them is Robert L. Dilenschneider, of the communications company that bears his name. In 2011 the Dilenschneider Group sponsored lectures in conjunction with the Carnegie Council for Ethics in International Affairs in New York. Bob organized a second series in Stamford, Connecticut, in the fall of 2012, hosted by Mayor Michael Pavia, who has stated that he wants to make his city the most civil in America. As Bob has said, "We and our nation's leaders need to recognize the gravity of our current predicament and reassess the trajectory of our national discourse."

I was honored to speak before a full house at the Ferguson Library in Stamford on the subject of Civility in Politics, which was a longer lecture than you might imagine. Other speakers in the series included Dr. James Cuno, president and CEO of the J. Paul Getty

Trust; Emmy-winning news anchor Ernie Anastos; Bill Bratton, former police commissioner in Boston and New York and former police chief of Los Angeles; Joel Klein, the former chancellor of the New York City Department of Education; Edward T. Reilly, president and CEO of the American Management Association; Allen Goodman, president and CEO of the Institute of International Education; and Fay Vincent, former commissioner of Major League Baseball.

It is a group that represents so many facets of American life: art, the media, politics, management, education, law enforcement, and sports. There is no realm of our daily activity that cannot be improved by civility and improved by compromise. Nationally there is a groundswell of support in this country for a change in our mode, style, and tone of discourse, and no entity would benefit more from that than Congress.

Our incivility perpetuates the stasis we have found in Washington. If all we do is attack the other side and never articulate our ideas; if we only put forward our proposals and don't consider the merits of theirs; if we only insist on our way rather than compromising; if we only respect our political allies and not our opponents as well, then nothing will ever change for the better. We're in this together because America is not defined by just the red or the blue, but by the red, white, and blue. The obstacles we face are only insurmountable if we continue to speak without listening.

Chapter 14

How We Can Change Congress

As the practice of civility in our society has diminished and as the polarization and dysfunction in Congress worsened, I have been consistently asked what we could do to alter the dynamic; unhappily, I had to say, there is no magic wand. But there are a number of practical changes that can be made to various components of our political system and processes that would result in a more productive Congress. The changes can be divided into two broad categories: Senate rules and congressional procedures, and campaign finance and political reform.

SENATE RULES AND CONGRESSIONAL PROCEDURES

The Senate is unique in its balance between the primacy of the majority and the accommodation of the minority. Regardless of which party is in the minority, any suppression of its ability to debate and help shape legislation is tantamount to silencing millions of voices and ideas that are critical to developing the best possible solutions.

I begin with Senate rules and congressional procedures because, frankly, that's where the current legislative and deliberative logjams are most evident, and can be corrected most readily.

The problems I have witnessed and described regarding filibusters, filling the amendment tree, failure to pass annual budgets, and circumventing the committee process demonstrate the crux of our institutional problems. In order to address these problems, there are nine significant reforms I believe would give senators and members of Congress the tools they need to be successful:

- Institute filibuster reform
- Create a more open amendment process
- Eliminate so-called secret holds on legislation
- Pass "No Budget, No Pay"
- Require biennial budgeting
- Restore the authorization process
- Adhere to five-day workweeks
- Establish a Bipartisan Leadership Committee
- Return to the regular order of doing legislative business through committees

Filibuster Reform

The solution to filibuster reform has been elusive, because it's important not to undermine the long-standing rights and principles that are considered fundamental to the institution—so the appropriate balance must be achieved. After the 2012 election and into the first weeks of 2013, however, there was discussion about the majority party introducing a new rule in the Senate to eliminate the filibuster by a simple majority vote as opposed to the sixty votes that are required today. This would have been as damaging as the so-called nuclear option that was considered by the Republican majority for judicial nominations in 2005.

The late, former Senate Majority and Minority Leader Robert Byrd (D-WV) was an expert in Senate procedure. He understood that the Senate is, as he said, "the one place in the whole government where the minority is guaranteed a public airing of its views," and a place "for open and free debate and for the protection of political minorities." In that light, in my farewell address to the Senate, I urged all of my returning colleagues to follow the "Gang of 14" template and exercise a similar level of caution and balance.

In July 2012, I wrote a letter to Majority Leader Reid and Minority Leader McConnell to "express my grave concerns with the Senate's dysfunction" and urge that they "begin a collaborative process of developing a strategy to address procedures currently being employed that are undermining the ability of the Senate to produce results—before the current perversions of the standing rules of the Senate permanently become the 'new norm.'" I also had discussions with Senator Carl Levin (D-MI) about his proposals, and my desire to address filibuster rules in a balanced fashion for both the majority and the minority.

So it was a step in the right direction that, in January 2013, the Senate chose not to leap into the procedural abyss and eliminate the filibuster altogether. Instead, both sides reached an agreement on temporary changes in which the minority would agree not to filibuster what are called "motions to proceed"—essentially to request the consent of the Senate to formally move to consider a particular bill on the floor—in exchange for a guarantee that the minority would be allowed to offer at least two amendments to that particular legislation. A group of eight senators, four Republicans and four Democrats (including Senator Levin along with Senator McCain), designed a solution that achieved the kind of balance we had discussed.

Nevertheless, I continue to believe that more can and must be done to reform the application of the filibuster as it is now practiced. For example, senators can still prevent legislation from moving forward by filibustering motions to send a bill to a House-Senate conference where differences between the chambers' versions are reconciled. The value of a conference committee is that it provides a formalized venue for grappling with differences between the two chambers and parties—and to short-circuit that process is to short-change our opportunities to forge consensus.

I serve on the board of the Bipartisan Policy Center. It was founded by four former Senate Majority Leaders—Howard Baker, Tom Daschle, Bob Dole, and George Mitchell—and is among those urging that House-Senate conferees sit down and attempt to find common ground on legislation, and I agree. Currently, there is an opportunity to filibuster the actual vote on a House-Senate conference agreement, so in my view there's no reason we shouldn't immediately eliminate the filibuster on sending bills to conference.

Another reform that should be instituted is barring the Minority Leader from objecting to legislation or a nomination on a colleague's behalf; the Brookings Institution has proposed this. Right now a senator doesn't even have to appear on the floor if he or she wishes to object to a measure or motion. Changing that practice would require a personal commitment from a particular senator to filibuster a measure. Others have proposed that the Senate should require so-called live or talking filibusters. Originally, a senator had to stand and speak to maintain the filibuster, as was immortalized in the movie *Mr. Smith Goes to Washington*—now all that's required is a mere threat of a filibuster to trigger a cloture vote, since no senator is required to actually go to the floor and address the chamber. If the temporary rules changes that were instituted ultimately prove ineffective, this is an option that could be considered.

A More Open Amendment Process

The filibuster agreement that the Senate reached in early 2013 to allow the minority two amendments was a step in the right direction, but it remains entirely insufficient. The Senate is predicated on minority rights and open debate—it was specifically designed not to be the House of Representatives and, therefore it should be unacceptable for a ceiling of just four amendments—two from the majority and two from the majority—to become the norm. The primary goals for the Senate should be less obstructionism for the consideration of bills on the floor as well as a robust and open floor amendment process, with the possibility for limiting the number of amendments considered to a specific bill in due course, by virtue of agreement between the Majority and Minority Leaders. The American people should insist that their voices not be silenced with restrictions on amendments.

Eliminate So-called Secret Holds on Legislation

We should also end the practice of "secret holds," which are an informal custom that, as the Congressional Research Service states, aren't "recognized in the Senate's rules or procedures." The holds take the form of a written "notice of intent to object" to bringing a bill or nomination to the floor; the notice is sent to a leader of a particular senator's party. A hold request can be ignored, and a motion made on the floor for the Senate to proceed to the bill nonetheless but under the current rules, the senator who sought the hold can filibuster that motion (or the actual bill, if the motion to proceed to the floor is successful).

The Senate banned secret holds in January 2011 through a resolution that passed with a 92-4 vote. Under the measure, a senator's name is supposed to be published in the *Congressional Record* within two days of the senator placing the hold. But because holds are made informally, they are difficult to regulate, and in the words of Dan Friedman at the *National Journal*, "Enforcing the ban is up to the party leaders, who are not particularly supportive . . . that means senators retain largely the same power to anonymously stall action." And the public has a role to play in this as well: it can apply pressure and demand a transparent accounting of—and thus accountability for—who is behind the delay, and why.

"No Budget, No Pay"

It is vital that the Senate introduce measures that will return the institution to its original role as a body that deliberates, debates, amends, and produces budgets that establish federal spending priorities. Passing a budget should be a matter of course. The federal budget establishes a level of spending for each of the major functions and agencies of government. Circumventing the budget process eliminates the necessity for Republicans and Democrats to work through their differences in agreeing to a package. It also removes an indispensable aspect of establishing well thought-out priorities for federal investments and expenditures. A return to passing budgets would also focus Congress on reversing the trend of spending more than we earn, thus putting America back on track to reducing its sky-rocketing debt and annual deficits.

It is crucial that Congress has a budget that establishes spending limits for government agencies, and that's why I cosponsored a measure in the Senate called "No Budget, No Pay," which was advocated by the group No Labels. As the name implies, salaries for senators are withheld if a budget is not passed, or if each of the twelve individual, annual appropriations bills isn't completed by the end of the fiscal year (September 30). The year 2011 was the first in the history of the Budget Act that not one of the twelve appropriations bills was enacted. One of the challenges, as *Roll Call* has pointed out, is that roughly half of current senators arrived in the institution after 2005, the last year Congress completed its appropriations responsibility—so they've never even experienced how the process is supposed to work. I would also propose that if the budget resolution doesn't pass by the statutory deadline of April 15, then recesses routinely scheduled for the House and Senate after that date be suspended until the budget is enacted.

In 2013, as part of the passage of legislation extending the debt ceiling until May 19, the Congress did adopt a version of No Budget, No Pay for that fiscal year. We should all urge them to make the legislation permanent and applicable to future years as well.

Biennial Budgeting

I have been a longtime champion of biennial budgets, indeed, since the beginning of my congressional tenure, because not only would it help restore budgetary discipline but also, given the complexities of our federal budgets and the enormity of our deficits and debt, it would provide us additional time to engage in aggressive oversight of existing programs. Biennial budgeting would afford Congress the opportunity to first evaluate the fiscal decisions it has already made and then adjust in the second year how we spend taxpayer dollars. Many states follow this track of biennial budgeting so that they are able to determine what is working efficiently and what isn't. Congress would benefit from the same approach.

Restore the Authorization Process

The traditional process for considering legislation is to refer bills to House and Senate committees overseeing various functions of government. These committees, often referred to as authorizing committees, have developed expertise in the areas under their jurisdiction. Recently, however, there has been a trend that finds budgetary and funding legislation being developed by the majority leadership in each House, taking the legislative drafting out of the committee of jurisdiction.

Even worse, without budgets to guide spending decisions, many of the annual spending bills funding the government (referred to as "continuing resolutions" since they continue the funding of government for the fiscal year) are developed by the Appropriations Committee and the leadership without significant input from the committees that were formed to review and recommend policy in the various functions of government. The bills the subcommittees work through oftentimes are never brought before the full Senate for debate.

This tendency to commonly utilize continuing resolutions also generates tremendous uncertainty as they are often extended for something less than the full budgetary year—meaning that agencies are subjected to fiscal fits and starts and are unable to appropriately plan their expenditures. In turn, this adversely affects those individuals who depend on these programs. By short-circuiting the established processes, we are shortchanging the American people.

To reverse the trend of excluding consideration of budget proposals by authorizing committees, the Bipartisan Policy Center rec-
ommends two important actions: that the leadership commit fully to
restoring the authorization process in Congress, and that appropriations committees refrain from authorizing substantive changes in
government programs in appropriations bills. Authorizing committees are the panels specifically established for rank-and-file members
to debate issues within their jurisdiction, analyze how government
programs and initiatives are functioning, and craft policy that addresses the nation's needs in a timely fashion. They approve the establishment of programs and that federal money can be spent for
them. The Appropriations Committee in both Houses (known as the
"appropriators") actually allocates the funds (and sometimes chooses
not to provide any funding).

Authorizations are usually established for a specific period of
time. Too often they are allowed to lapse, but still receive funding
(even as many components of the programs may be outmoded, in-
efficient, or ineffective) or are extended repeatedly without any
update—as occurred twenty-three times since 2007 with the Federal
Aviation Authority bill. As the Bipartisan Policy Center promotes,
majority party leaders in each house, in consultation with their committee chairmen, should meet at the outset of a new Congress and
agree on a timetable for considering major reauthorization bills. Furthermore, given the fact that it's the authorizers who have the expertise in their respective policy areas, majority party leadership
should work to strengthen their role and relevance by enforcing rules
against what's called "authorizing in appropriations bills" to the exclusion of the committees with the policy expertise.

Adhere to Five-Day Workweeks

Congress needs to work longer hours on legislative business. The
House and Senate should institute five-day Washington workweeks
from January through the first week in August (with five weeks allo-

cated to spend back in the senator's or member's state interspersed during this period), from September until Thanksgiving (except in election years, when Congress would be in recess from the second week of October through the second week in November), and in the first two weeks of December. The 170 days Congress spent in session in 2011 and the 153 days in 2012 were not sufficient to consider legislation required to address the nation's multiple and consequential problems. And for those 170 days in 2011, the Senate spent an average of just 6.5 hours per day in session—the second lowest since 1992.

To enforce the rule, representatives' and senators' salaries would be reduced by a proportionate amount for every day that the Senate or the House falls short of this goal. We should also return to a routine of a synchronized recess schedule between the Senate and the House. I applaud groups like the Bipartisan Policy Center and No Labels for championing this commonsense change that should serve to provide additional time to address the critical issues while also fostering more opportunities for senators and representatives to interact socially with each other in Washington.

Establish a Bipartisan Leadership Committee
Another worthy No Labels idea is a Bipartisan Leadership Committee. As it stands, engagement between and among party leaders only takes place on an ad hoc basis. *Everything* is separate—we sit separated on the committees, separately on the Senate floor, we have separate weekly policy luncheons and other separate discussion groups. Despite informal attempts over the last few years where senators have reached out to sit next to members of the opposite party at the annual State of the Union address, there are no regular, formalized occasions where legislators meet—which only serves to amplify the partisanship.

No Labels' proposal is that congressional party leaders form a bipartisan congressional leadership committee to discuss legislative agendas and substantive solutions. The group would meet weekly, possibly monthly, with the President. It would include the President pro tempore, the Speaker, and the Senate and House Majority and Minority Leaders, with four open slots for any two members of the Senate and House to be determined on a rotating basis in each Congress. I believe this proposal has great merit, but I would have the other four additional slots be the other four formal members of leadership: the majority and minority whips in the two houses rather than four rotating members.

This bipartisan, bicameral leadership approach has been used in the Maine legislature for decades, and if applied at the federal level, perhaps it could open the channels of communication in the same way. It's amazing the positive things that can happen when you get people talking in a room together!

CAMPAIGN FINANCE AND POLITICAL REFORM

Enhancing the efficiency of the Senate through rules changes is only part of the solution. We must ensure we also have a political system that is designed to reflect the views of the broad electorate by producing elected officials committed to having both houses of the legislative branch of our government reach agreement on significant issues facing the country. The reforms I believe would have the most impact are:

- Abolish so-called Leadership PACS
- Establish campaign finance reform
- Institute more open primaries
- Establish redistricting commissions

Abolish Leadership PACs
The current, seemingly singular preoccupation with fund-raising of most senators and members of Congress has become a major distrac-

tion from conducting normal business in Washington. The emergence of Leadership PACs has created enormous added pressure to raise additional money—further fueling what's become a permanent campaign cycle.

Leadership PACs are separate committees that can be established by senators and members of Congress in addition to their reelection committees—regardless of whether they are running for, or serving in, a leadership capacity in Congress. They allow more money to be raised than would otherwise be permitted to support other candidates or causes. PACs represent yet another outlet for contributions to officeholders beyond the senator's or House member's campaign committee. As a matter of fact, as of the beginning of 2012, I was one of only five senators who had not formed a Leadership PAC—and three of the five have now retired from the Senate. I propose that Leadership PACs be banned at least for those who are not truly in official positions of leadership in the Congress. There are other sources of funds for candidates without taking the time away from legislating necessary for members and senators to raise the level of funds expected in Leadership PACs.

The current, 24/7 scramble to raise money not only unduly influences agendas and the issues on which legislators deliberate, but also contributes to an alarming reduction in the number of days actually spent legislating. At this point, congressional scheduling is now at the mercy of fund-raising events. In January 2013, Congressman Rick Nolan (D-MN), who had just been reelected after a thirty-two-year hiatus (having left the House in 1981), stated that his leadership had told newly elected Democrats that they should allocate thirty hours per week for fund-raising calls!

There used to be a time when we would separate politics and policy at least for the first year after the election, to attempt to synchronize our legislative agenda on issues crucial to the nation before the campaign season of the second year. Now we are experiencing a perpetual focus on campaigns and fund-raising.

Establish Campaign Finance Reform

The institutional changes would go a long way toward improving the performance of both the individual houses of the legislative branch and the Congress as a whole by allowing more members to focus on the job they were elected to perform. Fixing the rules within Congress, however, only addresses a portion of the challenges facing our government and our political system. Money in political campaigns flows like water. Financing methods have expanded and morphed to take advantage of any and all loopholes. The massive expenditures have changed campaign finance and they impact elections. And the blizzard of attack ads have further polarized the electorate. Political committees used to be formed to contribute to candidates who supported their cause under strict campaign finance guidelines. Now many of those groups are shifting to minimally regulated independent expenditure organizations to directly impact election outcomes themselves.

The *Citizens United* decision has upended the financing of campaigns—creating even greater imbalance and triggering unbridled, undisclosed spending. Before *Citizens United* in 2010, corporations could not make direct contributions to candidates. They could fund advertising for or against a candidate, but only through individual contributions from their employees or members to political action committees. There are restrictions on how much an individual can contribute to a PAC, which result in de facto limits on how much the PAC can raise. PACs are also limited in how much money they can contribute to a particular candidate, and they bring transparency to the political process because their contributions and expenditures are subject to disclosure requirements. After *Citizens United,* those limitations and disclosure requirements disappeared for so-called electioneering advertising and independent expenditures, unleashing a torrent of millions of dollars in basically unrestricted campaign activity.

It's one thing to have a vigorous exchange of ideas. But when a select few individuals and organizations "own the microphone," the average citizen's voice is effectively drowned out by a cacophony of high-priced media blitzes. This imbalance is compounded by the exploding phenomenon of "outside" organizations that pour extraordinary financial resources into a state to influence an election not based on the interests of that state, but on the parochial, political objectives of that group. Oftentimes, outside groups spend more on campaigns than the candidates themselves, and that's not right.

I've long been involved in the fight to restore Americans' confidence in our system of financing campaigns. In 1998 I spearheaded an effort, along with Senator Jim Jeffords from Vermont, to devise an amendment to the McCain-Feingold campaign finance reform bill, named after Senator John McCain (R-AZ) and then-Senator Russ Feingold (D-WI). Jim and I worked to apply new campaign finance limits and disclosure requirements so that neither side would gain an unfair advantage and thereby help garner the support of more than half of the Senate.

Our amendment said, if you're running so-called issue ads thirty days before a primary or sixty days before a general election, and you use the name of a federal candidate, or the words "vote for" or "vote against" a particular candidate, you're deemed to be airing an advertisement intended to influence the outcome of an election. As a result, you're required to disclose your major funders and utilize only voluntary, individual donations through PACs rather than corporate or union treasury money—the same as for any other campaign ad. Senators McCain and Feingold wholeheartedly supported our effort, and we offered our amendment to their legislation on the floor of the Senate in 1998. The measure was adopted on a bipartisan vote, which allowed the McCain-Feingold bill to achieve majority support in the Senate for the very first time. In 2002, McCain-Feingold, including what became the Snowe-Jeffords provision, was passed and signed into law as the Bipartisan Campaign Reform Act, or BCRA.

After this successful effort, I was especially troubled by the Supreme Court's puzzling *Citizens United* decision. For the past century,

Congress had recognized the pernicious effect of undue corporate and labor union spending on political campaigns. The Supreme Court even recently has held that the nation had a compelling interest in ensuring that corporations do not corrupt the political process by exerting undue influence. In a majority opinion in 1990, Justice Thurgood Marshall characterized "the corrosive and distorting effects of immense aggregations of wealth that are accumulated with the help of the corporate form and that have little or no correlation to the public's support for the corporation's political ideas."

Yet in the *Citizens* decision, the Court abruptly abandoned a century of precedents and overturned the Snowe-Jeffords campaign advertising restrictions in BCRA. In so doing, the Court undermined existing law and further distorted the national political debate by giving corporations and unions unrestricted power to flood the airwaves with campaign ads with essentially no restriction. At the time, I characterized the decision as "a serious disservice to our country."

It is essential that Congress revisit the issue of campaign finance reform to counter the massive amounts of third-party advertising that are disproportionately and too often anonymously influencing our elections and fueling the fires of partisan discourse. It must explore and examine new means of achieving this end that will protect First Amendment rights to free speech while preserving the integrity of campaigns and elections. There have been recent proposals in Congress to address the overall issue—but the whole point of how we arrived at the Snowe-Jeffords measure and the McCain-Feingold legislation was to provide a level playing field for both parties, and if attempts are made that are unbalanced and don't incorporate input from both sides from the beginning, they won't be politically feasible. Whether a comprehensive, equitable approach is possible in Congress today is debatable. Therefore, I believe a national, bipartisan campaign finance reform commission should be established to sift through the enormous complexities and develop concrete recommendations for congressional consideration and enactment. Ultimately, there is no reason we cannot debate and pass at least individual measures—if not a broad, sweeping package—that are carefully balanced to apply fairly across the board.

More Open Primaries

As the electorate has become more polarized, ideologically moti-vated voters have concentrated their time and energies on party in-volvement and primary candidates and elections. At the same time, those closer to the center in each party are less likely to feel welcome and thus less inclined to get involved. The result, as I discussed in chapter 12, is either that good legislators and candidates are defeated in primaries, or incumbents who may otherwise be inclined to pur-sue bipartisan solutions have little political incentive to do so.

Today, the methods by which primaries are conducted vary from state to state. There are essentially four types: closed primaries, open primaries, "blanket" or "top-two" primaries, and semi-closed primaries.

In a closed primary, only those registered members of a certain political party can vote in their party's primary. This has the advantage of ensuring that those who belong to a different party won't make mischief by participating in the opposite party's primary election—for example voting to nominate an individual they believe would be weaker against their own general election candidate. In some states, independent voters or those affiliated with another party are allowed to register with a party, or switch affiliations on election day. They then remain a member of that party unless they either unenroll or switch back to their original party.

In an open primary, as the term denotes, independents and vot-ers registered with any party are allowed to vote in any primary, but only one primary per election cycle. The concern expressed about this system is, again, the potential for voters in one party to "sabo-tage" the other's primary.

Louisiana, Washington state, and, most recently, California have instituted variations on a "blanket" or "top-two" primary, in which all candidates for the general election participate in a single primary election regardless of party, and any registered voter may cast a ballot. The top two vote earners in the primary then become the two candidates for the general election.

In my view, the fatal flaw of the "top two" approach is the demonstrated and substantial potential for both candidates in the general election to hail from the same party. That's not an equitable system especially in districts or states that are dominated by one party, which would deny the other any opportunity to participate in the general election. One could argue that, in such instances, the majority party candidate is likely to prevail in the general election regardless—but I believe the general electorate should still have the option of voting between (or among) candidates of different, or even multiple, political affiliations (or nonaffiliations).

I favor some form of open or semi-open primary, in which unaffiliated voters may participate in whatever primary they choose in each election cycle, while individuals enrolled in a particular party must vote in their party's primary. I believe the benefits of a semi-open primary outweigh the concerns of inappropriate participation by members of the opposing party. In many states a plurality of the voters are not enrolled in a party, even though most probably lean toward one party or the other, so an open primary system that allows independents to vote in primaries will further engage them in the nominating processes of each of the parties. It seems reasonable to argue that if an independent or unenrolled voter happens to strongly support a candidate in a particular party, they should be able to vote for that candidate to be the nominee in the general election.

Many Democrats and independents in Maine have supported me over the years, and if I had run in 2012, they would have wanted me to be successful in my primary so they could have an opportunity to vote for me again in the general election. Under Maine law they would have had to enroll in the Republican Party in order to vote in the Republican primary. The semi-open approach would have afforded independents the opportunity to vote for me in the Republican primary without requiring them to relinquish, even if just temporarily, their independent status.

Whether you support a fully or semi-open primary system, I would encourage you to contact your state legislators to urge them to adopt one of them. In order to increase voter participation in our primaries, changing state election laws may be an uphill battle in states with legislatures dominated by one party over the other, but change begins with letting your voices be heard, and if elected state officials hear from enough of their constituents, it can and will make a difference.

Redistricting Commissions

Much attention has been focused on "redistricting," for the reasons I discussed in chapter 12. A number of states have removed at least some degree of decision-making on the composition of congressional districts from the hands of their state government. According to the National Conference of State Legislatures, currently "[t]here are 12 states that give first and final authority for legislative redistricting to a group other than the legislature," and "[o]nly six states give first and final authority for congressional line drawing with a commission." The composition of these commissions varies, and most of them include appointments made by legislative leaders.

These commissions aren't necessarily the ultimate answer for redistricting—but I would argue they provide a more promising alternative than leaving the issue solely in the realm of the state legislatures. Stanford University political scientist Bruce Cain recently released an analysis of redistricting commissions—he argues that redistricting can never be fully depoliticized, but he discusses a potential means of "lessening the partisan edge" by "incorporating the [current] New Jersey bargaining system into the independent citizen commission system."

He believes the New Jersey system has several virtues that separate it from other commissions, such as the impartial tiebreaker, who is likely to encourage the parties to seek the middle ground.

New Jersey has a twelve-member bipartisan panel, six chosen by the chairs of each party. If the commission is unable to agree on a plan, the state Supreme Court can appoint a thirteenth, tiebreaking member. In 2011, after the panel was unable to agree on a new electoral map after four days of deliberations, the chairman, John Farmer Jr., chose the GOP version. "I think it is fair to say I have exasperated all my colleagues at this table in an effort to drive compromise and bring both parties together," the *Philadelphia Inquirer* reported.

Professor Cain concludes, "In the end, political thickets can be pruned even if they cannot be removed entirely." I agree—and believe that redistricting commissions deserve further exploration as a step in the right direction for tempering the politicization of redistricting and, in turn, tamping down political polarization in Congress.

In Maine, and similar to New Jersey, a bipartisan electoral advisory commission is appointed, which increases the chances for compromise solutions. The state House majority and minority leaders choose three members each; their Senate counterparts two; each of the two state party chairs can serve or they can appoint someone in their place; two members of the public are chosen, one by each side; they in turn select a fifteenth member, and finally the two parties agree to appoint one individual to serve as the chair. In 2011, the commission disagreed over where to redraw the line between the state's two congressional districts, but in order to avoid a strictly party-line vote, with the neutral chairman breaking the tie, party leaders came together to approve a plan that was passed by 140-3 in the state House and 35-0 in the Senate. Maine voters subsequently voted to make redistricting subject to a two-thirds majority, ensuring that any plan would need bipartisan consensus in order to pass.

In 2013, when new members were appointed to the commission to redraw the state legislature's district boundaries, the independent chairman, Michael Friedman—who'd also been the neutral chair for the congressional redistricting process—joked that he was qualified for the job because, as he was quoted as saying in the *Port-*

land Press Herald, "I've taken [both parties] to the woodshed a few times." Such is the effort at consensus-building that best serves the requirements of this vital and sensitive task, and that effort is best served by redistricting commissions.

The bottom line is that there is no single remedy that will correct the processes and procedures of our system, and the suggestions in this chapter are far from an exhaustive list of the steps necessary to make our government work again. But they represent a solid starting point for reforming our political system and congressional rules and processes. The question is, how do we provide the impetus for our elected officials to take this path?

The answer is, a relentless citizens' movement demanding that they seek the common ground these perilous times demand.

In other words, it's up to each and every one of us to take back our government—and we have the power to make it happen.

Chapter 15

Fighting from the Grassroots

THE REFORMS I DISCUSS in chapter 14 would greatly enhance Congress's ability to adopt a more results-oriented approach to addressing our nation's problems. Together with an increase in civility, we could go a long way toward laying the groundwork for reducing dysfunction. We could go a long way, but only so far. In order to resolve our problems of congressional inaction, we must alter the rules of Congress and electoral politics and provide sufficient political incentives for our elected representatives to engage with their colleagues across the political aisle. We need to not only preach civility, we must also reward it.

Our representatives and senators must understand that compromise is not a dirty word—it's the essential ingredient in governing. The American people understand this intuitively. Consider Frank Luntz's poll: In 2012 he found that 65 percent of respondents wanted Congress to compromise on the major issues facing the country. As Congress failed to do so, its approval rating tracked between 9 percent and 13 percent throughout most of 2012 and the first part of 2013. The conclusion is indisputable: people were registering their highest disapproval for Congress's unwillingness to find consensus.

Every American should understand that today's political atmosphere does not have to be tomorrow's. If we look at this moment in time as an anomaly and not the norm, we can begin to grasp that reversing the current status quo is not an insurmountable task. And the instruments for change are at our fingertips—quite literally.

As I have witnessed firsthand over my forty years in the state and national legislatures, only when there are political consequences for a failure to act will our elected officials buck their party or congressional party leaders and come together. Ultimately, their constituents rightfully expect them to seek accommodation with the other side when their party does not have the votes to prevail. Those of us who believe in consensus-building across party lines must organize and speak out in sufficient numbers so our elected representatives have the political incentive to break from party orthodoxy and stalemate to seek common ground.

We must be heard!

I've witnessed the impact that voters can have on a legislator's actions. When constituents contact their federal, state, and local representatives, members and their staffs listen. Personal visits, emails, and phone calls to Washington or the local field offices all have an effect. Each interaction is tracked in every office and on the big issues tabulated at least daily if not hourly. But when there are fewer constituents who are motivated enough to get involved and express their opinion on issues, then those who do will have a disproportionate impact on congressional actions.

Groups who are well organized and effective in making their opinions known on particular issues can leverage their involvement to participate to an even larger extent. And there's infinitely greater potential to maximize the impact on congressional decision-making for those who are able to utilize the modern tools of social media. Regardless of ideology or the specific issue under discussion, those who are most adept at utilizing today's tools of communication are the ones who will have the largest and loudest voice and, therefore, in all probability, the most influence.

On the right of the political spectrum, we saw how the Tea Party formed a grassroots effort in 2009 around the principle of excessive government spending and built a groundswell through use of social media. And on the left in 2011, Occupy Wall Street's extremely sophisticated social-media-based activism—encapsulated by its slogan, "We are the 99 percent"—organized activities in communities across the country and around the world.

So how do we create a powerful, grassroots movement that will deliver political rewards for consensus-building? It will require leadership from visible and credible leaders who are Republicans, Democrats, and independents. Well-regarded activists can give credibility to the movement and make participation patriotic rather than partisan, and become the rallying point for each group.

Social media provides an online community that is instantaneous and easy to access. It acts as a message multiplier to boost the power of the individual exponentially. We're astoundingly interconnected in ways unimaginable just twenty years ago. Indeed, in the Arab Spring we witnessed the power of Internet-based communications to help topple decades-old dictatorships.

Only when elected officials understand that a significant number of their constituents are demanding bipartisanship will they be willing to engage in this essential practice. In my view, the fastest way to accomplish that goal is to support the efforts of existing national groups that advocate the type of bipartisan approach I've expressed in this book. Joining the existing groups' networks will enhance our voices and allow those of us who support consensus-building to become a political force that can impact decision-making in Congress.

What all of the groups currently lack is a sufficient number of followers to create the critical mass necessary to have an impact on Congress. Together, however, they have the potential to be a significant, positive influence on the governmental process.

Although I am certain there are many organizations throughout the country worthy of support—indeed, they are too numerous to mention—the following are the major groups I'm familiar with that merit your attention and, I hope, your participation. I urge you to browse their websites, visit them on Facebook, and follow them on Twitter. They have different purposes but all are looking to address the issues resulting from the lack of civility and bipartisanship, and how that failure is undermining our government's ability to prepare us for a better and more prosperous future.

BIPARTISAN POLICY CENTER

Led by its president, Jason Grumet, the Bipartisan Policy Center (BPC) in Washington, D.C., has been a leading bipartisan think tank providing indispensable analysis on pressing issues such as the debt ceiling and our nation's deficit. As I have said earlier, I am on the board of directors and a senior fellow at BPC—and the fact that four distinguished former Majority Leaders would establish an organization designed to promote bipartisanship and civil dialogue speaks volumes about the urgency of their mission. BPC draws on the depth and breadth of experience of its contributors from the highest levels of Congress, the administration, and the academic realm.

Just as Congress should, BPC approaches their policy analysis, negotiations, and dialogue by engaging individuals with different points of view to sit down together and work through the issues civilly and effectively. Through BPC's "Bridge-Builder Breakfasts," roundtables, summits, and policy discussions, the leaders and staff at BPC have forged comprehensive and bipartisan solutions to some of the most current issues facing this nation.

BPC's Economic Policy Program has led to initiatives like the Debt Reduction Task Force, cochaired by a formidable team of foremost experts: former Senate Budget Committee Chairman Pete Domenici; and former Office of Management and Budget Director Dr. Alice Rivlin. The Task Force produced a multiyear federal budget in 2010 and Domenici and Rivlin testified together in this capacity before the Senate Finance Committee in 2012. Their voices and expertise will be instrumental as, hopefully, Congress tackles our unprecedented levels of deficits and debt.

BPC's Democracy Project held a number of discussions beginning in 2011 on "How to Fix Congress," as well as a roundtable discussion series on Congress. Out of these bipartisan dialogues, the BPC and the Woodrow Wilson Center together produced a list of vital reforms, many of which I have championed: from the elimination of Leadership PACs and the adoption of a biennial federal budget to a full restoration of the authorizing process to committees and a more open amendment process on the floors of both houses. As BPC has said, the culture in Washington "is not conducive to bipartisan compromise or serious problem solving."

A cornerstone initiative at BPC is the Commission on Political Reform, which I am proud to cochair with former Congressman and Secretary of Agriculture Dan Glickman (D-KS)—as well as former Senate Majority Leaders Tom Daschle and Trent Lott; and former Secretary of the Interior, Republican Senator, and Governor of the state of Idaho, Dirk Kempthorne (R-ID). At the Ronald Reagan Presidential Library in California, we launched our monumental effort to address the key challenges facing the nation, including extreme partisanship. We also scheduled town-hall style "National Conversations on American Unity" at the National Constitution Center in Philadelphia; Ohio State University in Columbus; the Edward M. Kennedy Institute and John F. Kennedy Presidential Library and Museum in Boston; and finally, in Washington, D.C.

My fellow commissioners and I are examining the causes and consequences of the political divide and are working to develop specific policy reforms aimed at gaining acceptance from Republicans, Democrats, and independents. And our work is putting a premium on public engagement, which is why we are embarking on a significant social media campaign to raise awareness about these issues via platforms like Twitter and Facebook.

NO LABELS

The organization No Labels has been a refreshing voice of common sense in our political quagmire. Founded in 2010, No Labels is fighting tooth and nail to bring the nation's leaders and decision-makers together to forge solutions for the American people. They welcome "people left, right and everything in between as long as they are willing to collaborate with one another to seek a shared success for America." This is precisely the message and mechanism for change in our government that I believe Americans want—and deserve.

Over the past three years, No Labels has worked to promote an agenda that can fix Washington while simultaneously building a strong core of supporters who can pressure members of Congress to make these necessary changes. They've put forward two detailed action plans to reform both the U.S. Congress and presidential administrations, and they have already made great strides raising awareness of their campaign.

As I mentioned, I strongly support their common sense proposals for "No Budget, No Pay," which would force Congress to complete the appropriations and budget process each year under threat of losing their paychecks if they don't pass them on time, and enforcing the five-day congressional workweek in Washington, D.C., at least three weeks out of the month, both of which I discussed in chapter 14. No Labels is suggesting reforms that can truly make government work again.

The key to No Labels' success has been their inclusivity. From the beginning, its founders sought out a broad coalition of thinkers for their organization to ensure that it is truly a bipartisan effort. In January 2013, No Labels announced its new, bipartisan leadership team of Jon Huntsman, former Republican governor of Utah; and my former colleague, U.S. Senator Joe Manchin (D-WV).

No Labels has held Citizen Trainings where they work to educate the public about what people can do to make a difference. Americans can log on to the No Labels website and easily sign on to support their various proposals. The organization offers a variety of ways for people to share its message through social media, through a letter to the editor to the local paper, or by contacting their members of Congress with a prewritten letter calling for a specific proposal, which can be edited as the voter sees fit.

MAIN STREET PARTNERSHIP

Main Street was founded in 1998 by then-Congressman Amo Houghton (R-NY); my husband, Jock, served as chairman, and I was proud to be a member of the group since its inception. Jock and I went on a number of fund-raising trips with Amo, who is a longtime, wonderful friend, in the late 1990s to build support when Main Street was getting its start. We traveled throughout the country along with board member Sarah Chamberlain Resnick, who is also now chief operating officer, to promote the partnership. The group was the first of its kind designed to be a leading voice in the Republican Party calling for common ground, inclusiveness, and the development of pragmatic bipartisan solutions that, while representing the centrist wing of the GOP, worked for the entire nation.

The organization has urged leaders in our nation's capital to cut wasteful or ineffective discretionary spending, advocated for innovation in the health care sector to utilize new technologies, and supported the use of renewable energy and alternative energy sources. As of January 2013, Main Street—with fifty-four members currently serving in Congress and another twenty-one retired members whom they continue to work with—is being led by former Republican Ohio Congressman Steve LaTourette. Main Street's most recent and primary focus has been on building centrist support for a balanced package of debt reduction legislation to address the nation's fiscal issues. Main Street released a consequential report, "From Fiscal Cliff to Fiscal Tsunami," to that effect in early February 2013, offering a number of prescriptions to fix the economic crisis.

Main Street has been fighting for centrists in Congress since its foundation, providing indispensable support for those willing to work on policy for the good of the country. Each year, Main Street holds a National Dinner, where they recognize the work of centrists in Congress. Jock and I have both attended a number of times. Indeed, it was an incredible privilege to be presented with their award named in honor of Amo, and an even greater honor for me to present the award to other centrists.

THIRD WAY

Founded in 2005, Third Way is what I refer to as a center-left-leaning think tank in Washington, D.C. Third Way has put its focus on the "vital center," or what I often refer to as the "sensible center." With a mission to advance moderate policies, Third Way's policy teams have influenced debates on energy, the economy, national security, and social policy time and again.

Third Way is also behind what I believe has turned into an impressive and important practice during the annual State of the Union address: bipartisan seating. Following the horrific shooting rampage in Arizona in January 2011 that killed six people and wounded thirteen others, including incredibly courageous former Congresswoman Gabby Giffords (D-AZ), who served as an honorary chairwoman of Third Way, the group's president, Jonathan Cowan, sent a letter to congressional leaders urging them to promote civility on Capitol Hill. One of his suggestions was to encourage members to sit next to at least one person of the opposing party during that year's State of the Union address.

Within four days, I had joined sixteen other senators in signing on to another letter to leaders initiated by my colleague Senator Mark Udall (D-CO). In 2011, as ranking member of the Senate Committee on Small Business and Entrepreneurship, I was pleased my seatmate was my Democratic counterpart, Chair Mary Landrieu.

A year later, the practice expanded; and as ranking member of the Senate Commerce Subcommittee on Oceans, Atmosphere, Fisheries, and Coast Guard, I sat next to the chair of the subcommittee, Senator Mark Begich (D-AK). As I said then, I hoped that senators would use this as a stepping-stone to pursue a similar form of bipartisanship. Third Way, while encompassing more support from the Democratic side, has maintained its moderate approach just like the Main Street Partnership has on the Republican side.

CAMPAIGN TO FIX THE DEBT

Bipartisan organizations also exist in support of specific causes, such as our nation's debt crisis. The nonpartisan group Fix the Debt, which I've joined and with whom the Main Street Partnership is working closely, has worked tirelessly to coalesce individuals representing a diverse range of public and private sector experience across the political spectrum, to address our burgeoning national debt in a timely manner.

The campaign—which includes more than one hundred CEOs, former governors, members of Congress, cabinet secretaries, mayors, and ambassadors—was founded by Erskine Bowles, former director of the Small Business Administration and Clinton White House chief of staff; and former Republican Senator Alan Simpson. Maya MacGuineas, the president of the Committee for a Responsible Budget, who describes herself as a "die hard independent," spearheaded the establishment of Fix the Debt and was instrumental in driving its membership. Fix the Debt's cochairs also represent the political spectrum with my former Republican colleague Judd Gregg, former Democratic Pennsylvania Governor Ed Rendell, and Independent New York City Mayor Michael Bloomberg.

Fix the Debt's "Citizen's Toolkit," which can be downloaded from their website at www.fixthedebt.org, offers an in-depth manual for individuals to build a grassroots movement in their community to raise awareness about this historic problem and to put the pressure on our elected officials to solve it. With comprehensive instructions on how to hold effective community meetings on the debt crisis and ways to develop a motivational personal story that can convince others to get involved, the organization's work to engage everyday Americans on the debt debate is unparalleled.

Fix the Debt has also spread their message online through social media. For anyone unfamiliar with social media platforms like Twitter, Facebook, YouTube, or Flickr, Fix the Debt provides a "Social Media 101" to help people set up their accounts, cultivate their online network, and craft targeted messages to help get the word out. Simply put, the organization has made a complicated and convoluted issue like our nation's debt easy to understand and has disseminated information to apply pressure on lawmakers. It is precisely this community-level engagement across our nation that can become the movement necessary to wake Washington up to the fact that action must be taken.

THE NATIONAL INSTITUTE FOR CIVIL DISCOURSE

Colleges and universities are getting involved in this national effort. The National Institute for Civil Discourse (NICD) at the University of Arizona was established shortly after the 2011 shootings in Tucson. NICD is a center that encourages civility in political campaigns and public policy deliberation. A nonpartisan center for advocacy, research, and policy regarding civil discourse consistent with First Amendment principles, NICD has worked tirelessly since it was founded to foster an open exchange of ideas. And I could not have been more honored and privileged to join NICD's Advisory Board, and especially to serve with Gabby Giffords and her husband, Mark E. Kelly, who first approached me to share their enthusiasm for the organization and its value, and to invite my participation.

Indeed, the goals of the institute parallel my long-held belief that only by finding common ground can we achieve the results necessary for the common good. To that end, NICD has already received critical information that will greatly influence our national dialogue. The institute is continuing to collect crucial research on a wide range of issues, such as the problems that incivility in political discourse poses for our democracy.

Scholars at the University of Arizona are exploring these implications and finding that incivility in some campaign contexts can suppress voter turnout. In another case, their data shows that contentious, "in-your-face" political debates serve to "diminish the legitimacy of political actors whose views differ from the observer." Other data indicate that many voters find uncivil political discourse offensive and distrustful and suggest that person- or trait-based attack ads are ineffective.

What does this all mean for our political system? The efforts under way at NICD are making important strides in providing the essential evidence we need to prove that political strategies perpetuating polarization and incivility simply don't work. With the facts on our side, the Americans who feel the way I do can stand up to the caustic campaigning and help convince everyone from political operatives to incumbents running for reelection that the electorate demands a more sophisticated level of dialogue and discourse.

THE VILLAGE SQUARE

In places like Tallahassee, Florida, efforts are taking place from the ground up. In Tallahassee, local community members set up their own organizations in response to the bitter partisanship seen in all levels of government. A contentious debate developed on a local referendum over a coal plant and escalated into a divisive campaign. Two community members, Allan Katz, then a Democratic city commissioner, and who has also served as U.S. ambassador to the Republic of Portugal, and his friend Bill Law, a Republican who was then president of Tallahassee Community College, organized "The Village Square." On my visit to Portugal to discuss the Eurozone crisis, Ambassador Katz informed me about this group and its indispensable purpose.

Allan and Bill were disturbed by the divisiveness rampant in their community, so they took it upon themselves to build a bipartisan organization to change the dialogue. As the organization reports, events like their quarterly series "Dinner at the Square" have "drawn a wide range of citizens and sell-out crowds to civil fact-based dialogue on some of the most divisive issues of our time."

The Village Square has tackled a wide range of issues for the Tallahassee community, from Florida's fiscal crisis and property taxes to constitutional amendments and the health care debate. What better example is there of the impact two people with an extraordinary idea can have on their community? As they say on their website, "It's a crazy notion, but we think it might catch on." I couldn't agree with them more.

OLYMPIA'S LIST

In order to take a personal and direct role in effecting change, I've established my own political committee, called "Olympia's List," to support candidates who, above all else, believe as I do in building consensus and using elective office to its fullest potential. Our public discourse should not be concerned about whether an idea is a Republican or a Democratic one, but whether it's a good idea. It's not about what's in the best interests of a single political party, but about what's in the best interests of the people of the United States of America—all of us.

I will be supporting elected officials and candidates who demonstrate not a commitment to party, but a commitment to solving our nation's problems by working across the political aisle. And I encourage Americans who share my views to visit www.olympiaslist .org and join my team.

All of these organizations, and countless others, provide the institutional structure that we, as Americans, can utilize to truly change and inject a greater sense of civility into our political systems and our society. For instance, Jock and I are serving on the board of the University of New Hampshire's Warren B. Rudman Center for Justice, Leadership and Public Policy, established to honor Rudman's "legacy of advancing sound public policy, civil discourse, efficient government, fiscal responsibility and integrity." Citing that "Warren's years of bipartisan leadership in the U.S. Senate is a model for future leaders who seek to govern in the America's best interests," the Center will not only "train future lawyers who exemplify those foundational values"—justice, leadership, and public policy—but also serve as a forum where "emerging challenges and potential solutions" will be rigorously but respectfully discussed.

All the groups I've highlighted form the underpinnings for a movement to bring civil dialogue, compromise, and consensus-building back to government. Voters at times wonder if they can have a positive impact on political campaigns and in government at the local, state, and national levels. My message is they *can*, and one prime way to do so is by supporting organizations like the Bipartisan Policy Center, No Labels, Third Way, Main Street Partnership, the National Institute for Civil Discourse, local community ventures like the "Civility in America" series in Connecticut and the Village Square in Florida, or organizations like my own—Olympia's List. What is required is creating the critical mass behind these groups that will allow them to more profoundly influence the course of events in Congress. Together, bolstered by the participation of millions of Americans, they have the potential to be a significant, positive force to reshape our government.

My travels across this great nation started me on this journey that has taken my fight for bipartisanship from within the United States Senate to outside the institution. I was struck by how people from all walks of life—in states from Maine to California to Texas; from Florida to Tennessee to New York and Washington, D.C., irrespective of their own strong views or wherever they were on the political spectrum, wanted to know: Why is it so bad in Washington? How did it get this way? Can it be fixed? Some people just shook their heads; they were at a loss for words in expressing the depths of the political breakdown.

Even as they might identify themselves as Democrats, Republicans, or independents, they consider themselves Americans first—and therefore, they ultimately place "nation" above "party." They advocate for their positions as the right course for our country but understand that, in the end, no single political philosophy or approach can prevail 100 percent of the time—and that an unyielding adherence to ideology is a recipe for deadlock.

That's why the overwhelming majority of men and women I've encountered are profoundly disheartened by the breakdown in Washington that prevents the greatest nation on earth from solving its most fundamental problems. If you've read this book, you're likely among that number—and the motivations for your disillusionment are the same as those that contributed to my decision to leave the institution I love. But to you, I want to offer assurance of one indisputable fact:

It doesn't have to be this way.

Those who seek to divide us either by creating wedge issues or through hyperpartisan rhetoric would have you believe they are representing the vast majority of Americans, but they aren't. Yes, we are a nation of incredibly diverse backgrounds and viewpoints that form the bedrock of our strength, ingenuity, and eternal promise—and distilling this vast array of ideals and opinions will never be easy. Yes, America was purposefully founded as a cauldron of passionate beliefs. But regardless of what the polarizing forces and the political classes would have you believe, it is possible to move forward from our differences.

What has driven me in my post-Senate life is my unwavering confidence in America's ability to fix whatever ails us. I have witnessed firsthand how necessary and effective change can be formulated when the President, the leadership, and the men and women of the House and Senate share a commitment to bringing it about. So to the American people who distrust the institution of Congress, to the forty-three senators new to Congress since 2008 who have only ever experienced dysfunction I say, Congress can be fixed! It can be done!

I'm convinced from my service in both the U.S. House and U.S. Senate that those serving today want to do what's right for America. What's required is that they hear from you that compromise is essential, and will be supported by their constituents on both sides of the political aisle. As Americans, we are the beneficiaries of one of the most remarkable documents in the history of humankind—the Constitution of the United States of America, which endows us with the power to control and determine the course of our governmental institutions. We must now harness that power by mobilizing those among us who share a vision of a problem-solving and bipartisan Congress.

When I spoke on Civility in Politics at Stamford, Connecticut, during my final months in the Senate, the venue for the event, the Ferguson Library, was filled to overflowing. The people weren't there for the messenger; they were there for the message. These were people who cared about civility and were clamoring for change—like the rest of America. For forty years I have fought day and night for the people I have represented in Maine and for all Americans. Now I intend to do so again to make certain our elected leaders get the signal loud and clear that the American people want them to find common ground—to fight their way toward it—confident in the truism that there is nothing we can't accomplish together.

Including making our government work again.

Acknowledgments

As all elected officials know, success is never based on their efforts alone. That has been especially true for me. It has been my family, friends, supporters, and most of all the people of Maine who have allowed me the privilege of serving in public office for the past four decades.

First among them has been my husband, John "Jock" McKernan. Even as he was building his own successful career in politics—first in the Maine legislature and then in Congress and as governor of Maine—and now in business, Jock has been a sounding board, confidant, adviser, and soul mate for more than half of my life.

I also could not have attained any measure of achievement without my extraordinary family—they have truly provided the bedrock for whatever accomplishments I have been able to build. Jock's mother used to say to me, "For an orphan, you sure have a large family!" But as I've often said, their enthusiasm and numbers have been the secret to my electoral success. To a person, they have always been there to help, whether on my campaigns, attending numerous events, or just dealing with the normal—and sometimes not so normal— travails of life.

My brother, John Bouchles, has been unceasingly supportive of all that I have done. After my parents died, my aunt Mary was an inspiration to me. Her children, my cousins, are like additional siblings to me: Toni Spirounias, her late husband, Charlie, and their daughters, Evangelea and Maria, and their husbands, Matt and Jim; Duke Goranites and his wife, Charlene, and their daughters, Eleni, my godchild, and Angela, and their fiancées, Seth and George; Georgia Chomas and her daughters, Mary and Thea, and their husbands,

Kerry and Steve; Kiki Harrington and her husband, John, their son, Jim, and daughter, Mary, and their spouses, Marah and Nolen; and Peter Goranites and his wife, Rosemary, and their sons, Jeffrey and Jared. They have always provided me with the love and support we all need in our lives—and I'm pleased to say we are blessed with a next generation, which is thriving as well!

I thank my brother-in-law, Bob McKernan, for his support, advice, and the creative and effective media he consistently produced for my campaigns—as well as the support of his wife, Kim, and our nephews, Kyle and Ryan.

And I could never adequately express the appreciation I have for my former in-laws, Carlie and the late Barbara Snowe—and their daughter, Gretchen, and her husband, Chuck, for their unwavering love and support through the years.

Representing more than one million people is an undertaking you cannot accomplish alone, and I'm deeply indebted to the more than four hundred staff people who have worked in my offices in Maine and Washington, D.C., over my thirty-four years in Congress. Specifically, I thank my long-serving chiefs of staff: Kirk Walder; Kevin Raye, as well as his wife, Karen; Jane Calderwood; and John Richter, who has been with me for twenty-three years and was indispensable in completing this book and finding the right words to bring my experiences to life for our readers. I also want to thank John's wife, Patty (who also worked for me for many years), and their son, Jason, for all they have done and the lengthy hours they have endured over the years.

I would also like to make special mention of my long-tenured staff: Pat Doak, the late Dave Lackey, Matt Walker, Amy Pellegrino, Patrick Woodcock, and Wally Hsueh in my Washington offices; and in Maine: Gail Kelly, Peter Morin, Mark Kontio, Cheryl Leeman, Linda Lyon, Sharon Campbell, Renee Goodwin, Diane Jackson, and Brian Whitney. In total they have served me for more than 150 years!

I've also been incredibly fortunate to have a long-standing and talented campaign team, the nucleus of which has been Jock, Bob, our close friend and Jock's former chief of staff, Sharon Miller, Kim Gore, Lucas Caron, Sandy Tuttle, Ted O'Meara, and our pollster, Bill McInturff. In every campaign we have added additional talented people, and I want to thank all of them. The 2012 campaign was no exception—with Justin Brasell, Jan Love, Martin Sheehan, and Cheryl Russell. And I couldn't have done it without the volunteers and my steadfast supporters over the years who made all the difference in my campaigns.

Among those who have been especially helpful and personally supportive over the years is my good friend, former Secretary of Labor Lynn Martin, with whom I served in the U.S. House. Lynn has unfailingly given me not only great advice, but unwavering encouragement. And Jock's close friend and former law partner Bob Moore has for decades provided thoughtful counsel as we've undertaken major decisions.

I especially want to express my most profound appreciation to the people of Maine, who gave me the extraordinary honor of serving them at the highest levels of our government in the United States Senate—and I will be eternally grateful for the trust they invested in me.

As a result of the outpouring of support I received following my announcement that I would not seek a fourth term in the Senate, Jock suggested that I write a book. When I called my friend Bob Barnett of the firm Williams & Connolly, and with whom I had worked when the women of the Senate wrote the book *Nine and Counting* in 1999, he said he'd already been contacted by a number of publishers who wanted to be notified if I decided to pursue such a project. Bob has been indispensable in my successfully navigating the process of the publishing of this book and continues to be an incomparable counselor and adviser as I make my transition into private life.

This book would also never have been completed without the tireless efforts of my collaborator, Ian Jackman, who was instrumental in helping me to organize my thoughts into what I believe is now a compelling "call to action." His experience writing books was invaluable as we transformed my experiences and beliefs into the right description of how things used to work in Congress, why they haven't in recent times, and what can be done about it. I also thank his wife, Kara; daughter, Lindsay; and son, Sam—for accepting Ian's long hours on this project and numerous trips to Washington and Maine.

My former press secretary, Brandon Bouchard, burned the midnight oil doing exhaustive research to make certain my recollections were correct and appropriately described. And without Lynda Griffith, I'm sure we never would have been able to keep our efforts on track; she continues to keep Jock's and my lives as organized as they can be given our schedules!

As critical as I believe my message is, it would never be heard without the willingness of Harvey Weinstein to provide me with the platform to make my case. I thank Harvey for unhesitatingly embracing the value and the importance of the subject matter of this book, and for his enthusiasm for publishing it.

I also appreciate the efforts of his editorial director, Amanda Murray, whose advice improved the final product immensely—as did the ongoing guidance we received from editor Ruth Fecych, who refined the language and the organization of the material covered in this book.

I thank David Steinberger, the CEO of Perseus Books Group, for his support and encouragement throughout this project. David and his team understood that it was crucial that the imperative of fixing Congress be disseminated in the spring of 2013. Finally, I want to thank Georgina Levitt, publishing director of Weinstein Books; Lynn Goldberg and Angela Baggetta of Goldberg McDuffie Communications; Richard Aquan for the cover design; production manager/packager Christine Marra of *Marra*thon Production Services; and copy editor Tom Pitoniak.

Renowned American poet and son of New England Ralph Waldo Emerson said, "Because all things have contributed to your advancement, you should include all things in your gratitude."

For everything I have in life, including this book, I couldn't be more grateful.

Index